Administering

Targeted Social

Programs

in Latin America

From Platitudes to Practice

WORLD BANK

REGIONAL AND

SECTORAL STUDIES

Administering Targeted Social Programs in Latin America

From Platitudes to Practice

MARGARET E. GROSH

The World Bank
Washington, D.C.

The World Bank Regional and Sectoral Studies series provides an outlet for work that is relatively limited in its subject matter or geographical coverage but that contributes to the intellectual foundations of development operations and policy formulation.

The complete backlist of publications from the World Bank is shown in the annual *Index of Publications*, which contains an alphabetical title list and indexes of subjects, authors, and countries and regions. The latest edition is available free of charge from Distribution Unit, Office of the Publisher, The World Bank, 1818 H Street, N.W., Washington, D.C. 20433, U.S.A., or from Publications, The World Bank, 66, avenue d'Iéna, 75116 Paris, France.

Margaret E. Grosh is an economist with the Poverty and Human Resources Division of the Policy Research Department at the World Bank.

Cover design by Sam Ferro

Library of Congress Cataloging-in-Publication Data

Grosh, Margaret E.
    Administering targeted social programs in Latin America : from
platitudes to practice / Margaret E. Grosh.
        p. cm.
    Includes bibliographical references.
    ISBN 0-8213-2620-1
    1. Human services—Latin America.   2. Latin America—Social
policy.   I. Title.
HV110.5.G76   1994
361'.0068—dc20   93-40676
                                                           CIP

Contents

Boxes

Figures

Tables

Acknowledgments

A great many people have helped me get this study from its beginning to its end. George Psacharopoulos encouraged me to start the work. He, Julian Schweitzer, Emmanuel Jimenez and almost everyone I worked with for the past two years have gracefully accommodated the delays in other tasks that I incurred in finding time to finish this one. Judy Baker assisted through most of the project. Her help extended beyond both the call of duty and her term of employment on the study. Judy Baker, Rodrigo Cisneros, Haydee Garcia, Gerard Laforgia, Antonio Sancho, Juan Diego Trejos, Isabel Vial and Gustavo Yamada wrote the case studies that form the basis of much of the synthesis provided here. Fiona Mackintosh helped in all aspects of substance and process as editor. Barbara Diallo, Marta Ospina and Maria Eugenia Quintero did the document processing and layout. Participants in two courses sponsored by the Economic Development Institute, as well as those in several internal World Bank seminars, have helped me to clarify my thoughts and their presentation. I benefited from exceptionally detailed, thoughtful and constructive comments from Harold Alderman, Paul Glewwe, Emmanuel Jimenez, Steen Jorgensen, Linda McGinnis, Philip Musgrove, Kimberly Nead, Sandra Rosenhouse, Julian Schweitzer, Dominique van de Walle and Jacques van der Gaag, as well as from the case study authors and three anonymous reviewers. I will remain in their debt far into the future. Any remaining flaws are mine, and are probably due to my inability to absorb all of the excellent advice so generously provided.

1

Introduction

The conceptual issues of targeting are well understood. Whether, how and how much to target social services or subsidies to the poor depends on balancing the benefits and costs in a given set of circumstances. The benefit of targeting is that it can concentrate expenditures allocated to poverty alleviation or social programs on those who need them most. This saves money and improves program efficiency. The costs are the administrative costs of identifying potential beneficiaries, possible economic losses due to disincentive effects and any loss of political support for the program. It is often assumed that, as the accuracy of targeting and hence the benefits increase, the associated costs will increase as well (see Besley and Kanbur 1990 for a clear exposition of the issues).

Knowledge of the size of the tradeoffs faced in real programs, however, is scarce. Latin American governments have recently become markedly more interested in targeting their social expenditures than they were in past decades. Now that serious attempts are being made to target social expenditures, practical questions are arising about how best to do so. Which targeting mechanisms provide the best targeting outcomes? What are their administrative costs? What are their administrative options and requirements? These, and a host of subsidiary questions, are the focus of this study. It is designed to fill the gaps in our knowledge of the practicalities of administering targeted programs. It should also help to determine whether expectations of targeting success or administrative failure are realistic and what it takes to make targeting work.

This book[1] synthesizes information drawn from 23 case studies commissioned for this comparative work[2] and from other sources on seven additional programs. The programs were selected on the basis of three criteria. First, programs that would represent a mix of targeting mechanisms and benefit types were sought. Second, programs for which incidence information would be available were given priority. Third programs for which a case study could be produced at low cost were preferred. While the resulting mix of case studies is neither scientifically chosen

1

nor exhaustive, it is, to the author's knowledge, the most complete compilation of comparable quantitative information available in the literature.

Of the 30 social sector programs in 11 Latin American countries reviewed here, eight deliver food commodities or subsidies, three deliver school lunches, five deliver food stamps, three deliver free or reduced-cost health services or health insurance, three deliver student loans or fee waivers, three deliver cash, two provide jobs, two provide daycare and one provides mortgages. Most have national coverage, and most are government programs, though a few are run by nongovernmental organizations. About half have either been newly established or have had their implementation substantially reformed in the past five years. Several of the new programs were specifically motivated by increases in poverty in the 1980s or by the need to mitigate the social costs of macroeconomic adjustment programs. According to the terminology developed in Chapter 4, 17 of the programs use individual assessment mechanisms, seven use group mechanisms and six are self-targeted. Table 1.1 provides a brief guide to the programs included.

The study focuses on the targeting outcomes and the administrative costs, options and requirements of targeting mechanisms in a variety of social programs in Latin America. It is designed to shed much-needed light on how administrative considerations affect whether and how to target social programs. In order to maintain this focus, the study leaves aside many topics that are important and that are often the dominant themes in discussions of targeting and social programs. Specifically, this study does not attempt to cover the political and economic incentive considerations in the choice among targeting mechanisms. Nor does it address the issue of which services or benefits a government should provide, or attempt to measure the net benefits of services after accounting for the direct and indirect effects of expenditures on them and of the taxes that support them. Thus, the study supplies information on only a few dimensions of the complex issue of which services to provide and whether and how to target them. In concentrating on the administrative issues involved in the implementation of alternate targeting mechanisms, the study is able to cover a large variety of programs. To have tried to cover the omitted issues here would have detracted from the purpose of this work and would have necessitated reducing the number of case studies we covered to the few for which full evaluations are available.

This study assumes that all the programs were aimed generally at the poor and that targeting a food supplement program is much the same as targeting a cash transfer program or an education program. All of these interventions have an element of income transfer that should be directed to the poor. All of these programs are made more effective by concentrating their benefits on those who need them most. All face the same problems in balancing improvements in targeting outcomes against the costs of targeting. And regardless of the sector of intervention, the menus of targeting options are similar.

Table 1.1 Inventory of Programs

Country	Full Program Name	Type of Program Benefit	Number of Beneficiaries per Year	Scope	Total Annual Cost per Beneficiary (US$)	Targeting Mechanism
Belize	Belize Hospital Fee Waivers	Hospital Fee Waivers	—	National	—	School Worker Evaluation
Bolivia	Bolivia Emergency Social Fund (ESF)	Employment	48,000 person months per year	National	—	Self-selection (by employment)
Chile	Subsidio Unico Familiar (CAS-SUF) (Unified Family Subsidy)	Cash Transfer	887,000	National	$39	Proxy Means Test
Chile	Pensiones Asistenciales (CAS-PASIS) (Pension Assistance Program)	Cash Transfer	292,000	National	$32	Proxy Means Test
Chile	Viviendas-Basicas (CAS) (Basic Housing Program)	Cash Transfer (Mortgage)	20,500	National	$4,100	Proxy Means Test
Chile	Programa de Alimentacion Escolar (PAE) (School Feeding Program)	School Lunch	570,000	National	$75	Geographic (by school)
Chile	Programas Especiales de Empleo (PEM & POJH) (Special Employment Programs)	Employment	117,000	National	$170-380	Self-selection (by employment)
Chile	Programa Nacional de Alimentacion Complementaria (PNAC) (National Food Supplement Program)	Food Supplement	1,240,000	National	$40	Self-selection (by health services)
Colombia	Colombia Institute of Credit and Training Abroad (ICETEX)	Student Loan	48,000	National	$700	Means Test
Costa Rica	Centros de Nutrition (CEN/CENAI) (Nutrition Centers)	Daycare, Food Supplement	58,000	National	$265	Nutritional Risk

(continued)

3

Table 1.1 (continued)

Country	Full Program Name	Type of Program Benefit	Number of Beneficiaries per Year	Scope	Total Annual Cost per Beneficiary (US$)	Targeting Mechanism
Costa Rica	Comedores Escolares (School Lunch Program)	School Lunch	450,000	National	$22	Geographic (by school)
Costa Rica	Programa de Asegurados por Cuenta del Estado (Program for State-sponsored Health Insurance)	Free Health Insurance	299,000	National	$132	Social Worker Evaluation
Costa Rica	Pensiones no Contributivas (Non-contributory Pensions)	Cash Transfer	74,000	National	$350	Social Worker Evaluation
Costa Rica	Becas Universidad de Costa Rica (Scholarships at the University of Costa Rica)	University Tuition Waiver	25,000	U. of Costa Rica	$88	Proxy Means Test
Dominican Republic	Hospital Fee Waiver	Hospital Fee Waiver	—	Selected Hospitals	—	Social Worker Evaluation
Dominican Republic	Proyecto Materno - Infantil (PROMI) (Mother-Child Project)	Maternal and Child Health	36,000	3 Rural Regions	$61	Nutritional Risk
Honduras	Bono de Madre Jefe de Familia (BMJF) (Food Stamps for Female-headed Households)	Food Stamps	125,000	9 States	$40	Means Test
Honduras	Bono Materno - Infantil (BMI) (Food Stamps for Mothers and Infants)	Food Stamps	60,000	3 Health Regions	$50	Self-selection (health services)
Jamaica	Food Stamps Program (Means Tested)	Food Stamps	200,000	National	$55	Means Test
Jamaica	Food Stamps Program (Health Services)	Food Stamps	200,000	National	$40	Self-selection (health services)
Jamaica	Student Loan Program	Student Loan	2,520	National	$784	Means Test

4

Jamaica	Nutribun Program	School Feeding	153,000	National	$37	Geographic (by school)
Mexico	Leche Industrializada Compania Nacional de Subsistencias Populares (LICONSA) (National Subsistence Commodities' Industrialized Milk Program)	Subsidized Milk Ration	10,000,000	National (Urban)	$20	Means Test and Nutritional Risk
Mexico	Tortivales	Free Tortilla Ration	13,500,000	National (Urban)	$26	Means Test
Peru	Comedores Populares (Soup Kitchens)	Communal Soup Kitchen	2,450,000	National (Urban)	$23	Geographic (by neighborhood)
Peru	Programa de Alimentacion y Nutricion para Familias de Alto Riesgo (PANFAR) (Nutrition and Feeding Program for High Risk Families)	Food Supplement	513,000	National	$17	Nutritional Risk
Peru	Vaso de Leche (Glass of Milk)	Food Supplement	2,900,000	National	$9	Geographic (by neighborhood)
Venezuela	Programa Beca Alimentaria (Food Scholarship Program)	Food Stamp	2,300,000	National	$175	Geographic (by school)
Venezuela	Programa Hogares de Cuidado Diario (Daycare Program)	Daycare	106,000	National	$565	Geographic (by neighborhood)
Venezuela	Programa Alimentario Materno Infantil (PAMI) (Maternal Child Feeding Program)	Food Supplement	500,000	National	$180	Self-selection (health services)

— Not available.

5

There are, of course, ways in which targeting differs depending on the type of intervention involved. Perhaps most importantly, the target groups themselves may differ. A basic health intervention may have as the target group those who are sick. A safety net program may aim to reach those who are poor. A program with hybrid objectives may aim to reach those among the poor who are sick. In evaluating programs, for maximum accuracy, it is important to distinguish clearly whether they are aimed at the sick, the poor or the poor who are sick (with obvious parallels for nutrition and education). Here, however, the target group is taken to be the poor.

Note

1. An earlier version of this study, Latin America and the Caribbean Technical Department, Regional Studies Program, Report #215, in Spanish is available from the World Bank Latin America and the Caribbean Information Center.

2. These are compiled in Grosh (1992a), Vol.2. The depth of the information contained in each study varies according to how well documented the programs are and the extent to which they have been evaluated. In the case of the many very new programs included, no evaluations have yet been done of their incidence, coverage or impact. But the models they provide of new targeting mechanisms and the problems involved in starting new programs are valuable nonetheless. Half of the case studies are in English and half are in Spanish. There is at least one case study in each language for most of the targeting mechanisms discussed.

2

In Theory:
Costs and Benefits of Targeting

What Is Targeting?

In this book, targeting refers specifically to the identification of those who will or will not be eligible for a social program. Targeting carries with it the idea that some groups of individuals should be excluded from receiving the program benefit. Policymakers are most often concerned with delivering welfare transfers (either cash or in-kind) to the poor. In contrast, in health programs, it may be the ill or those who are at risk who are targeted.

The choice of and identification of those in the target group can be thought of separately from the actual delivery of the service to them. Consider a targeted school lunch program. The targeting aspect of the program consists of choosing those who should receive the free lunch and those who should be excluded. The service delivery aspect of the program includes decisions about how many calories to provide in each lunch, what food to buy and how to hire cooks. Conceptually, the distinction is fairly clear, though in practice, decisions about one aspect often have implications for the other. Since targeting is only one aspect of a social program, judging the success or failure of targeting is not equivalent to making judgements about the program as a whole. A program may choose the right children to feed, but if it serves them expensive foods or too few calories, the school lunch program will not be successful.

Benefits of Targeting

The goal of targeting is to concentrate resources on those who need them most. A cash transfer given to a rich person, for example, does not reduce poverty and thereby wastes the resources of a poverty alleviation program. If benefits go only to the poor, the level of benefit given to each recipient can be higher or the cost of the program can be reduced.

Let us take an example. Suppose a country has 15 million people, of whom 3 million are poor. It has a budget for poverty programs of $150 million. If it used that money in an untargeted program, then each poor person would get $10. Of the $150 million, four-fifths would go to the nonpoor. If the country had a perfectly targeted program, the resources would go only to the poor. With a $150 million budget, each poor person would get $50, much more than in the case of the untargeted program. Another alternative would be for the government to continue to give each poor person $10 and thus to save $120 million.

The possibility that targeting can save money may lead to a further benefit—the possibility of reducing inefficiencies in the economy (deadweight losses) caused by the taxes that finance the subsidy. Measuring the benefits of deadweight losses requires a full analysis of the tax system, which is beyond the scope of this study. Rather, we let the budget savings serve as a minimum estimate of the total savings to the economy.

Good targeting also means that most of the poor are reached by the program. If many were left out, the program's impact on poverty would be reduced commensurately. Thus good targeting improves both the cost-effectiveness of a program and its impact on welfare.

Costs of Targeting

While targeting is beneficial in that it increases the efficiency of poverty and social programs, it also has costs. Broadly, there are three kinds of costs: administrative, incentive and political. Only by assessing the costs and benefits of each targeting mechanism is it possible to determine the targeting outcome for which it is best to aim.

Administrative Costs

Targeting requires some mechanism to distinguish between the poor, so that they can be given a benefit, and the nonpoor, so that they can be prevented from getting the benefit. This mechanism incurs costs. In general, the more exact is the sorting of the poor from the nonpoor, the more likely it is that the administrative costs of targeting will be high.

For example, to identify the poor and the nonpoor perfectly, the welfare of every individual in the population would have to be examined. This examination would include careful consideration of seasonal and in-kind income, household composition, local prices, the value of assets and so on and would require that this information be verified. This is hard to do and would probably be very expensive. Indeed, it has not been attempted. An imperfect means test would examine the incomes only of those who applied for a program and would ignore issues such as seasonal and in-kind income and verification. This would be cheaper to administer, but would separate the poor from the nonpoor only imperfectly. A mechanism that would have even lower administrative costs would be one that gave benefits to everyone living in regions that are poorer than average. However, this would miss out all the poor people in the wealthy regions and would give benefits to the wealthy individuals in poor regions.

The extent of administrative costs it is worth incurring in order to improve the incidence of a program depends not only on how well the mechanism sorts the poor from the nonpoor, but also on the value of the benefit to be delivered. While it is not worth paying $10 per person to screen out ineligible candidates for a program that provides only $5 in benefits per person, it is worth paying $10 per person to screen out ineligible candidates for a program that provides $100 in benefits per person.

Administrative costs will vary by the type of mechanism used, the level of existing information and the institutional capacity with which the country starts as well as the local costs of the personnel and equipment needed to carry out the targeting. Quantifying these costs for a range of programs and countries is a major emphasis of this work.

Incentive Effects

Targeting schemes can have incentive effects that are side effects of their principal goal of sorting the poor from the nonpoor. They result from changing the implicit prices and rewards faced by households or individuals and, therefore, their economic behavior.[2] Some of these changes will be positive for the economy, and some negative. This study does not attempt to quantify incentive costs for all the programs reviewed here. Rather, this section is designed as a brief sketch of the issue so that the reader will be aware of the "forest" that surrounds the "trees" that will be studied in detail.

Three major negative incentive effects that offset the benefits of targeting are frequently discussed—labor-leisure choice, relocation and unproductive use of time or resources. How likely it is that any of these disincentives will arise and to what extent depends on the degree of perfection of the targeting, the size of the benefit and the special features of the program.

The labor-leisure choice problem is an issue encountered in programs targeted according to an income criterion. Imagine a program that uses a means test and has an eligibility threshold of $250 of income or less. The benefit given is $50. All those persons who, in the absence of the program, would earn from $250 to $299 would be better off working less so that they could fall under the $250 threshold and receive the $50 transfer. Their income would thereby be higher *and* they would have more leisure. As individuals, they would be better off, but society as a whole would lose the output of the work they no longer do. Since program planners usually do not value the leisure of participants, this would be counted as a loss. Furthermore, the number of beneficiaries would increase from the original number whose incomes were below the threshold to include those who would work less in order to become eligible.

This problem is even more severe if the amount of benefit depends on the individual's income. If the poverty line is $250 and the program promised to raise income to that point, then no one under the poverty line would want to work, as they would face a 100 percent marginal tax rate on their earned income (see Besley and Kanbur 1990 and Kanbur, Keen and Tuomala 1992 for a more detailed treatment).

The labor-disincentive problem has been an important concern in industrial countries. In reviewing the evidence for the United States' Aid to Families with Dependent Children (AFDC) program, Moffitt (1992) reports that few female heads of household who were ineligible for AFDC benefits seemed to lower their hours of work in order to become eligible; this effect may increase the case load by 5 percent at the most. However, he reports clearer evidence that AFDC recipients themselves reduce the number of hours that they work. Econometric models of the labor disincentive provide a range of estimates of the effect of a reduction in work effort of between 1 and 10 hours per week. The midpoint disincentive estimate of 5.4 hours per week would imply a 30 percent reduction in work effort.

The labor-leisure choice problem may be less important in many poverty programs in developing countries than it is in the case of the AFDC. First, means tests are rare. The labor disincentive problem does not arise when characteristics that are less subject to manipulation than income (such as age or sex) are used to target programs instead of means tests. Second, the means tests used in programs such as those reviewed here are imperfect. When screening is imperfect, workers may not have such strong incentives to reduce their work effort. Third, because very few programs have graduated benefit levels, the high marginal tax problem does not often apply. Finally, the small size of the one or two fixed benefit levels means that the number of people whose incomes fall between the eligibility threshold and the threshold plus the benefit (in other words, those who would have an incentive to change their behavior) are few.

Relocation is another incentive that can be undesirable. If benefits are targeted geographically, people can have an incentive to move from places not covered by the program to those that are. Imagine a country with two regions, one with an average income of $100 per person and another with an average income of $300 per person. The government might decide to target a program to all those in the first region. If the poorer people in the rich region then move to the poor region in order to get the benefit, program costs would increase. This would be justified because more of the poor would be covered. But if rich people from the rich region were to move to the poor region so that they too would get benefits, then program costs would be increased without justification. If, in addition to incurring private costs to those who move, the relocation caused problems such as congestion in service delivery mechanisms, reduction in the number of benefits available per eligible person or unemployment, the net costs to society could be large.

The extent of relocation effects depends on the size of the private benefit gained relative to the private costs of moving. In developing countries, the overall package of services and amenities in cities may help to draw people to urban areas from rural areas. Whether one individual program targeted to poor areas (rural areas or urban slums) would cause sizable or deleterious relocation effects is more doubtful. In the United States, the choice of residence within urban areas is clearly affected by differences in service quality, especially of public schools.

Other examples of unproductive behavior prompted by targeting mechanisms can be found. If food supplements are based on children's nutritional status, mothers might have an incentive to underfeed their children before weighing to ensure that they are underweight and the family will continue to get the food. Dreze and Sen (1989) speculate that this may occur. In Chile, field workers sometimes cite this happening in the PNAC program, but there is no scientific evidence that it does happen (Vial, personal communication). If eligibility for programs were based on features of housing quality (such as the number of rooms in a house or the availability of running water and sewage treatment facilities) or the ownership of durable goods (such as cars, televisions and refrigerators), then families who could afford these things might choose not to have them in order to stay eligible for the program's benefits. Where gasoline is subsidized and lines for it are long, people have an incentive to buy large gas tanks so that they can get the most subsidy for each trip through the queue.

In contrast to the negative incentive effects just reviewed, targeted programs can also cause positive incentive effects. The most common such effect for the programs reviewed here is that linking food stamps or food supplements to maternal-child health care can encourage the use of preventive health care services. In the Honduran food stamp program, for example, children under the age of five and pregnant or lactating women in poor areas can receive food stamps if they receive regular preventive check-ups at the public health clinic. Thus, these people have an incentive to avail themselves of more preventive health care. In fact, use of services increased by 131 percent in the pilot clinics when the program began. Although this effect on the use of services is not documented in all cases, similar mechanisms are used for the Chilean PNAC, Venezuelan PAMI, Honduran BMI, Jamaican Food Stamps, Peruvian PANFAR and Dominican PROMI (see Chapters 5 and 7).

Little attention has been given in the targeting literature to such positive incentive effects. In the Latin American programs reviewed in this study, the targeting criterion was more often one that would encourage the use of basic health or education services than one that would provide a high marginal tax rate and thus discourage work effort. It is to be hoped that as these programs mature and they are evaluated, our knowledge of their positive incentive effects will deepen.

Political Economy

Targeting raises important issues of political economy. The one that is most frequently discussed is the link between targeting, political power and the consequences for the program's resources. Another important issue is how the interests of the different actors involved in administering the program will shape how it is implemented. Again, this study was not designed to cast new light on these issues, so this section must suffice to remind the reader of their importance in making a full evaluation of any program.

Many discussions of targeting (see, for example, Besley and Kanbur 1990, Alderman 1991 and Ravallion 1992) assume that an individual's political support for a program is determined by whether or how much that individual may benefit from it and that the poor have little political voice. Thus, if a program is well targeted to the poor and the poor are relatively disenfranchised, the program may have little political support and a correspondingly small budget. In contrast, a program that provides enough benefits to the middle class may garner their support and thus enable it to have a bigger budget. Even after allocating a share of the benefits to the middle class, the budget left for the poor may still be bigger than it might be if the budget depended only on their political support. Thus, good targeting might sometimes run counter to the interests of the poor.

Before targeted programs are judged to be altogether politically unsustainable, it is important to consider whether serious attempts have been made to offset the handicap and, indeed, whether the postulated basis for support is accurate.

Let us examine the Colombian and Sri Lankan food stamp programs to see how a change in targeting and other factors can affect a program's size. These two programs are frequently cited as illustrations of the phenomenon whereby good targeting leads to program shrinkage. Although the relatively weak political voice of the poor may have affected the fate of these programs, strategic and circumstantial factors apparently also contributed to the programs being reduced. This suggests that, if governments can manipulate factors of political economy in the interest of dismantling a program, program designers should also be able to manipulate these factors when designing a program.

In Sri Lanka, subsidized rice rations were available to the whole population until 1978. At that time, as part of a program of broad economic liberalization, the government undertook to reform the subsidy system and ultimately to reduce its fiscal burden. In a preliminary move, the value of the subsidy was increased. Then, in the first major reform step, rice rations were limited to those with a self-declared income of below Rs 300 per month (which constituted about half the population). Eighteen months later, the rice ration was replaced by a food stamp that was initially worth 15 to 20 percent more than the ration had been. Once denominated in rupees rather than kilos, the real value of the food stamps eroded steadily with inflation.

Many who discuss the case paint a clear picture of how good targeting led to the erosion of the program's political support and, in turn, to the erosion of its real value. Hopkins (1988) draws an additional lesson by showing how details of the reform process were crafted to improve its political viability. In each of the two major reform steps, the value of the subsidy was first increased, countering possible opposition to the change in the form of the benefit by an increase in its value. The reform program was started in a time of growth so consumers were not especially anxious about their subsidy benefits. The cabinet ministers who were least committed to the reforms were placed on the technical committees that were to develop the concrete proposals. In this way they came to hold a stake in the reforms. The erosion of benefit levels by inflation was gradual, there were no political flashpoints around which to catalyze interests. Finally, the major issues on the political stage had changed from those of economic policy to regional and ethnic issues. While good targeting may have contributed to the program's shrinkage, it was not the only factor.

The Colombian food stamp program (1975–82) is another example that is often cited of good targeting leading to a program's demise. By most accounts, the food stamp program was successful in terms of efficiency, management and nutrition criteria. Yet after a change in government, it was discontinued. In addition to its effective targeting to the rural poor who have a weak political voice, one may speculate about the role of other factors. The program was new, having been initiated by the previous administration. Thus, it might have been viewed as something of a stepchild by the incoming government of the opposition party. Moreover, its very newness implies that the beneficiaries may not have had time to consider the program to be part of their "rights" under the basic social contract. This presumably contributed to the quiescent acceptance of the withdrawal of the program. Furthermore, the administration of the program was moved to the Ministry of Agriculture whose interest was more in food production than in household nutrition or health. The food stamps did not serve the ministry's traditional client groups. Finally, the program's external support had drawn to a close, so it became more of a burden on the Colombian government.

The political support for a program may also be influenced by the taxpayer-voter's assessment of its effectiveness. On this basis, even when the taxpayer-voter is unlikely to benefit from any of the program options personally, s/he is more inclined to favor the well-targeted programs, as they require a lower tax burden to sustain them. Furthermore, any altruism or social conscience that s/he may feel will prompt the taxpayer-voter to support targeted programs.

In some cases, an important part of the support for a program may come not from those who receive the benefits but rather from those who supply the inputs. For example, the influence of the farm lobby and the need to distribute excess farm commodities have always driven United States food programs, both domestic and international (see Atkinson 1991, Ballenger and Harold 1991, and Hopkins 1988). In such cases, the interests of the supplier lobby, either alone or in combination with the beneficiary lobby, may be sufficient to sustain the program.

In addition, the implementation of a program may be affected by those more directly involved with the program itself, such as the managers, staff, central planners and international funding agencies. This facet of political economy is less often discussed, but is clearly important.

In the Jamaican food stamp program, for example, one part of the program is targeted through primary health clinics to children under the age of five and to pregnant or lactating women. Health care workers have refused to do the extra work of registration or to distribute food stamps on the grounds that they are already overworked and underpaid. The makeshift arrangements whereby staff from the Ministry of Labour, Welfare and Sport register participants at clinics are cumbersome, and the extra time and transport costs the potential beneficiaries must incur discourage some from participating. Thus, nurses' interests worked to exclude intended beneficiaries from the program.

A contrasting example is the part of the Honduran food stamps program that is run through the school system. Primary school teachers identify participants on the basis of enrollment, a simple means test and household headship. Measuring income is highly inexact, and determining whether a household is female-headed leaves some room for interpretation. Given that parents protest when their children do not benefit, teachers have an incentive to interpret the guidelines very liberally. Thus, the teachers' interest is to give food stamps to many children, while the program administrators may wish to exclude those who are not as needy as others.

Factors of political economy will affect decisions about whether and how to target programs. Furthermore, these factors may influence long-run support for these programs and the way in which their designs are implemented on the ground. While clearly important, these issues are not addressed in detail in this study.

Note

1.   These are—in addition to the incentive effects inherent in the receipt of subsidy— changes in savings, private transfers and the labor-leisure choice from the income effect of the subsidy.

3

Methods for Judging Outcomes

To judge whether the benefit of a good targeting outcome is worth the administrative, incentive or political economy costs incurred in achieving it, it is necessary to measure these costs and benefits and to weigh them against one another. Because the focus of this study is on program administration and its link to targeting outcomes, this chapter will discuss only how to measure administrative costs and targeting outcomes. The first two sections explain these in some detail. The sections are meant as a primer for the reader unfamiliar with the techniques. The third section of the chapter describes the methods and data used in this study and discusses their limitations and consequences.

Issues in Measuring Targeting Accuracy

To measure the accuracy of a targeting initiative, it is necessary to define the target group, to find out the number of targeting errors and to aggregate that information. There is an entire literature on these themes (see, for example, Ravallion 1992 and Gill, Jimenez and Shalizi 1990), but a brief summary of the issues is provided here.

Defining the Target Group

The first task is to ensure that the group to be targeted is precisely defined. If the program is aimed only at the poor, a poverty line must be set. Since most poverty programs in developing countries use some proxy for poverty to establish eligibility, no rigorous poverty line is defined. This does not necessarily hinder the business of delivering a targeted service, but it may distort assessments of the success of targeting.

For example, many programs are targeted to children under the age of five who use public health clinics. The use of public health clinics is the proxy for poverty. It is, however, inexact. Some nonpoor children use the clinics. Whether a food ration given to such a child constitutes a targeting error depends upon whether the goal was to reach the poor or to reach the children. Even if there is a consensus that reaching only poor children is the goal and that giving a ration to a nonpoor child is a targeting error, a precisely defined poverty line may still not be drawn.

Concepts of Targeting Accuracy

The information used to determine program eligibility is usually only a very inexact proxy for the individual's real welfare. Thus, some poor people will be missed by the program, and some nonpoor people will be served. This problem gives rise to the need to measure targeting accuracy.

One way of classifying targeting outcomes is to look at all individuals at once and to divide them into four categories as shown in Figure 3.1. Those who are poor and do receive benefits are a targeting success. In this example, 30 percent of the population falls into this category. Those who are not poor and do not receive benefits are likewise a targeting success (here, 40 percent of the population). Those who are poor but do not receive benefits are counted as an error of exclusion or type I error (here, 10 percent). The nonpoor who do receive benefits are counted as an error of inclusion or type II error (here, 20 percent). This categorization is most often used in technical literature and may be somewhat unfamiliar to program managers.

Figure 3.1   Program Outcomes

	Poor	Not poor	
Served	Success	Type II (inclusion) error	
	30	20	50
Not served	Type I (exclusion) error	Success	
	10	40	50
	40	60	100

Another way of measuring the same phenomenon is to calculate leakage and undercoverage rates. Rather than looking at all individuals at once, this approach starts by looking at subgroups.

Leakage is calculated by looking at all those who are in the program. (In Figure 3.1, this is equivalent to looking only at the top row.) Then, the number of non-poor beneficiaries is divided by the total number of people served. In this case, the leakage rate is 40 percent (20/50).

To estimate undercoverage, we start by looking at the poor who ought to be in the program. (In Figure 3.1, this is equivalent to looking only at the left column.) Then, the number of the poor who ought to be in the program but who were erroneously left out is divided by all those who are poor. In this case, the undercoverage rate is 25 percent (10/40). The complement of undercoverage is coverage, that is, the percentage of those who ought to be served who are served. This is sometimes called the participation rate. Here, it would be 75 percent (30/40).

Reporting Targeting Accuracy

Calculating errors of inclusion and exclusion is the most complete way of evaluating targeting outcomes. However, it requires a firmly-defined poverty line, which may not exist. It also requires knowing as much about those who do not benefit from a program as about those who do, which is also not always possible. Furthermore, comparisons among programs with different poverty lines are somewhat difficult to interpret. We will, therefore, review a somewhat simpler way of judging targeting outcomes.

INCIDENCE. Incidence looks at the division of total benefits across the income distribution. If a poverty line is fixed, then the errors of inclusion can be calculated from the incidence information. But even without fixing the poverty line, it is possible to judge which of two programs has better incidence and lower leakage.

Table 3.1 shows a typical incidence comparison. It is interpreted as follows. Of all people receiving benefits in Program A, 30 percent are in the poorest quintile (that is, the poorest 20 percent) of the population. Twenty-five percent of the beneficiaries of Program A are in the second poorest quintile of the population. The row will add up to 100 percent, or all the beneficiaries of the program. Of all the people in Program B, 45 percent are in the poorest quintile of the population and so on.

Table 3.1   Incidence of Two Programs: Population Quintiles

	Poorest				*Richest*	
	1	*2*	*3*	*4*	*5*	*National*
Program A	30	25	25	15	10	100
Program B	45	30	12	9	4	100

If we knew that the poverty line was set to include the first and second quintiles, then we could say that 55 percent of the benefits of Program A go to the target group and that 45 percent of them leak away to the nontarget group. For this poverty line, Program B's leakage would be just 25 percent of the benefits. With or without precisely defined poverty lines, in this example, it is possible to say that Program B has more progressive incidence than Program A.

When poverty lines differ, incidence can be a better means of making comparisons than strictly calculated errors of inclusion. Suppose that these programs are in different countries with different poverty lines. Country A has set its poverty line to take in the first and second quintile, while in Country B, only the first quintile would fall below the poverty line. In this case, Program A's leakage (benefits accruing to quintiles 3–5) would be 45 percent of benefits whereas Program B's leakage (benefits accruing to quintiles 2–5) would be 55 percent of leakage. Expressed this way, Program B performs less well than Program A, but purely because it is being judged by a higher standard.

In this book, we label as progressive a distribution of benefits that gives a higher proportion of benefits to the poor than the proportion of the population that they represent.[1] Careful calculations of incidence will take into account whether the value of the benefit received differs by each individual, especially where there are systematic differences among income groups. With general food price subsidies, for example, most individuals may benefit, but the rich buy more food and thereby benefit more than the poor. Meaningful calculation of incidence for price subsidies, therefore, requires that the value of the benefit be factored in, as well as the access to it. Except in the case of food subsidies, this is usually not done. For distributions of health care use or public education, it is usual merely to see who uses the systems rather than also factoring in whether the value received is equal. The implicit assumption of equal value is required by limitations in the readily available data. Where the poor tend to receive services of lower value (for example, poorly equipped and overcrowded schools) than the nonpoor, the incidence may seem more progressive than if the benefits were measured more accurately. We will show the importance of these issues in Chapter 8.

Our discussion so far has implicitly assumed that the person who directly receives the program benefit keeps its full value. It may be, however, that the receipt of the subsidy causes changes in the behavior of the recipient or other individuals that shift some of the value of the benefit to persons other than the direct beneficiary. Cox and Jimenez (1992) provide an example of the possible importance of this factor in a program similar to those studied here. They predict that, in Peru, private intrafamily transfers may fall by as much as 20 percent when the elderly members of the family receive social security. The social security program thus provides an indirect benefit to the younger generation who reduce their support to their elders, and the older generation's welfare is improved by less than the amount of the social security payment. Few studies of welfare programs in developing countries carry out the economic modeling required to account for benefit shifting, but methods are available to do so and are often used in evaluating taxes in industrial countries. McLure (1975) is a basic reference from the tax literature on these issues. Selden and Wasylenko (1990) and Gill, Jimenez and Shalizi (1990) review the implications of this benefit shifting in government transfer programs.

The discussion has also ignored the source of revenues. To consider the tax side would entail studying the incentive effects of the taxes and the distribution of the tax burden, which can be studied with methods parallel to those for the subsidies they support. A common simplifying assumption is that the issue under study is alternate uses of existing revenues, rather than the decision about whether to raise taxes to finance a new program. (Pechman 1985 provides a simple description of the common simplifications in incidence analysis.) We invoke that assumption here.

PARTICIPATION RATES. Participation rates indicate what fraction of the population benefits from a program. If participation rates among the poor are low, then even if the incidence of a program is excellent, it may not be very effective in combatting poverty because it does not reach very many of the poor. Just as incidence gave us insight into leakage (errors of inclusion), participation rates give us insight into undercoverage (errors of exclusion).

Table 3.2 shows a typical representation of participation rates. It can be interpreted as follows. Of all those in the poorest quintile, 94 percent receive benefits from Program C. Of those in the richest quintile, 26 percent participate in Program C. Overall for the nation, 69 percent of the population participate. The average, not the sum, of the individual quintile participation rates will give the national participation rate.

Note that, from the participation rate, it is possible to derive incidence if the benefits received are uniform. To derive quintile participation rates from incidence tables, it is necessary to know at least the average participation rate.

Three cautionary notes must be made about interpreting participation rates, especially before inferring that low participation rates imply high errors of exclusion.

First, participation rates are most frequently reported using the whole population of each quintile as the denominator. This shows how large the program is so that we can infer whether the program is big enough to have an impact on reducing poverty. However, basing the participation rate on the whole quintile's population implies that the program set out to cover the whole of the poor population. In fact, most programs have set more specific target groups. For example, the program may be targeted to those among the elderly who do not receive social security

Table 3.2   Participation Rates for Two Programs: Population Quintiles

| | *Poorest* | | | | *Richest* | |
	1	*2*	*3*	*4*	*5*	*National*
Program C	94	89	78	58	26	69
Program D	43	35	27	24	16	29

pensions. In that case, rather than the whole quintile, only the elderly who do not have pensions in each quintile are the denominator that should be used. Or the program may be aimed at pregnant women. Even if all pregnant women are reached, because they constitute a small proportion of the total population, participation rates based on the full quintile would be quite low. One might infer that errors of exclusion are large, but this would be a mistaken conclusion based on having used the wrong denominator.

Second, even when the participation rate is low based on an appropriately defined group, caution is needed before inferring that the targeting mechanism inherently leads to high errors of exclusion. It may be that the design is adequate but that administrative and financial constraints lead to worse than ideal outcomes. Take the case of a program that gives out food supplements through health clinics. There is a concern that the poorest people may not come to clinics. Low participation may stem from the fact that the poorest people often face physical, economic or cultural barriers to gaining access to health care. This is an inherent problem of piggybacking a targeted program onto the health care system. But if participation rates are low because the program budget will only cover the first 200 children to sign up in each clinic (thus requiring the clinic to turn down many more who also come to the clinic), this is a financial constraint that is not inherent in the program's design. Raising participation rates (lowering errors of exclusion) would require not a change of targeting mechanism or an improvement in the coverage of the health care system, but more complete financing for the program so that it could fulfill its design.

Finally, in evaluating a country's poverty strategy it is best to consider the joint effect of its various poverty programs. Each may serve only part of the poor population, but if in combination they cover the poor adequately, the fact that each individual program provides only partial coverage may not matter.

QUINTILE CALCULATION AND INTERPRETATION. There are some technical points about how the quintiles[2] are calculated that are important in interpreting results, especially when comparing studies that may have used different techniques.

Individual versus household quintiles. Individual quintiles (or deciles) are calculated by estimating a welfare level for each person and ranking them from highest to lowest. The ranked population is divided into five (or ten) groups of equal size. These are sometimes referred to as population quintiles. Quintiles can also be formed on the basis of households. Households' welfare levels are calculated, and the households are ranked and divided into groups. Because poor households tend to be larger than nonpoor households, the poorer individual-based quintiles will contain fewer households than will the wealthier quintiles. The poorer household-based quintiles will contain more individuals than will the wealthier quintiles.[3]

The apparently greater progressivity when using household quintiles stems from the tendency of poor households to be larger than average. Imagine an economy made up of two households—a poor household with seven members and a rich household with three members. Suppose every person used health care services once. Rank and divide the population into two halves, first on the basis of individuals and then of households. Looking at the distribution by individuals shows that the poorest half of people (five persons) accounted for half (five) of the health visits. Incidence is neutral. Divide the population on the basis of households. The poorest half of households (seven persons) used 70 percent of the health care (seven visits). Incidence is progressive.

The apparent incidence of a program will look different depending on how the quintiles are calculated. For example, the incidence of the public health services in Lima in 1990 is shown in Table 3.3 which reports both individual and household-based quintiles. In both cases, per capita household income was the welfare measure used. The household quintiles make the service look much more progressive than the population quintiles. In this example, using individual quintiles, 11 percent of all public health users fell in the poorest quintile. Using the household quintiles, 29 percent of all public health users fell in the first quintile.

Which kind of quintile is more appropriate? For benefits rendered to individuals, such as health care, individual quintiles are more appropriate. Many programs, however, benefit households. The provision of water or housing subsidies are examples. In those cases, using household quintiles may be appropriate, although analysts debate the point heavily. All agree, however, that it is essential to interpret appropriately whichever quintiles are used. Otherwise, it is easy to draw mistaken conclusions, especially in comparing reports that use quintiles that are calculated differently.

Welfare measure. There are also different options for which welfare measure to use to rank households or individuals. Ranking can be based on income or on expenditure. This may or may not include the imputation of the use value of owner-occupied housing or durable goods. It may or may not be based on adult equivalence scales. It may or may not be posttax and take into account program benefits. Usually, studies are internally consistent, but in comparing studies, the reader should take into account the differences in technique.

Table 3.3   Incidence of Lima's Public Health Care Utilization under Alternate Quintile Definitions

	Poorest				*Richest*
	1	*2*	*3*	*4*	*5*
Per Capita HH Income					
Population Quintiles	11	22	25	23	19
Household Quintiles	29	18	25	15	13
Household Quintiles					
Total Household Income	22	19	23	20	16
Per Capita Household Income	29	18	25	15	13

Source: Author's calculations based on LSMS survey, Lima, Peru (1990).

One of the most important differences to check for is whether households are ranked on the basis of total household income or per capita household income. Since poor households are relatively large and frequently have more than one earner, they may look better off using total household income than using per capita household income. Let us go back to our ten-person, two-household world. Suppose that in the seven-member household, both parents and one of the children work. The total household income is $70 and per capita is $10. In the small household, only one person works making total household income $60 and per capita $20. Ranked by total household income, the big family is in the top half of the income distribution and the small family in the bottom half. If the households are ranked by per capita household income, the ranking is reversed.

Table 3.3 shows how different the incidence of Lima's public health care looks depending on the welfare measure used. The incidence looks less progressive when total household income is used than when per capita household income is used. Some big families with several earners are put farther up the welfare distribution with total household income than they would be if household income per capita were used. Since health care is used by individuals, the shift in the placement of these households can account for disproportionate numbers of health care users.

Life cycle effects. Making adjustments to account for the life cycle of earnings can change the interpretation of some results. James and Benjamin (1987) show that when accounting for life cycle earnings, the conclusion that public expenditures on university education are more regressive than those for secondary education is tempered. Parents of children of university age (expected to be age 40 to 59) are, on average, older than parents of secondary age children (expected to be 35 to 54) and, therefore, more advanced on the parents' age-earnings cycle. James and Benjamin control for this effect by defining quintiles separately for the two age cohorts. In the case of Japan, controlling for age does change the strength of the conclusion that university expenditures are regressive. With current income quintiles, 43 percent of university students fall in the richest quintile. With lifetime cohort quintiles, 30 percent of university students fall in the richest quintile (see Table 3.4).

How large an effect life cycle earnings have on incidence calculations will depend on how steep the age-earnings profile is. Since it is usually less steep for those with lower levels of education and less skilled jobs, it may be somewhat less important in developing countries than in Japan.

How much life cycle earnings affect the setting of program priorities depends partly on how good capital markets are. If families can borrow when they are young and pay back when they are older, then it does not matter much whether the blend of social services is concentrated on those needed by families at the young end of the age-earnings cycle. But if borrowing is constrained, the program mix will matter. Prenatal care and child immunizations will be needed during the young and poor end of the age-earnings cycle and will do no good if postponed. Higher education, on the other hand, will not become an issue until the family is near the height of its earning power. This would be a reason to give more priority to social interventions that benefit younger children rather than older children, even when the interventions are equally important by other criteria.

Table 3.4 Distribution of Students in Japanese Public Education by Current and Lifetime Cohort Quintiles

	Family Income Quintiles				
	1	*2*	*3*	*4*	*5*
Based on Current Family Income					
High School	14	15	17	25	29
University	7	12	7	30	43
Based on Lifetime Cohort Quintiles					
High School	19	17	18	21	24
University	12	12	19	27	30

Source: James and Benjamin (1987), Tables 1 and 3.

Average versus marginal incidence. When thinking about expanding a targeted program, it is important to distinguish between average and marginal incidence. Average incidence is based on those who are currently in the program. Marginal incidence is based on the welfare of possible new entrants into the program. If program coverage were to be expanded, the new entrants might be very similar to those already in the program or they might be somewhat different, depending on how the expansion is to be carried out. Let us take three examples.

First, consider a food supplement scheme that distributes food to infants receiving health care in health posts of the simplest kind that have no doctors. These are found mostly in rural areas or in squatter settlements around major cities. If the program is expanded by increasing the amount of food distributed to the current participants, then the marginal incidence will be the same as the average incidence.[4]

The same food supplement scheme could be expanded by extending its coverage to more sophisticated clinics with doctors and higher quality services, which tend to be concentrated in downtown areas of major cities. In that case, the new entrants in the program may be less poor on average than the original participants. Thus, the marginal incidence would be less progressive than the average incidence.

By contrast, consider the expansion of a sewer system within a city. Before expansion, the system mostly serves the nonpoor who live in the city center. The poor peripheral areas are not reached. The average incidence is, therefore, quite regressive. But expanding the system would bring in a whole new tier of poor people. Thus, the marginal incidence of the expansion could be quite progressive, certainly more so than that of the average incidence before expansion.

The Tradeoff between Leakage and Undercoverage

Lower leakage (inclusion error) is preferable to higher leakage. Lower undercoverage (exclusion error) is preferable to higher undercoverage. Comparing leakage and undercoverage, however, is more difficult. In general, the higher the priority that is given to raising the welfare of the poor, the more important it is to eliminate undercoverage (errors of exclusion). Conversely, the higher the priority that is given to saving limited budget funds, the more important it is to eliminate leakage, that is, to minimize inclusion errors.

In practice, poverty and social programs aim to raise the welfare of the poor as much as possible within their budget constraints. Both kinds of error are, therefore, important, and a firm preference for one over the other is rarely stated by program planners. It is interesting to note that great concern for minimizing errors of exclusion has been a traditional argument in favor of universal subsidies, especially of food prices. With the tighter budgetary constraints of the 1980s and 1990s, many governments are moving toward more targeted programs that will presumably reduce leakage but will introduce the risk of excluding some poor people.

The best way of formalizing the choice between different rates of inclusion and exclusion errors is by using the impact on poverty as the criterion on which to make the decision. The mechanism that most reduces poverty for a given transfer budget is preferred.[5] This approach requires choosing a poverty measure from among the many that are available. We use the Foster-Greer-Thorbecke (FGT) class of poverty measures because it has all the axiomatically desirable properties and contains common and easily understood variables (see Box 3.1 for a brief explanation of the measure and Foster, Greer and Thorbecke 1984 for details).

Now, let us examine an example of how the impact on poverty can be used to weigh the tradeoff between errors of inclusion and errors of exclusion. Grosh and Baker (1992), using Jamaican household survey data, simulate how uniform transfers compare with proxy means tests based on household characteristics such as location, housing quality, family size and ownership of durable goods.

In the simulation, the poverty line is set so that before the transfers, 30 percent of the population is poor. A uniform transfer to all persons would then have an error of exclusion of 0 and an error of inclusion of 70 percent of the population. The proxy means test correctly identifies 17.3 percent of the population as poor and 61.7 percent as nonpoor (see Table 3.5). The error of exclusion would be 12.7 percent of the population, and the error of inclusion would be 8.3 percent of the population. With a budget of J$1 million in this sample economy of 16,000 persons, the uniform transfer can give a benefit of J$73.15 per person. The targeted program with the same budget can provide J$293.68 to recipients. Which is better?

In this example, the gain from reducing leakage and concentrating benefits on the poor outweighs the problem of erroneously excluding some poor from the program. Before the transfer, 30.0 percent of the population were poor ($P_o = 30$). After the uniform transfer, 28.8 percent of the population would be poor. After the (im)perfectly targeted transfer, 27.9 percent of the population would be poor. Thus, the targeted option reduces poverty more than the untargeted program. For the other poverty measures, the improved impact from targeting is even greater.

A Yardstick by Which to Judge Targeting Options

The literature on the principles of targeting usually contrasts targeted services with a benefit that is universally provided. The universal benefit is usually

Box 3.1 Foster-Greer-Thorbecke Poverty Measures

The formula for the FGT poverty index is:

$$P_\alpha = \frac{1}{n} \sum_{i-1}^{q} \left(\frac{Z - y_i}{Z}\right)^{\alpha}$$

where
Z = poverty line
y_i = income of the ith person
q = the number of poor
n = the total population.

The n people in the population are ranked by welfare from poorest to richest: $i = (1, 2 \dots q \dots n)$. The parameter α represents the sensitivity to the income distribution among the poor. When $\alpha = 0$, the FGT measure collapses to the Headcount ratio or the percentage of the population that is below the poverty line. This measure can give estimates of how many of the poor should be served by poverty programs, but is insensitive to differences in the depth of poverty. Suppose the poverty line is $100. There are ten people in the economy and two are poor. The Headcount index will give the same result ($P_0 = .2$) if there are two poor people with incomes of $95 as it would with two incomes of $5, yet clearly, in the latter case poverty is more severe.

When $\alpha = 1$, the FGT index becomes the Poverty Gap, a measure of the depth of poverty. This measures the total income shortfall as a percentage of the poverty line. Thus, in the case of the two poor people with incomes of $95, $P_1 = 0.01$. With two poor people earning $5, P_1 would be 0.19.

The drawback to the Poverty Gap measure is that it will estimate the poverty to be the same when one poor person has an income of $90 and the other an income of $10 as it would when both have an income of $50. Yet most people would agree that the suffering of the extremely poor person with only $10 is worse than that of the poor person with $50 or $90. This is overcome for $\alpha > 1$. Let us use $\alpha = 2$. Then the first case gives $P_2 = 0.082$ and the second gives 0.025. The drawback to using $\alpha = 2$ is that the measure is hard to interpret.

stylized as an equal lump-sum transfer to all individuals. Its incidence is exactly neutral.

In practice, the incidence of "universally provided" services can be far from neutral. Food price subsidies, for example, are usually regressive. The poor buy less food than the rich and thereby obtain less subsidy. Free university education is another example of a service that is theoretically available to all but that in fact benefits mainly the rich. Poor young people rarely have access to the high quality schools that would prepare them for university, and in any case few can afford the loss of income entailed in staying out of the labor market for the length of time it would take to earn a degree. In contrast to these examples of regressive "universal" services, public primary health care is often quite progressive in incidence. Although the nonpoor are eligible to use the services, they are more likely to go to private doctors or to be affiliated with the separate social security system.

Table 3.5   Weighing Type I and II Errors

	Before the Transfer	*Uniform Transfer*	*Imperfect Targeting*
Targeting Accuracy (percent)			
Poor correctly identified		30	17.3
Non-poor correctly identified		0	61.7
Error of exclusion (Type I)		0	12.7
Error of inclusion (Type II)		70	8.3
		100	100
Poverty Outcome			
Benefit per recipient (J$)		$ 73.15	$ 293.68
FGT ($\alpha = 0$)	0.30	0.29	0.28
FGT ($\alpha = 1$)	0.10	0.10	0.08
FGT ($\alpha = 2$)	0.05	0.04	0.03

Source: Grosh and Baker (1992).

This realization that "universally provided" services are not necessarily neutral in incidence has two implications for targeting. First, although we can use a hypothetical lump sum transfer with neutral incidence as the yardstick against which to measure targeted program options, we should bear in mind that the "untargeted" option may, in fact, be much more or less progressive than the neutral yardstick. In discussions about whether or not a targeted program is well targeted, it is sometimes useful to compare its incidence to whatever "universal" service is the most likely alternate use of funds. Second, the common reference to "targeting universally provided services" is not the contradiction in terms it first seems. Rather, it refers to some feature of service provision intended to improve its equity. Some of these will be discussed in Chapter 8.

There is a continuum of targeting from the perfect through the imperfect to none. In this work, we use the general term of targeting to apply to any actions that try to concentrate benefits on the poor end of the income distribution. Most of these schemes are, in fact, quite imperfectly targeted. Rather than always using the cumbersome term "imperfect targeting," we use the general term "targeting" and distinguish the hypothetical case of perfect targeting.

Issues in Quantifying Administrative Costs

To quantify administrative costs it is necessary to identify all of the costs which have an effect on delivering and targeting services. There are both conceptual and practical difficulties with this, as discussed in this section.

In Theory

This study distinguishes two levels of administrative costs that have a bearing on targeting services, and the case studies sought to separate them out. *Total administrative costs* include all costs necessary to *deliver* the targeted benefit. Only part of these, which we will call *targeting costs*, are incurred in the screening process that determines *who* benefits. Consider, for example, a means-tested welfare program. The time that a social worker spends interviewing the client to determine whether she or he is eligible is the cost of targeting. The time and equipment needed to keep track of the beneficiaries once enrolled, to write checks for them and to distribute those checks are part of the general administration of the program and are not strictly related to its targeting.

In calculating targeting costs on a per capita basis, the result may be sensitive to whether the denominator used is the total number of program beneficiaries, the number of applicants or the number of newly approved beneficiaries. How different the results are will depend on the rates of program turnover and applicant rejection.

Let us illustrate, first, the case of program turnover. In most programs, admission is granted for more than a year. Many food programs cover children from birth to the age of five. Several grant eligibility for an unspecified period. Of the means-tested programs, only the Honduran BMJF repeats means tests every year. Suppose a program has 1,000 participants, 900 of whom were admitted in previous years and only 100 this year, the year for which we know that $2,000 was spent on means testing. The targeting costs divided among all participants are $2 per person, but are $20 per person when divided among new entrants.

Next, we consider the influence of the rejection rate. Suppose the above program rejected half of its applicants. In order to admit 100 new entrants, it would have to means test 200 applicants. So the cost per applicant would be $10.

Which of these concepts and numbers should the analyst use? It depends on the purpose. The average cost per beneficiary will give a reasonable estimate of the recurrent costs of a mature program. The average cost per newly admitted beneficiary, however, will give better cost estimates if a new program is to be set up or a major expansion is planned. When comparing on going programs, the rejection rate will not be very important. High rejection rates may make per beneficiary costs look high, but since they also presumably result in good incidence, the effect "comes out in the wash" in the comparison of program cost effectiveness. A planner budgeting for a new means testing campaign will, of course, need to budget for testing applicants who will be rejected.

In Practice

In practice, quantifying administrative costs is not easy. The first problem is that complete, separate budget information is not available for many programs. In many cases, agencies do not keep separate budgets for the several programs they administer. This is especially common in the case of new programs that share overheads with older programs. The new programs are added on to existing administrative structures in order to gain efficiencies and to allow for rapid start-up. For example, a new welfare program may be added to the social security agency. At first, the agency's existing computers, vehicles, management, social workers and clerical staff are used to run the new program, though these resources, on the budget books, are allocated to established programs. So the administrative costs of the new program are difficult to separate out from those of old programs.

Likewise, many targeted programs are the result of the cooperative effort of several institutions. Therefore, the complete costs of all the groups involved may not be aggregated anywhere. The distribution of food aid is perhaps the most important and most complex illustration of this phenomenon. An international agency may donate food and keep track of its value. A national government agency may be responsible for clearing the food through customs and distributing it to a few major points around the country. Then, one or more nongovernmental organizations may be in charge of organizing local groups, setting up distribution rules, providing training and other program components and generally overseeing the use of the food. Many small community groups may be responsible for transporting the food from the major concentration points to their neighborhoods or villages. These groups will also handle the distribution to individual families or the daily preparation of the food. Nowhere are the total administrative costs aggregated.

A second problem in quantifying administrative costs is that it is often difficult to separate out the costs of screening the potential beneficiaries (the targeting costs) from the general administrative costs, which include both the costs of deciding whom to serve with the program benefits and the costs of providing them with the program benefits. Even where it is conceptually clear whether an action is related to screening potential beneficiaries or to delivering a benefit, this distinction is rarely made clear in the records. For example, the program analyst may know the salaries of social workers. But the analyst must then make a rough estimate, based on reports from program staff or field observations, of the proportion of time the social worker spends on means testing as opposed to doing other tasks.

Furthermore, it is sometimes not even conceptually clear whether specific actions are costs of targeting or costs of service provision. For example, consider a program delivered through health clinics and targeted by nutritional status. Originally, the children who attended the clinic were weighed for diagnostic reasons as part of the health service. Then a food supplement program was introduced that gave food to underweight children. Is the cost of weighing the children applicable to the delivery of the health program or to the targeting of the food supplement? In this case, the answer is debatable since the information serves both purposes. If neither the number nor the frequency of weighings change, it may be that the cost should be counted as one of health care provision rather than food supplement targeting since that was its original justification. But the food supplement program may encourage mothers to have their children weighed more often than is required for medical purposes, thus increasing the cost of that activity.

Methods Used in This Study

The following section describes the methods used in this study. It discusses how to determine the success of a program in providing benefits to only the target population; to quantify costs; to calculate the percentage of expenditures that reaches the target population; and the limitations of the methodology used.

Targeting Outcomes

To determine how well a program avoids giving benefits to the non-needy (errors of inclusion), we use incidence. In the tradition of Meerman (1979) and Selowsky (1979),[6] we assume that the full value of the benefit remains with the person who receives it.[7] In some of the case studies, the incidence numbers were the result of original calculations by the case study authors and in others the numbers were taken from published materials. In most of the case studies, household-based quintiles were used, with households ranked on the basis of household per capita income (or consumption). The exceptions are noted in Table 4.2. The incidence estimates come from nationally representative household surveys. The welfare variable is usually labor income. The rankings are postintervention.[8]

In the following discussion, the bottom two quintiles as seen in Table 4.2 are used as an approximate shorthand for the poor. Generally, our results would be the same if only the poorest quintile were used.

To determine whether a program satisfactorily reaches the needy (avoids errors of exclusion), we originally intended to use participation rates, but we decided against doing so for two reasons. First, they were available only for a very few programs so that it was not possible to determine any general trends. Second, it was apparent in several of the cases for which participation rates were available that the participation rates did not measure the general likelihood that the targeting mechanism would succeed or fail in reaching the target group. Rather, they tended to be complicated by administrative idiosyncrasies peculiar to each program and would have provided misleading conclusions about the risks of the targeting mechanism in general. The inability to study errors of exclusion was the major disappointment in this research.

Quantifying Administrative Costs

In quantifying administrative costs for this study, the case study authors were asked to distinguish targeting (screening) costs from total administrative costs. This was not always possible. Records that were incomplete or inseparable hindered the task of getting precise estimates. Despite the care and diligence of the case study authors, the cost figures are only approximate. Where a cost of $5 is shown, another analyst with different informants or judgments might easily come up with an estimate of $3 or $8. But the estimate that costs are in the order of $5, rather than $50 or $100, is probably accurate.

Share of Expenditures Benefitting Target Groups

Because participation rates were reported for so few programs, it was not possible to simulate their effect on poverty. Rather, we calculated the percentage of total program expenditure, including administrative costs, that benefit either the target population or the poorest two quintiles. An example will illustrate the procedure. In Jamaica in 1988, 57 percent of the transfer value of the Food Stamps Program accrued to the poorest two quintiles. But that does not take into account the administrative cost of the targeted program, which constituted about 9 percent of total costs. In order to adjust, take a hypothetical budget of $100 and subtract the $9 administrative overhead. That leaves $91 of transfer value. Fifty-seven percent of $91 is $52. Thus, 52 percent of the total program expenditures of the food stamp program accrued as benefits to the poorest two quintiles.

Methodological Limitations

While this study provides much more information on the magnitude of the administrative costs and incidence obtained in targeting social programs than has previously been available, it does have some methodological limitations. These must be borne in mind in interpreting the data presented. In any future work, it will be important to overcome some of the drawbacks that we faced.

The biggest problem was the *imprecision in calculating administrative costs*. As explained previously, the records on which the calculations reported here were based were not well suited to the task of calculating administrative cost numbers. Small changes in the assumptions, decisions or sources used in the calculations, especially of the targeting costs themselves, could alter the magnitude of the tradeoffs suggested here.

Let us illustrate this sensitivity in the case of food supplement or food coupon programs that are self-targeted through the use of health services. These programs often require the participants to get regular medical checkups. Should we count the time spent by the medical staff on these checkups as part of the cost of the food program or as part of the underlying health service? In the case of the Chilean PNAC, it is probably fair not to count it as a cost of the targeted food program, as the medical staff spend most of their time with participants just providing medical care while the program paperwork and the commodity distribution are done by other staff. In the case of the Honduran BMI, however, the nurses probably spend at least as much of their time with participants on paperwork related to food stamps as on medical care. In Venezuela and Jamaica, the program duties are divided up in a way that makes it easier to decide that medical time should be excluded. If the medical staff's time costs are counted for the Chilean and Honduran programs, the mean share of administrative costs as a percentage of total program costs is 10 percent for programs self-targeted through the use of the health care system.[9] If medical time is not included in either case, administrative costs average 6 percent for this category. If they are included for Honduras but not Chile, the mean is 7.5 percent. We have chosen not to include the time costs of medical staff in our results, though the decision is clearly debatable.

The next issue is that, in the interests of getting a broad overview of targeting experience, *we have compared many programs of different scales, providing a wide variety of kinds and levels of benefits and from countries with different poverty levels and institutional capacities.* Holding all these factors approximately constant and making allowances for varying local prices would give a more precise estimate of the effect of differences among the targeting mechanisms themselves. It is not, however, feasible to hold so many features approximately constant and get results that could be generalized to apply to a wide variety of settings. In this study, we chose to stress breadth of coverage rather than to limit ourselves to fewer but more similar cases.

If the confounding factors such as scale, benefit type and level are uncorrelated with the main variables of interest—administrative costs, targeting outcomes and targeting mechanisms—then our conclusions regarding the latter factors are valid. We bore this in mind in the selection of case studies and were largely successful in avoiding confounding correlations. Graphical presentation (such as those shown in Figures 4.2, 4.6 and 4.7), regression analysis and case-by-case comparisons were used to verify that the confounding correlations are not unduly problematic and that the conclusions are justified.

A further issue is that *many programs explicitly use more than one targeting mechanism.* In such cases, the programs were placed in the category that seemed likely to have the most influence on the targeting outcome and on administrative costs. These decisions were often based on qualitative information, and thus a degree of subjectivity could not be avoided.

For example, all children under the age of five who use public health services are eligible for the Chilean PNAC food supplements. In practice, their mothers must enroll them, bring them in for checkups regularly and queue for the ration. In the sense that those who are eligible can choose whether or not to participate, the program is self-targeted. All public clinics participate in the program, but as more public clinics were built in poor areas than in nonpoor areas, the clinics themselves and the PNAC that relies upon them are, to that extent, geographically targeted. Moreover, the level of benefit is differentiated according to nutritional risk, which is an individual assessment mechanism. We have classified the PNAC as a self-targeted program because that seemed to be the key feature in producing the low administrative costs and high participation rates.

A last, probably less important issue is *the differences in detail of how the incidence results were calculated.* Most of the results reported here are taken from literature that was not sufficiently explicit about how the calculations were done. Most appeared to be comparable, but there may be hidden surprises. We also made a conscious decision to compare some numbers that were calculated using slightly varying methods, as noted in Table 4.2.

We feel confident that our findings on the ranges for the incidence and the administrative costs of the targeted programs are robust to the shortcomings in the data with which we have had to contend. The correlation between the screening costs and the incidence outcomes may however, be sensitive to these shortcomings. This statement about the robustness of the conclusions is based on having reworked the details within many of the case studies with alternate assumptions or methods. We also recalculated the medians and ranges presented numerous times as the number of case studies, the results they contained and their classification by targeting mechanism evolved during the course of the study.

Notes

1.   This is a stricter standard than two others that are sometimes used. The first alternate definition compares measures of income inequality before and after the transfer and judges transfers that lower inequality to be progressive. Reductions in inequality can be achieved by providing transfers to the poor that are larger as a share of pretransfer income but smaller in absolute size than the transfers given to the wealthier. The second alternate definition includes the impact on the income distribution of both the transfer and the tax that finances it. Under this definition, a program can be called progressive as long as the poor receive a higher share of benefits than the share that they contribute to funding it.

2.   Quintiles mean that the units of observation have been ranked and divided into five groups of equal number. Quartiles divide the whole into four groups; deciles into ten. The general term is quantile. All the concepts explained here hold regardless of how many subgroups are formed.

3.   Note that the use of individual quintiles does not mean that all of the household's income is attributed to the wage-earner and that the dependents are counted with zero income. With both individual and household quintiles, the household's income is assumed to be shared among the members.

4.   This statement disregards any changes in participation decisions that might be caused by the increase in the gross benefits.

5.   Alternately, the budgetary impact of achieving a given poverty level may be calculated, and the lowest cost option selected.

6.   This book replicates only the first step in Meerman's and Selowsky's two-step methods. They use household surveys to determine how many units of government services households consume. Then they use budget information to estimate the cost of producing those services, which they allocate among households. We count the frequency with which beneficiary households fall into each quintile of the welfare distribution.

7.   If receiving the subsidy causes the behavior of the recipient or of any other individual to change in ways that alter net welfare, this will not be captured here.

8.   Since we do not have information either on the costs of participation or on any behavioral changes induced by participation in the program, it is not possible to compute the distribution of net benefits.

9.   In the rest of the book, we use medians rather than means, partly to avoid giving undue weight to outliers. In this paragraph, we use the mean, giving each program a weight of one because there are no serious outliers in this category and because discussing the median of a group of four is somewhat clumsy.

4

In Practice:
Program Costs and Outcomes

A wide variety of mechanisms is available for targeting social programs to the poor. This chapter sets out a taxonomy to classify them. It summarizes the administrative costs and targeting outcomes of 30 programs according to the taxonomy, giving the "big picture" of program experience in Latin America. General lessons are drawn. In subsequent chapters, more detailed attention is given to each mechanism's administrative options and requirements.

An Administrative Taxonomy of Targeting Mechanisms

In order to streamline the discussion, we group the different targeting mechanisms here according to the basic administrative requirement of each mechanism:

- *Individual assessment mechanisms* require program managers to decide whether or not to accept individual applicants on the basis of various criteria, such as means tests, the gender of household head or the nutritional status of the applicant.
- *Group (or geographic) targeting mechanisms* grant eligibility to groups of candidates who share some easily identifiable characteristic. In practice, many such programs use some form of geographic characteristic. School lunch programs that operate only in schools in poor areas or programs that allot benefits to states, municipalities or neighborhoods based on their average welfare level are examples.
- *Self-targeting mechanisms* rely on the individual decision of a potential candidate to participate or not. The service or program is theoretically available to all, but is designed in such a way as to discourage the non-poor from using it. Time costs, work requirements, stigma or a low quality service or product are the principal devices used to encourage self-targeting.

Within each category in the taxonomy of targeting mechanisms, there are several options. The most common are listed in Table 4.1.

Sometimes policymakers decide not to target, but rather to provide services to all. Such services are often called *universal*. Primary education, for example, is usually intended to benefit all children. Since features that cause a service to be self-targeting may exist independently of any explicit design decision, the line between self-targeted services and universal services can sometimes be fuzzy. Public health care is often intended to be universal, but, because it may lack quality or amenities, the nonpoor often opt to use private health care. Thus, an argument could be made that public health care is a self-targeted rather than a universal service, even though the low quality of public health services is rarely intentional or intended to induce self-targeting. Instead, it results from low budgets, inappropriate policies or inadequate management. In this paper, we will consider public health and education to be "universal" services.

There are, of course, other ways of grouping targeting mechanisms. Besley and Kanbur (1990), for example, contrast an unrealized ideal of perfect targeting with *indicator* targeting and *self-targeting*. (Besley 1989 uses the term *statistical* targeting rather than indicator targeting.) They define their indicator targeting mechanisms as those that are based on the aim of finding an indicator that is less costly to identify than income but that is correlated with it. They use a household's region or the age distribution of its members as examples. Conceptually, the methods classified in this paper under individual and group assessment fit under the rubric of indicator targeting.[1] In this study, it is appropriate to subdivide the indicator class of targeting mechanisms according to the administrative implications of how the various indicators would be used, since the topic of this monograph is the administrative costs of targeting schemes in practice.

Regardless of what taxonomy one chooses to use, there are two complications in categorizing real-life programs as we have seen in Chapter 3. Many programs explicitly use more than one targeting mechanism, and all programs implicitly have more than one targeting mechanism.

The Honduran Bono Madre Jefe de Familia is an example of a program that explicitly uses several different targeting mechanisms. It is targeted to children in grades 1–3 (group) in selected poor areas (geographic) from female-headed households (individual assessment) that pass a means test (individual assessment).

Table 4.1   Taxonomy of Targeting Mechanisms

Individual Assessment	Group Characteristic	Self-targeted
Means test	Students in uniform	Weaning food vs milk
Social worker evaluation	Armed forces	Employment programs
Proxy means test	By school	Time contribution
Gender of household head	By place of residence	Use of public health
Nutritional status	State	Services
Nutritional risk	Municipality	
	Neighborhood	

The final incidence of every program will depend on two implicit factors: the nature of the benefit and the decision of each individual about whether or not to participate—in addition to the effects of any explicit targeting mechanisms. For example, since university students tend to be drawn largely from the upper and middle classes, the potential beneficiaries of programs linked to university attendance are likely to be wealthy, whereas those eligible for public primary education services are usually somewhat poorer than average. Thus, programs associated with universities will tend to have regressive incidence, while primary programs will tend to have more progressive incidence. Furthermore, almost all programs require the beneficiaries to take some action to apply for or to collect the benefits. Some eligible persons will choose not to do so, judging the probable costs of participation to exceed the probable benefit. Therefore, it is necessary to take into account the effects that the nature of the benefit and individuals' decisions whether or not to participate have in determining who is in the applicant pool for a program before evaluating the additional effect that a formal screening mechanism will have in sorting the poor from the nonpoor.

Targeting Outcomes

Table 4.2 contains comparative information for each program in detail. Because the table is somewhat unwieldy, subsets of the information it contains are drawn out in medians and ranges and are shown in graphs in the following sections. The medians are calculated by ranking the programs by each criterion discussed and then taking the middle program. This avoids giving outliers undue influence. Any reader who is dissatisfied with the summary comparison may refer back to Table 4.2. The details of the universal services (general food price subsidies, public health services and public education) are shown in Tables 8.1, 8.2 and 8.3.

Three of the programs reviewed in the text have design features that constrain their ability to reach the poor—two are student loan programs and one is a housing program with a down-payment requirement. Because these features put them in a different class of program from the others reviewed here, they are excluded from the general summary comparisons in the text and graphs in the next subsections. Instead, they are discussed separately near the end of the chapter.

Incidence

TARGETED VERSUS UNTARGETED INTERVENTIONS. Targeted programs have much more progressive incidence than general food price subsidies. The share of the benefits of the least regressive food price subsidy accruing to the poorest 40 percent of households was 37 percent. For the least progressive of the targeted programs, 59 percent of the benefits accrued to this group (see Figure 4.1). The medians, of course, diverged even more. On average, 33 percent of the benefits of general food subsidies went to the poorest two quintiles. For the targeted programs, the figure was 72 percent.

Table 4.2 Administrative Costs and Incidence Outcome by Targeting Mechanism

| | Administrative Costs | | | | Incidence[a] (% of Beneficiary Households) | | | | |
| | Total Administration | | Targeting Costs Only | | Poorest | | | | Richest |
	% of total	US$/ben/ yr	% of total	US$/ben/yr	1	2	3	4	5
Individual assessment									
Means Test									
Jamaica: Food Stamps	10[b]	4	—	—	47	29	15	6	3
Honduras: Food Stamps for Female-headed Households (BMJF)	12	4.50	—	—	—	—	—	—	—
Mexico: Liconsa Milk Program	28.5	5.75	—	—	←— 64[c] ——→←			36 —→	
Mexico: Tortivales	12	3.12	—	—	—	—	—	—	—
Jamaica: Student Loan[d]	30	332	3.6	40	15	31	17	23	14
Colombia: Student Loan[e]	21	148	—	—	←— 23	48 —→		23	29
Social Worker Evaluation									
Dominican Republic: Hospital Fee Waivers	3.6	0.39	3.2	0.35	—	—	—	—	—
Belize: Hospital Fee Waivers	0.4	0.57	—	—	—	—	—	—	—
Costa Rica: Pension	3.5	12.50	0.4	1.36	39	20	15	15	11
Costa Rica: Health Insurance	5.0	6.50	1.0	1.30	55	19	13	9	5
Proxy Means Test									
Chile: CAS-SUF - Unified Family Subsidies	—	—	1.6	5	57	26	12	4	2
Chile: CAS-PASIS - Pension Assistance	—	—	1.4	5	50	23	17	7	3
Chile: CAS - Basic Housing	—	—	0.1	5	28	22	20	18	12
Costa Rica: University Tuition Waivers	16	14	8	7	—	—	—	—	—

36

Nutritional Risk									
Peru: PANFAR - Food Supplements	22	3.62	4.2	0.72	—	—	—	—	—
Dominican Republic: PROMI - Food Supplements	12.3	7.50	—	—	100	→	→	→	0
Costa Rica: CEN/CENAI - Daycare	9	23.16	1.6	4.17	44	26	16	12	3
Food packet	—	—	—	—	56	23	14	8	0
Geographic area									
By Neighborhood									
Venezuela: Daycare Centers	16.1	86.0	2.1	11.2	—	—	—	—	—
Peru: Glass of Milk	4.2	0.38	1.0	0.09	42	30	20	6	3
Peru: Soup Kitchens - CARITAS	8.9	1.95	1.0	0.23	37[f]	56	→	→	7
PRODIA	13.6	3.82	0.7	0.19					
By School									
Venezuela: Food Scholarship	4.0	6.92	—	—	—	—	—	—	—
Chile: School Feeding	5	3.70	0.0	0.01	53	26	12	6	3
Jamaica: Nutribuns	6.8	2.50	—	—	44	28	16	9	3
Costa Rica: School Lunch	—	—	0.4	0.08	33	29	20	12	6
Self selection									
Employment Programs- Work Requirements									
Bolivia: ESF[g]	3.5	8.50	—	—	31	46	19	4	0
Chile: Special Employment Programs	—	—	—	—	51[h]	20	13	9	3

(continued)

Table 4.2 (continued)

| | Administrative Costs | | | | Incidence[a] (% of Beneficiary Households) | | | | |
| | Total Administration | | Targeting Costs Only | | Poorest | | | | Richest |
	% of total	US$/ben/ yr	% of total	US$/ben/yr	1	2	3	4	5
Use of Health Services									
Chile - PNAC - Food Supplement	6[j]	7.60	—	—	41	28	18	10	3
Jamaica: Food Stamps - MCH	10[b]	4	—	—	44	31	18	5	2
Honduras: Food Stamps - MCH	6[i]	6.92	—	—	—	—	—	—	—
Venezuela: Food Supplement	3[i]	5.35	—	—	—	—	—	—	—

— Not available.

a. Unless otherwise noted, the quintiles are for households, using post-intervention per capita household income (or consumption) as the welfare measure.

b. Administrative costs for the means-tested and the MCH parts of the program are not separable.

c. Figures are for the poor, who make up one-third of households. Here this has been approximated by using the bottom two deciles.

d. Quintiles are for total household consumption.

e. Quintiles are based on the individual incomes of those in the working population.

f. 37 percent of benefits go to the extremely poor (the bottom 22 percent of the population), while 93 percent go to the critically poor (the bottom 54 percent of the population). By subtraction, about 56 percent of benefits go to the second and third quintiles.

g. Quintiles are based on the individual primary earnings of employed males in urban areas.

h. The CASEN survey provides figures for all employment programs aggregated. About half the workers were in the POJH, about 30 percent were in the PEM and the rest were in the many smaller programs.

i. Does not include medical time; does include time of the distribution clerk.

j. Does not include time of medical staff involved in growth monitoring (Chile, Honduras) and paperwork (Honduras). If medical time is valued, Chile's administrative costs would be 19 percent, and Honduras' would be 15 percent.

Figure 4.1 Share of Benefits Accruing to Poorest 40 Percent by Sector

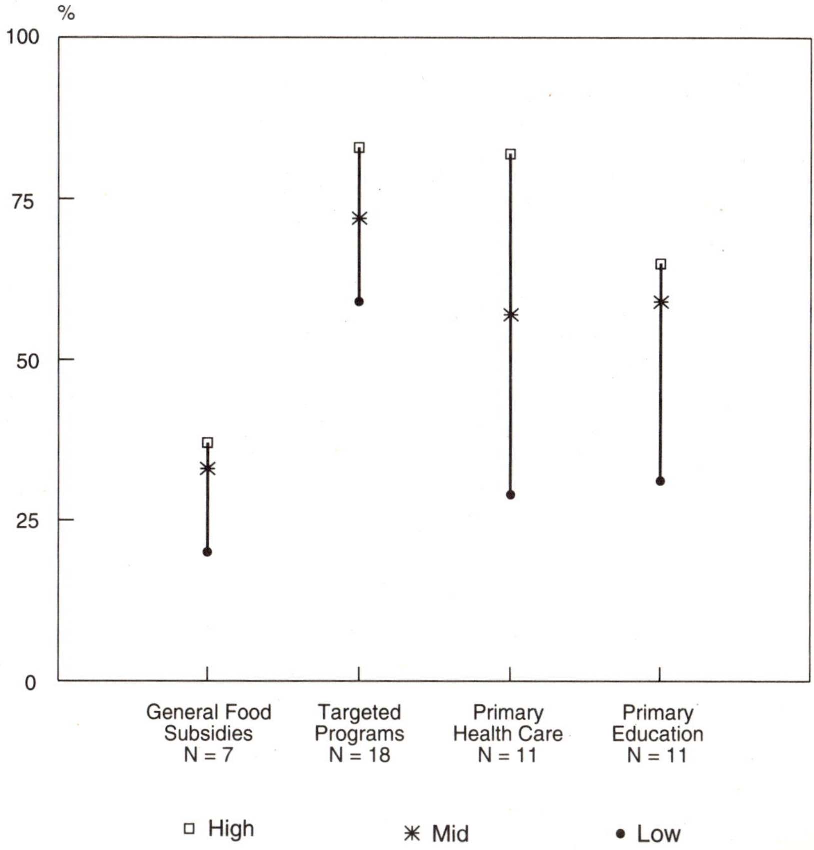

%

100

75

50

25

0

General Food   Targeted   Primary   Primary
Subsidies   Programs   Health Care   Education
N = 7   N = 18   N = 11   N = 11

□ High   ＊ Mid   • Low

On average, targeted programs also had more progressive incidence than public primary health and public primary education services, although there was a good deal of overlap in the ranges. The most progressive of the targeted programs gave 83 percent of benefits to the poorest two quintiles. For public primary health services, in the most progressive case, 82 percent of benefits accrued to that group. For public primary education, in the most progressive case, 65 percent of services were delivered to the poorest quintiles. For the median results, the ranking is clearer. The median share of benefits going to the poorest two quintiles was 72 percent for targeted programs. For public primary health care, it was 57 percent, and for public primary education, it was 59 percent. In the least progressive cases, the ranking was even clearer—in the case of targeted programs, 59 percent of benefits went to the poorest 40 percent of the population, in the case of the public health services, the figure was 29 percent, and in public primary education, it was 31 percent.

The fact that targeted programs had more progressive incidence than universal services was confirmed in country-by-country comparisons (see Figure 4.2). In

Figure 4.2 Share of Benefits Accruing to Poorest 40 Percent by Country and Sector

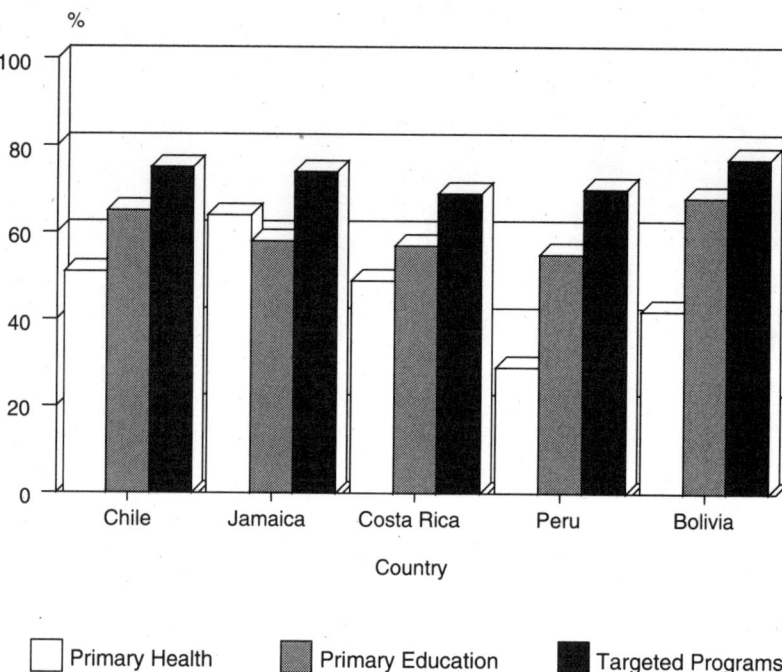

An average is shown for targeted programs; Chile, N=5; Jamaica, N=3;Costa Rica, N=5; Peru, N=2; Bolivia, N=1

every one of the five countries for which we have comparable information, the median incidence for targeted programs was more progressive than that for primary health and primary education.

Many of the targeted programs that we studied were food, food stamp or cash transfer programs that had broadly the same goals (income transfer, food security or improvements in nutrition) as the general food subsidies, but had much better incidence. Thus, a targeted food program may be a viable option for replacing a general price subsidy, though of course this will depend on an assessment of its other important characteristics such as its administrative costs, potential political economy effects and any behavioral changes it may induce. The fact that the targeted programs had more progressive incidence than public primary health or education does not imply that targeted transfer programs should replace basic health or education services, since the goals of each are clearly different. A sensible social sector strategy must obviously include strong health and education programs.

Although public primary health and education programs have different goals than those of many of the targeted programs, which may make it appropriate to judge them by different standards, they can provide something of a minimum benchmark for the incidence that should be expected of targeted programs. Most of the targeted programs we reviewed attain that minimum standard.

INCIDENCE BY TARGETING MECHANISM. Overall, a broad spectrum of incidence was apparent across the targeted programs that we studied. The share of benefits accruing to the poorest two quintiles ranged from 59 percent to 83 percent (see Figure 4.3).

There was little difference in incidence outcomes among classes of targeting mechanism. The incidence outcomes from a single mechanism as applied in different countries or programs on average were more diverse than the outcomes

Figure 4.3 Share of Benefits Accruing to the Poorest 40 Percent by Targeting Mechanism

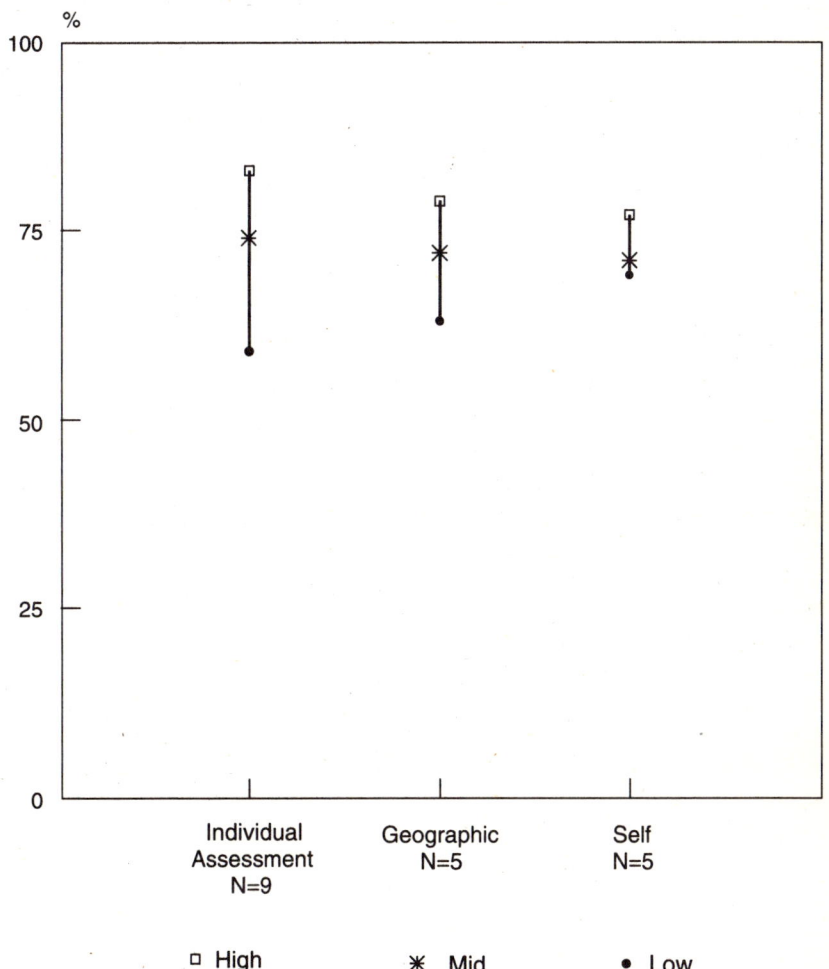

among different mechanisms. This is clear in Figure 4.3. The range of outcomes for the individual assessment mechanisms was much wider than for the other mechanisms, with 59 to 83 percent of benefits going to the poorest two quintiles. The median was 73 percent. For geographic targeting mechanisms, the range was from 62 to 79 percent of benefits went to the poorest two quintiles. The median was 72 percent. For self-targeting mechanisms, 69 to 77 percent of benefits accrue to the poorest two quintiles. The median was 71 percent.

CORRELATIONS OF INCIDENCE AND COUNTRY. The incidence achieved by the targeted programs differed little by country. In all five of the countries shown in Figure 4.2, the median share of benefits accruing to the poorest two quintiles was about 75 percent for the targeted programs. Although the distribution of benefits across the welfare distribution was similar across countries, the prevalence of poverty was not. In Chile, the programs explicitly aimed to help the poorest three deciles (Sancho 1991). In Jamaica, one-third of the population was considered to be poor at the time of this survey (Gordon 1989). In Peru, poverty was much more common, with 54 percent of the population considered to be poor.

Participation Rates

In the programs examined by the case studies, participation rates shed little light on inherent errors of exclusion resulting from the targeting mechanism. Participation rates were available for only a handful of programs, and in most of these, clear budgetary limits or ceilings were set on the number of participants or new entrants. An illustration of the problems confronted in trying to measure errors of exclusion is provided by the four programs that give food or food stamps to young children and pregnant and lactating women who use public health centers (the Chilean PNAC, Jamaica FSP, Venezuelan PAMI and Honduran BMI). For the two newer programs (the Venezuelan PAMI and Honduran BMI), no information on participation rates is available. For the other two programs, participation rates are shown in Table 4.3.

Table 4.3   Participation Rates in Two Clinic-based Programs

Program	Year	Quintile				
		1	*2*	*3*	*4*	*5*
Chilean PNAC	1987	94	89	78	58	26
Jamaican FSP - Women	1988	72	40	32	24	4
- Children	1988	61	45	35	26	11

Sources: PNAC—Vial, Camhi and Infante (1992), Table 14; FSP — STATIN and World Bank (1988), Table 4.4.

The participation rates in the maternal-child part of the Jamaican Food Stamps Program look low. This does not necessarily imply, however, that there is an inherent problem in Jamaica with reaching women and children through health clinics. At least part (probably a large part) of the low participation rate can be attributed to administrative procedures that discouraged participation by those women and children who did reach the health clinics. Lack of interinstitutional cooperation and tight administrative budgets resulted in registration being carried out in the clinics for only a few days per month in 1988, and not always on a very predictable basis. Furthermore, by 1988, the program was not as well advertised as it had been at its inception, so that mothers might have to show up more than once, first to find out about it and then to return with their children's birth certificates. In subsequent years, the participation rate fell even further when the number of days per month and the number of clinics carrying out registration were cut back even further. The errors of exclusion induced by these factors could be lowered by raising administrative budgets or by improving interinstitutional cooperation, but a change in the basic targeting mechanism itself is not necessary.

A different factor that would lead to low participation rates among eligible candidates is demonstrated in the Honduran Bono Materno-Infantil program. This program has a budget that will enable it to cover only about a third of the number of eligible children and pregnant or lactating women in the areas that have been designated as high priority. Apparent errors of exclusion are likely to be high because the targeting criteria and budget do not square. One way out of this problem would be to lower the number of regions in which the program operates or to lower the age limit for children. Either would tighten the targeting criteria to produce a number of eligible candidates that could be covered by the budget. The participation rates in this program will be low not only because the program lacks the administrative capacity to reach the poor, but also partly because policymakers have been unable to establish priorities.

Programs that rely on clinics to enroll beneficiaries also usually produce errors of exclusion caused by the fact that the poor have limited access to the public health care system. These errors are more structural or inherent. To reduce them might require building more clinics, establishing more community outreach programs, extending clinic opening hours or other actions that could be costly and outside the purview of the food stamp program. Since the persons excluded by this factor are often those most in need, this factor is a more serious concern than those induced by administrative choices.

In Jamaica, given the excellent coverage of the public health care system, errors of exclusion due to the poor not having access to the system are probably minimal. Ninety percent of Jamaicans live within ten miles of a clinic. And over 90 percent of children have been taken to public clinics at some time or another. Indeed, rates of clinic use and immunization coverage are no different for those who do receive food stamps than for those who do not. In Honduras, however, since the health system's coverage is much lower, the BMI will almost certainly have high errors of exclusion no matter how sensible and efficient its administrative operations may be.

The degree of concern that should be accorded to errors of exclusion should depend on whether those who are excluded are of relatively high or low priority in policy terms and on how hard it is to lower those errors. It sometimes seems that this distinction is not made and that concerns over errors of exclusion, therefore, can sometimes be exaggerated.

Administrative Costs

The range of total administrative costs (including the costs of screening potential beneficiaries and of delivering the program benefits to them) was from 0.4 percent to 29 percent of total program costs (see Figure 4.4). The median was 9.0 percent. In absolute terms, the total administrative costs of the targeted programs

Figure 4.4 Total Administrative Costs as Share of Total Costs by Targeting Mechanism

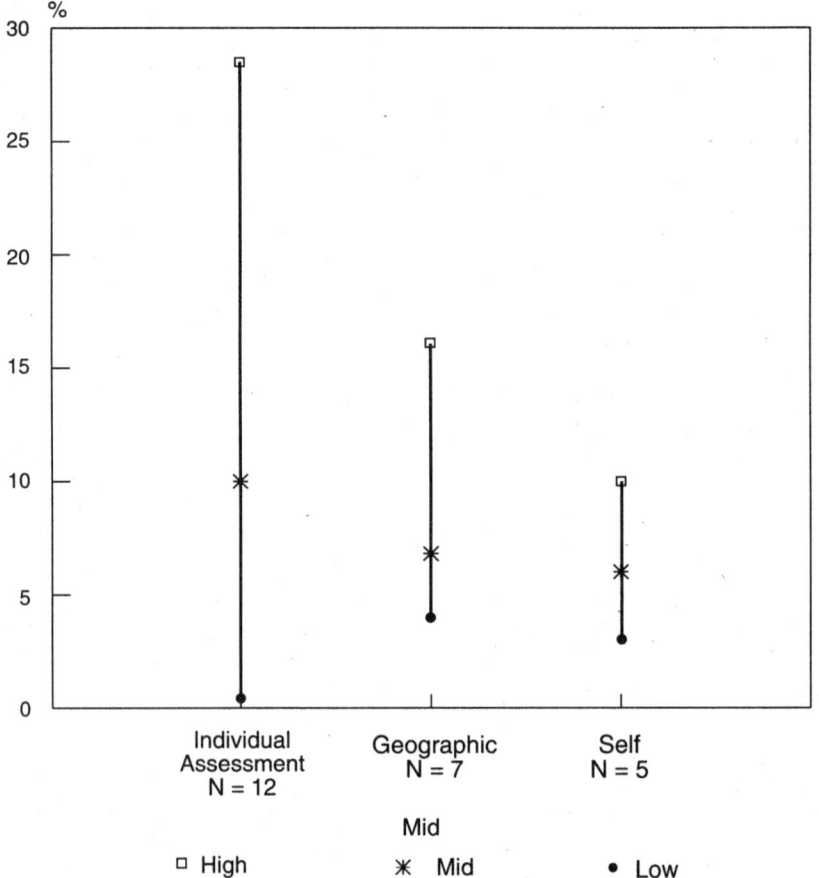

Figure 4.5 Targeting Costs as Share of Total Costs by Targeting Mechanism

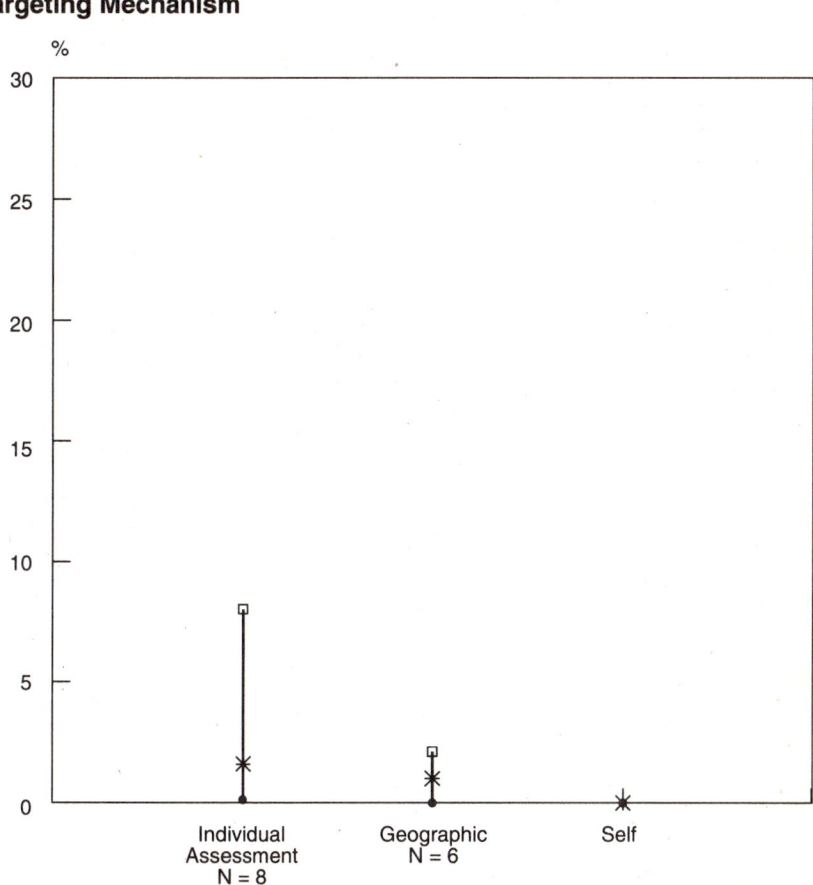

in our case studies were below US$25 per recipient per year, with one exception. The median cost was about US$5 per beneficiary per year.

In the case of individual assessment mechanisms the range of total administrative costs as a share of program costs was the greatest, from 0.4 to 29 percent. For geographic targeting, the range was from 4 to 16 percent. For self-targeting mechanisms, the range was from 3 to 10 percent. The median total administrative costs as a share of total program costs were 9 percent for individual assessment, 7 percent for geographic targeting and 6 percent for self-targeting.

Expressed in dollar terms, the total administrative costs of individual assessment mechanisms ran from US$0.39 to US$23.16 per beneficiary per year. Three-quarters of the programs targeted by individual assessment had total administrative costs that were below US$10 per year per beneficiary. Group targeted programs had administrative costs that ranged from US$0.38 to US$6.92 per beneficiary per year, with one exceptional outlier at US$86 per year. Self-targeted programs had administrative costs that ranged from $4.00 to $8.50 per beneficiary per year.

As discussed in Chapter 3, only a part of total administrative costs is, strictly speaking, due to targeting (or to the screening of potential beneficiaries). In the few cases where it was possible to separate out targeting costs, they accounted for only a small part of total administrative costs. Targeting (screening) costs ran from 0.4 to 8 percent of total program costs (see Figure 4.5). In dollar terms, the highest was only US$11 per beneficiary. The median targeting cost was only US$1.36 per beneficiary per year.

Concern over high administrative costs is perhaps the reason that is most commonly given for not adopting targeted programs. It is often cited as the reason to choose some mechanism other than those requiring individual assessment. These numbers show that the concern about administrative costs has been greatly overstated. In fact, a wide variety of programs have found targeting mechanisms that produce moderately good incidence and that cost very little when measured as a proportion of overall program costs.

The conclusion that total administrative costs are low must be somewhat tempered, however. In several of the programs, it appears that low administrative budgets have led to deficient program management. Spending more on administration within a given program framework might lead to better service quality incidence or both. The general level of administrative deficiency, however, seems no worse in the targeted programs than in most public social sector programs, including basic health and education programs.

The assumption that individual assessment mechanisms are much more expensive to administer than other options is not borne out by these data. The cost range for individual assessments is much greater than for the other mechanisms, but simple individual assessment mechanisms are no more costly than other options.

Correlations by Program Type

Administrative costs varied greatly by program type; incidence varied less. The university tuition and loan programs had both a higher median and a greater variance of administrative costs than most of the other interventions (from 16 to 30 percent—see Figure 4.6). The costs of the health fee waiver programs were more tightly clustered and much lower (0.4 to 5.0 percent). The administrative cost share of school lunch programs was similarly tightly clustered and fairly low (from 5.0 to 7.0 percent). For daycare programs, the spread and average costs were a bit higher (9.0 and 16 percent). The administrative costs of the cash transfer programs ranged from 3.5 to 12 percent. Only one job program had administrative costs, and these amounted to 3.5 percent. The spread was widest for the food distribution programs, from 4.2 to 28.5 percent.

In terms of incidence, correlation by program type was less marked. For all but the university programs, between about 60 and 80 percent of the benefits accrued to the poorest 40 percent of households. There was a heavy concentration around the center of the range (see Figure 4.7).

Figure 4.6 Total Administrative Cost Share by Type of Program

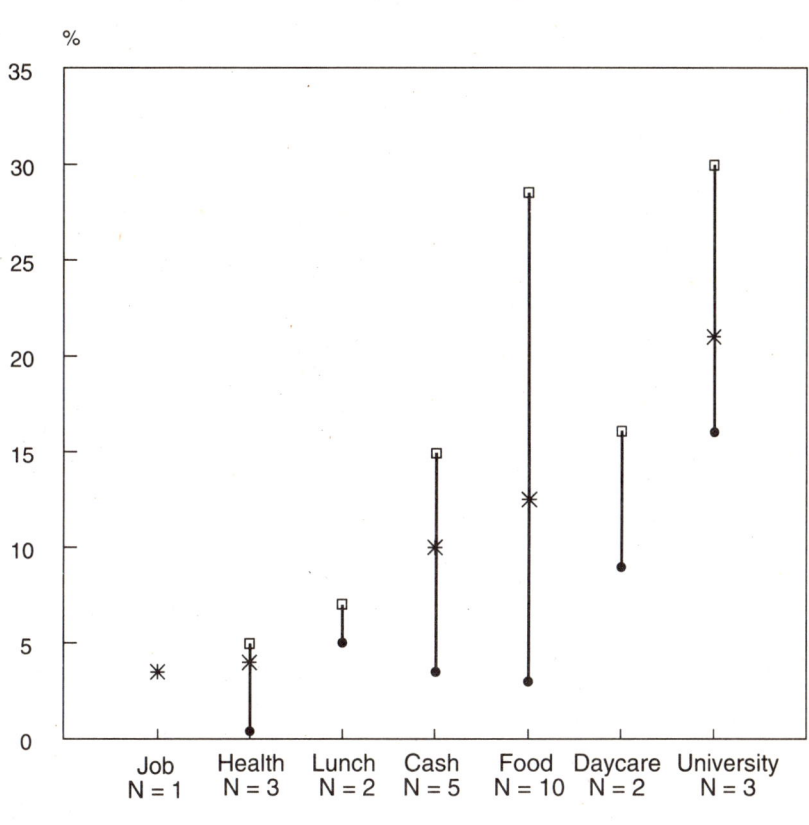

Linking Administrative Costs and Incidence

The relationship between incidence and administrative costs is complex. Generally, it is believed that higher targeting costs yield better targeting outcomes. The following section examines the relationship between incidence and administrative costs.

Correlations of Incidence and Administrative Costs

There was no apparent correlation between incidence and shares of total administrative costs, as is clear from Figure 4.8. This contradicts the usual hypothesis that better incidence requires burdensome administrative expenditures. The reason for this somewhat surprising result is that the screening costs of the

Figure 4.7 Share of Benefits Accruing to Poorest 40 Percent by Type of Program

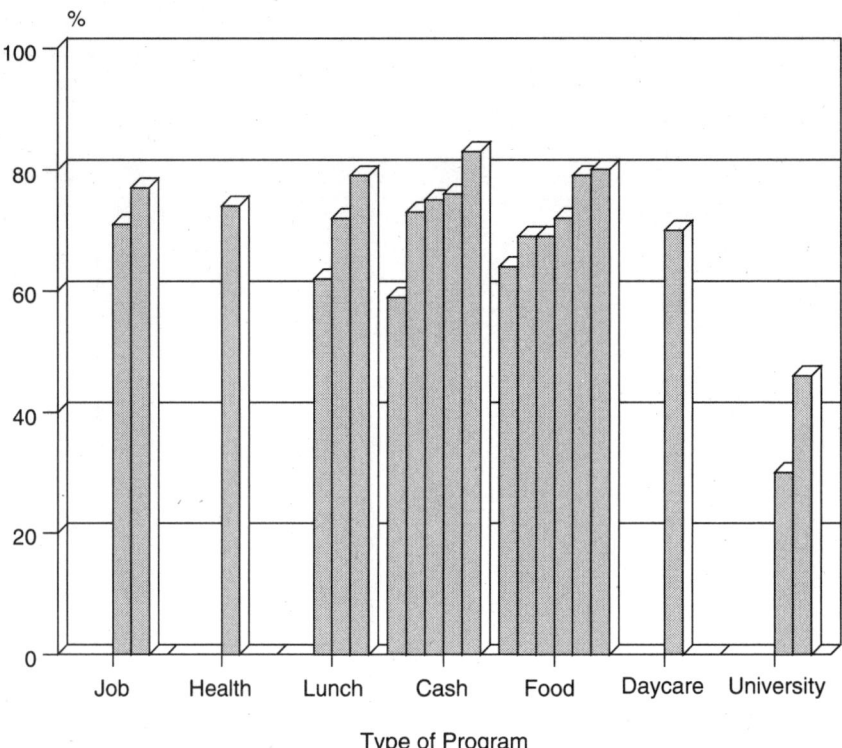

Type of Program

(imperfectly) targeted programs that we studied constitute only a small share of overall administrative costs. Even programs that use very simple geographic or self-targeting methods need administrative mechanisms capable of delivering the program benefit, so their overall costs are not much lowered by having no explicit targeting costs. There is also a great deal of variation in the scale, type, benefit level and the degree of adequacy of management among programs. These factors are important determinants of the share of administrative costs, for which we do not control in this comparison.

When isolating targeting costs, the correlation between higher screening costs and more progressive incidence becomes evident (see Figure 4.9). Both were quantified for 10 programs. The programs with targeting costs of about 1.5 percent of total program costs delivered about 80 percent of their benefits to the poorest 40 percent of households, while the programs with targeting costs of 0.5 percent of total program costs delivered about 60 percent of their benefits to the poor. This accords with the commonly held hypothesis that higher targeting costs should yield better targeting outcomes. The small number of programs and the imprecise measurement of targeting costs, however, demand caution in drawing inferences

Figure 4.8 Total Administrative Cost Share and Benefits Accruing to Poorest 40 Percent

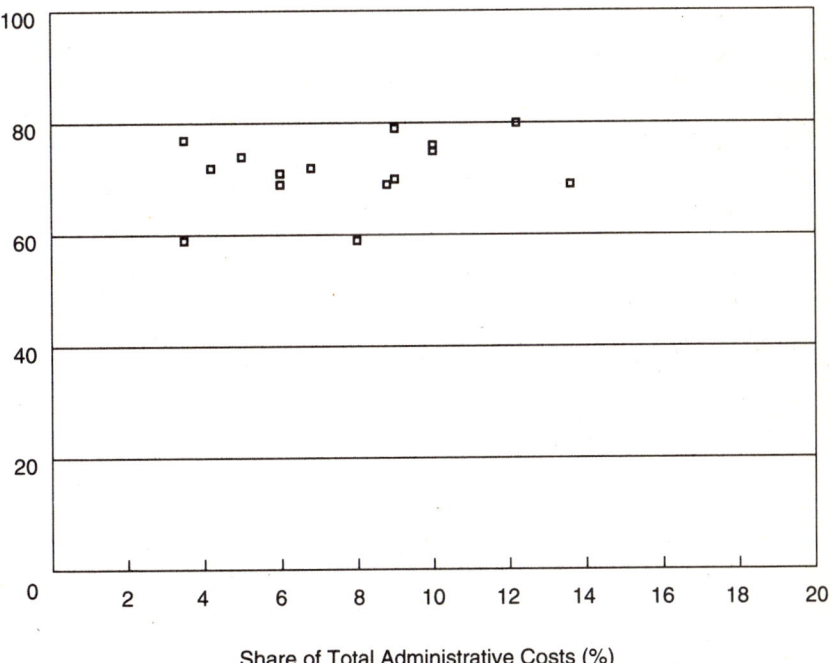

Share of Benefits to Poorest 40% (%)

Share of Total Administrative Costs (%)

about whether increasing screening costs further would provide similar improvements in incidence. But in these particular programs, the higher targeting costs are clearly offset by improvements in program incidence.

Share of Program Expenditures Accruing to the Poor

The share of each dollar that benefits the poor after discounting for administrative costs is a simple way of combining the incidence and administrative cost information. This is calculated as follows. First, the administrative share is subtracted from the budget. Then, the percentage of the remainder that goes to the poor is calculated. For example, the Liconsa program had administrative costs that amounted to 28.5 percent of total costs. So, for each dollar spent, only 72 cents was available to be spent on the beneficiaries. Of that, 64 percent (or 46 cents) went to the poorest two quintiles. So the share of total program *expenditures* going to the poorest two quintiles was 45 percent. This is different from the share of program *benefits*, which is the 64 percent from the incidence calculations presented in the previous subsection.

Figure 4.9 Targeting Cost Share and Benefits Accruing to Poorest 40 Percent

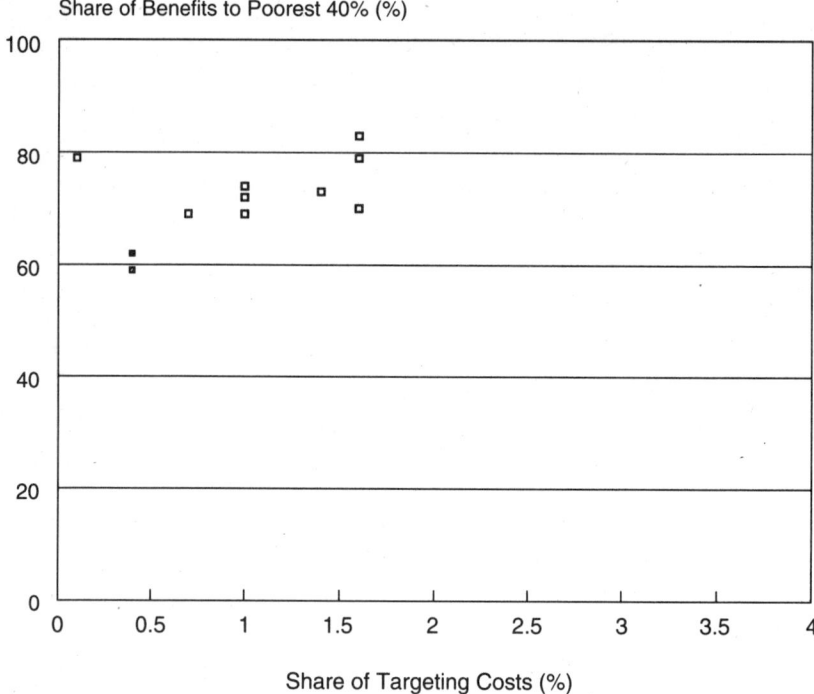

Share of Benefits to Poorest 40% (%)

Share of Targeting Costs (%)

The median of the range of program expenditures benefiting the poorest two quintiles was nearly identical for the three categories of targeting mechanisms. For individual assessment targeting, it was 68 percent, for geographic targeting, it was 67 percent and for self-targeting, it was also 67 percent. The range for the individual assessment mechanisms was broader than the ranges for the other two mechanisms, but there was broad overlap (Figure 4.10).

The median of the range of program expenditures benefiting the poorest two quintiles did not differ greatly by program type except in the case of the student loan programs, which rated low (see Figure 4.11). The fact that the results by share of program expenditure and by share of benefits that accrue to the poor are similar is not surprising. The incidence was similar and the administrative cost shares were low so that, although they varied by type of program, they did not have much effect on the ranking by the share of total expenditures that reached the poorest.

For this sample of programs, the benefit shares and program expenditure shares accruing to the poor differed little. Indeed, the Spearman's rank-order correlation for the rank of the programs on each of the two criteria was 0.93. The insensitivity of the ranking to the criteria was the result of two factors: administrative costs were fairly low and they were not correlated to incidence outcomes.

Figure 4.10 Share of Expenditures Benefiting Poorest 40 Percent by Targeting Mechanism

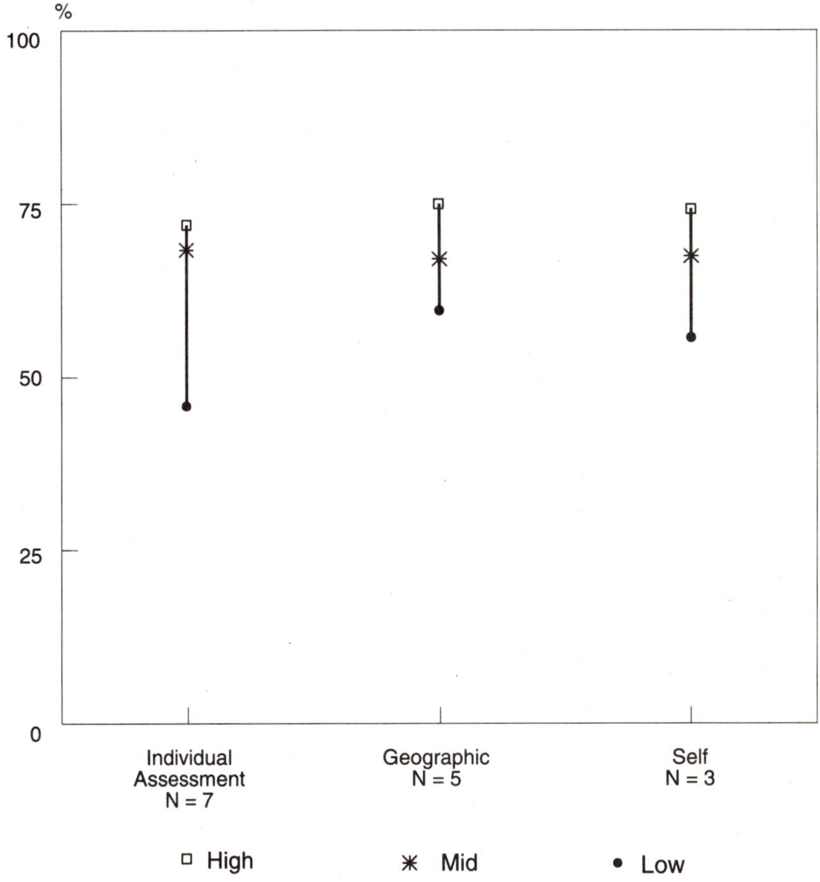

Outlier Programs

As was mentioned before, three programs (two university student loan programs and a housing program with a mortgage down-payment requirement) have been excluded from the preceding discussion on the grounds that they had design features that constrained their ability to reach the poor. This made them qualitatively different from the main body of programs reviewed, even though their targeting mechanisms were similar.

Although the three "outlier" programs did have significantly worse incidence than the others, this is not necessarily an indictment of their means testing mechanisms per se. In Chile, for example, the same proxy means test is used both for the Basic Housing mortgage subsidy and for the cash transfer (SUF) program. The Basic Housing program had the second worst incidence of all the programs we

Figure 4.11 Share of Expenditures Benefiting Poorest 40 Percent by Type of Program

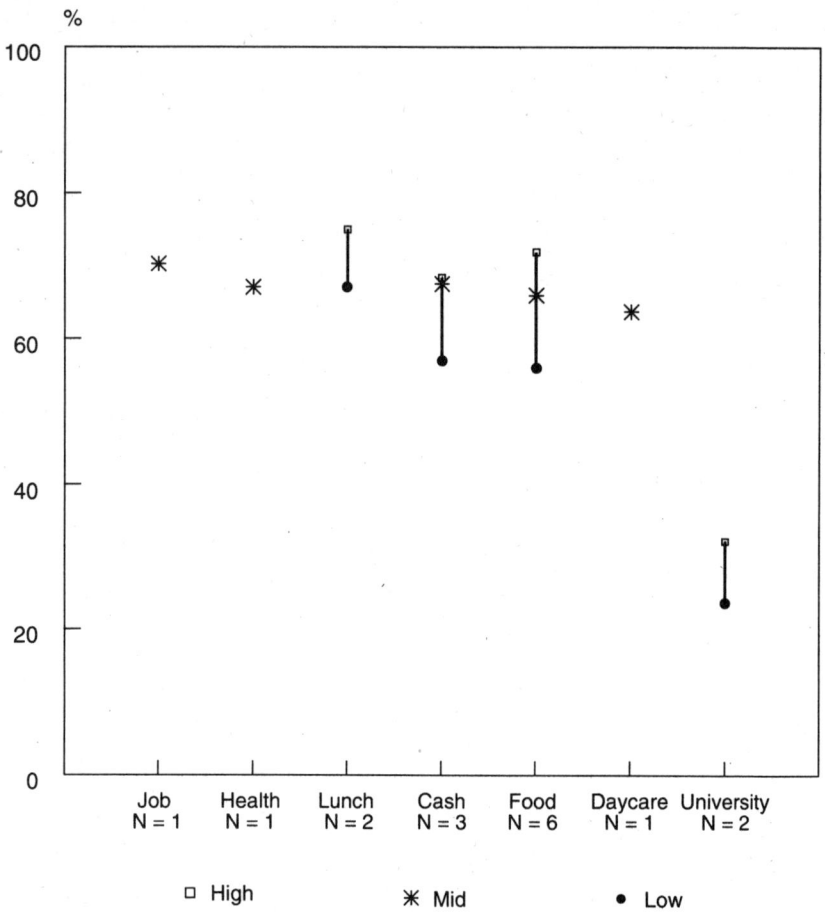

reviewed (50 percent of benefits accruing to the poorest two quintiles), while the SUF had the best incidence of any program reviewed (83 percent of benefits accruing to the poorest two quintiles). The difference in outcome apparently lies in the down-payment requirement for the mortgage subsidy. The contrast illustrates how important the kind of program benefit, and hence the composition of the pool of potential beneficiaries, can be in determining targeting outcomes.

In the case of Jamaica's student loan program, 46 percent of benefits accrued to the poorest two quintiles, and only 48 percent of the benefits of Colombia's student loan program reached the poorest *three* quintiles. The student loan programs also had very high total administrative costs compared with the other programs— US$332 per loan for Jamaica and US$148 for Colombia. Although the value of the benefits targeted was also very high, the shares of the administrative costs were still at the upper end of the spectrum, running at 20 to 30 percent of program costs. This is presumably explained by the fact that these costs included keeping track of students and their loans throughout all the years of school and repayment, in contrast to other programs whose administrative expenses only included keeping track of the beneficiary for one year of benefit at a time. In Jamaica, the cost of processing a loan application was taken as a proxy for the cost of targeting. It came to US$40 per loan or 3.6 percent of program costs. This was still the most costly screening of all the programs, although it was also among the most sophisticated.

Discussion and Conclusions

The programs reviewed here all tend to produce broadly similar outcomes. In terms of incidence, 60 to 80 percent of expenditures accrue to the poorest 40 percent of households across all the programs. Total administrative costs range from 5 to 15 percent of program expenditures, with screening costs ranging from 0.5 to 1.5 percent of program expenditures. This leads to the conclusion that, for programs with moderately good incidence, administrative expenses are not prohibitive. It is not possible, however, to infer from these data the extent to which administrative expenses would have to increase to achieve a dramatic improvement in incidence. Given the evidence of administrative inadequacy in the case studies, it seems reasonable to think that moderate increases in administrative expenses might help to achieve moderately better targeting or service delivery. But the fact that none of the programs come very close to perfect targeting probably means that much higher administrative expenses would be required to achieve radically lower leakage.

How applicable are these findings to countries that are substantially poorer, such as those in Sub-Saharan Africa? There is considerable debate about whether very poor countries should try to target their social programs. Those who question the value of doing so point out that leakage, defined as benefits given to the non-poor, is bound to be low even with untargeted programs if a large proportion of the population falls below the poverty line. Furthermore, the institutional capacity in very poor countries tends to be very limited, making targeting mechanisms even more difficult to administer.

That programs in poor countries like Bolivia and Peru managed to produce targeting outcomes equivalent to those for Chile and Costa Rica's programs suggests that targeting can still be useful in moderately poor countries with weak administrative capacities. It may even suggest that the incidence that can be expected from the targeted programs may have little to do with how poor a country is. For countries with greatly different institutional systems from those in Latin America, however, it may be extrapolating out of the range where valid inference is possible to expect the same results to be achievable. This is an empirical question that cannot be answered definitely until similar studies are done that evaluate targeted programs in other settings.

Nevertheless, it does seem that the benefits of targeting in very poor countries are qualitatively not so different from those that accrue in the countries studied here. Regardless of how large a proportion of the population is poor, some people will be poorer than others. It is presumably more desirable to reach those in the poorest quintile than those in the middle quintile of the welfare distribution, even if those in the middle quintile are poor according to an absolute standard.

The availability of suitable targeting options may, however, be scarcer in Africa than in Latin America. Targeted programs do require service delivery capacity even if very simple targeting methods are used. Many of the simple mechanisms involve tying into existing institutions or programs, especially in the health and education sectors. Improving the service delivery capacity in these sectors is clearly a high priority for its own sake. Where this is pursued, it may also help to improve the feasibility of targeted programs linked to the use of health and education services. Meanwhile, if administrative barriers are substantially greater in Sub-Saharan Africa than in Latin America, the choices about targeting may reasonably be different as well.

Finally, it is interesting to compare the Latin American programs to some in the industrial world. Five of the largest means-tested welfare programs in the United States are shown in Table 4.4. They account for nearly two-thirds of all means-tested public expenditures. Interestingly, the administrative costs of these programs as a proportion of total costs are similar to those for the Latin American programs—from 4.0 to 16 percent. Targeting accuracy, however, appears to be much better in the United States' programs. Error rates are calculated by periodically sampling beneficiaries and recalculating their eligibility and benefit levels. On the whole, errors are quite low. Overpayments or payments to ineligibles run from 3.0 to 16.0 percent. Underpayments run from 0.6 to 5.0 percent. This greater targeting

**Table 4.4   Administrative Costs and Error Rates
in U.S. Welfare Programs, 1985**

(percent)

	Administrative Costs	Error Rates, Overpayments and Payments to Ineligibles	Underpayments
AFDC	11.9	6.2	0.6
Supplemental Social Security	8.7	3.3	1.0
Food Stamp Program	15.6	8.3	2.3
Medicaid	5.1	2.6	2.6
Pell Grants (to university students)	4.2	16.0	5.0

Source: Compiled from Mackintosh (1989).

accuracy is presumably due to the fact that means testing is comparatively easier in the United States than in Latin America. In the United States, workers are largely employed in formal sector jobs with salaries that are regularly reported to the Internal Revenue Services. Verification is thus comparatively easy, though admittedly off-the-books earnings do occur and may be more common among the poor than among average workers. Since the economy is much more monetized, there is less need to value in-kind income. Finally, the use of computerized information systems, mail and telephone inquiries for verification and other sophisticated information technologies is much more widespread and is comparatively cheaper in the United States.

Briefly stated, our review of administrative costs and targeting outcomes in 30 Latin American social programs has led to three main conclusions:

1. Targeted programs have much more progressive incidence than general food price subsidies. They even have somewhat more progressive incidence than basic public health and education services.

2. The administrative costs of programs with moderately good incidence need not be excessively high.

3. It is not possible to rank targeting mechanisms a priori. There are no broad correlations between the targeting mechanisms and targeting outcomes, and there is only a weak correlation with administrative costs.

Given that we cannot make sweeping generalizations about one targeting mechanism as opposed to another in most circumstances, we look in some detail in the next four chapters at how each mechanism has worked in practice to see what did and did not work in each circumstance.

Annex: Data Sources for the Figures

The graphs in this chapter portray information from Table 4.2, except for Figures 4.1 and 4.2, which have ancillary sources as described below. The individual programs included in each bar of each graph are as follows. The acronyms can be found in Tables 1.1 and 4.2.

Figure 4.1 In addition to information from Table 4.2, this figure relies on Tables 8.1-8.3 of Grosh (1992a). The programs used to compile those tables are given here. *General food subsidies:* Algeria—separate figures for flour, pasteurized milk, semolina, powdered milk; Sri Lanka—sugar, average for wheat and bread; Jamaica — average for powdered milk, cornmeal, wheat. *Targeted programs:* Bolivia ESF, Chile CAS-PASIS, Chile CAS-SUF, Chile PAE, Chile PNAC, Chile POJH/PEM, Costa Rica CEN/CENAI daycare, Costa Rica CEN/CENAI food packets, Costa Rican health insurance, Costa Rican school lunches, Costa Rican pensions, Dominican Republic PROMI, Jamaica FSP (MCH), Jamaica FSP (means-tested), Jamaica Nutribuns, Mexico Liconsa, Peru Comedores, Peruvian Glass of Milk. *Public primary health care:* Argentina 1980, Chile 1983, Colombia 1974, Costa Rica 1984 and 1986, Dominican Republic 1980 and 1989, Jamaica 1989, Peru 1985, Uruguay 1983 and 1989. *Public primary education:* Argentina 1980, Chile 1983, Colombia 1974, Costa Rica 1984 and 1986, Dominican Republic 1980, Dominican Republic 1989, Jamaica 1989, Peru 1985, Uruguay 1983 and 1989.

Figure 4.2 *Bolivia:* ESF. *Chile:* PAE, PNAC, CAS-SUF, POJH/PEM, CAS-PASIS. *Costa Rica:* CEN/CENAI-food packets, health insurance, CEN/CENAI-daycare, pensions, school lunches. *Jamaica:* FSP (MCH), Nutribuns, FSP (means-tested). *Peru:* Glass of Milk, Comedores.

Figure 4.3 *Individual assessment:* Chile CAS-PASIS, Chile CAS-SUF, Costa Rica CEN/CENAI daycare, Costa Rica CEN/CENAI-food packets, Costa Rican health insurance, Costa Rican pension, Dominican Republic PROMI, Jamaica FSP (means-tested), Mexico Liconsa. *Geographic:* Chile PAE, Costa Rican school lunches, Jamaica Nutribuns, Peru Comedores, Peru Glass of Milk. *Self:* Bolivia ESF, Chile PNAC, Chile POJH/PEM, Jamaica FSP (MCH).

Figure 4.4 *Individual assessment:* Belize hospital fee waivers, Dominican Republic PROMI, Costa Rican CEN/CENAI, Costa Rican health insurance, Costa Rican pensions, University of Costa Rica tuition waivers, Dominican Republic hospital fee waivers, Honduran BMJF, Jamaican FSP, Mexico Liconsa, Mexico Tortivales, Peru PANFAR. *Geographic:* Jamaica Nutribuns, PAE, Glass of Milk, Beca Alimentaria, Peru Comedores-CARITAS, Peru Comedores-PRODIA, Venezuelan daycare centers. *Self:* PNAC, FSP, BMI, ESF, PAMI.

Figure 4.5 *Individual assessment:* Chile CAS-PASIS, Chile CAS-SUF, Costa Rica CEN/CENAI, Costa Rican health insurance, Costa Rican pensions, Dominican Republic hospital fee waivers, Peru PANFAR. *Geographic:* Chile PAE, Costa Rican school lunches, Peru Comedores-CARITAS, Peru Comedores-PRODIA, Peru Glass of Milk, Venezuelan daycare program.

Figure 4.6 *Jobs:* Bolivia ESF. *Health:* Belize hospital fee waivers, Costa Rican insurance, Dominican Republic hospital fee waivers. *Lunch:* Chile PAE, Jamaica Nutribuns. *Cash/food stamps:* Costa Rican pensions, Honduras BMI, Honduras BMJF, Jamaica FSP, Venezuela Beca Alimentaria. *Food:* Chile PNAC, Costa Rica CEN/CENAI, Dominican Republic PROMI, Mexico Liconsa, Mexico Tortivales, Peru Comedores-CARITAS, Peru Comedores-PRODIA, Peru Glass of Milk, Peru PANFAR, Venezuela PAMI. *Daycare:* Costa Rica CEN/CENAI, Venezuelan daycare centers. *University:* Colombia ICETEX, University of Costa Rica tuition waivers, Jamaica SLB.

Figure 4.7 *Jobs:* Bolivia ESF, Chile PEM/POJH. *Health:* Costa Rican health insurance. *Lunch:* Chile PAE, Costa Rican school lunches, Jamaica Nutribuns. *Cash/food stamps:* Chile CAS-PASIS, Chile CAS-SUF, Costa Rican pensions,

Jamaica FSP (MCH), Jamaica FSP (means-tested). *Food:* Chile PNAC, Costa Rica CEN/CENAI, Dominican Republic PROMI, Mexico Liconsa, Peru Comedores, Peru Glass of Milk. *Daycare:* Costa Rica CEN/CENAI. *University:* Colombia ICETEX, Jamaica SLB.

Figure 4.8 Bolivia ESF, Chile PAE, Chile PNAC, Costa Rica CEN/CENAI, Costa Rican health insurance, Costa Rican pensions, Dominican Republic PROMI, Jamaica FSP (MCH), Jamaica Nutribuns, Peru Comedores-CARITAS, Peru Glass of Milk, .

Figure 4.9 Chile CAS-PASIS, Chile CAS-SUF, Chile PAE, Costa Rica CEN/CENAI daycare, Costa Rican health insurance, CEN/CENAI food packets, Costa Rican pensions, Costa Rican school lunches, Peru Comedores-CARITAS, Peru Glass of Milk, Comedores-PRODIA.

Figure 4.10 *Individual assessment:* Costa Rica CEN/CENAI daycare, Costa Rica CEN/CENAI food packets, Costa Rican insurance, Costa Rican pensions, Dominican Republic PROMI, Jamaica FSP (means-tested), Mexico Liconsa. *Geographic:* Chile PAE, Jamaica Nutribuns, Peru Comedores-CARITAS, Peru Comedores-PRODIA, Peru Glass of Milk. *Self:* Bolivia ESF, Chile-PNAC, Jamaica FSP (MCH).

Figure 4.11 *Job:* Bolivia ESF. *Health:* Costa Rican insurance. *Lunch:* Chile PAE, Jamaica Nutribuns. *Cash/food stamps:* Costa Rican pensions, Jamaica FSP (MCH), Jamaica FSP (means-tested). *Food:* Chile PNAC, Costa Rica CEN/CENAI food packets, Dominican Republic PROMI, Peru Comedores-CARITAS, Peru Comedores-PRODIA, Peru Glass of Milk. *Daycare:* Costa Rica CEN/CENAI. *University:* Colombia ICETEX, Jamaica SLB.

Note

1. A possible exception may be the means tests, as these try to measure income directly rather than its correlates. However, since the means tests reviewed here are so simplistic in their definitions of income and are based on uncertain information, it may be more plausible to think of the resulting figure as a correlate or predictor of true, full income similar to other indicators than to think of these simple, imperfect means tests as the ideal.

5

Individual Assessment Mechanisms

Individual assessment targeting mechanisms are frequently thought to be impractical. The reluctance to use them is based on the fear that they may be very costly and require more organizational, administrative or logistical capacity than many programs can realistically muster, even with adequate administrative budgets. Also, administrators tend to doubt that they would be allocated adequate administrative budgets, especially as many of the welfare programs reviewed here were started up in times of general government cutbacks and retrenchment.

This concern over the administrative requirements and cost of individual assessment mechanisms, though based on good sense, appears to have been somewhat exaggerated. The entire class of individual assessment mechanisms need not be discarded out of hand. Nor should standards be set too high. For example, highly accurate, sophisticated means tests may well be too hard or too expensive for developing countries, but less precise, simple means tests may be a workable option.

Within the general class of individual assessment instruments, there is a broad spectrum of possibilities. Some have minimal cost and logistical requirements; others are more demanding. As shown in the previous chapter, the range of the total administrative costs of the individual assessment mechanisms that are most frequently used is under US$10 per beneficiary per year. The targeting costs of the most complex forms of means testing encountered in this study ranged from US$7 to US$40 per beneficiary. Even these mechanisms are a good deal cruder than sophisticated targeting mechanisms, as used in, for example, the United States' food stamp or AFDC programs. It is this standard that is hard to envision in a developing country context.

This chapter will review five kinds of individual assessment mechanisms—means tests, social worker evaluations, proxy means tests, gender of household head and nutritional status or risk. For each case, the general pros and cons will be explained and some of the options for setting up the mechanisms will be explored. A general theme throughout is that the details of the context and the program implementation are important determinants of what is workable and what outcomes will result. Table 5.1 presents a summary of the individual assessment mechanisms and Table 5.2 presents information on how individual assessment mechanisms can be verified.

Means Tests

A "true" means test is one that is based only on income and wealth. Proxy means tests and social worker evaluations, which contain elements in addition to or instead of income, have a great many similarities with "true" means tests, but are considered separately below.

In addition to the logistical requirements implied in the necessity of examining each candidate, the means test is difficult to do well because income is hard to define and measure, because the respondent has the incentive to lie and because it is difficult to verify the respondent's answers. A true means test can be carried out to many levels of accuracy and sophistication. Means testing, however, is frequently thought of only in terms of its more sophisticated versions.

A good evaluation of income requires that the value of income from such sources as informal sector or household enterprises, from home-produced goods and from owner-occupied dwellings should be calculated. It also requires that the data should be adjusted for seasonality or irregularity in flows and for local prices. Defining household income requires sorting out the obligations of individuals whose association with the household may be somewhat fluid or unclear. These are complex technical questions that can keep economists arguing endlessly. Perhaps even more daunting is the task of trying to verify respondents' claims. In an industrial country in which most poor people are employed in salaried jobs and are registered with the national tax system, it is comparatively simple. In countries where the poor do not work in permanent, salaried jobs and tax records are scarce, the task can be extremely difficult.

In developing countries, food stamp programs that use means tests have, therefore, chosen options at the very simple end of the scale. They make no real attempt to value in-kind, informal sector or home-produced income, nor do they verify income. Basically, they ask the respondents what their income is and record that figure. The smaller university student loans programs have means tests that, at least on paper, are more sophisticated.

In Food Stamp Programs

JAMAICAN FOOD STAMPS. One part of the Jamaican Food Stamps program is means-tested. Social workers from the Ministry of Labour, Welfare and Sport visit the household and fill in a short form with the candidate's address, family information and income. The visit to the house allows the social worker to verify whether the apparent living conditions are in accordance or are grossly at odds with the reported income, but the characteristics of the dwelling and ownership of durable goods are not formally used in the evaluation of eligibility. During the first years of the program, a single eligibility threshold was used regardless of household size. Recently, a two-tiered threshold was adopted, with one level being for single-person households and another for larger households. Also during the first years of the program, no regular review of eligibility was conducted. Rather, an ad hoc "cleaning of the rolls" was performed periodically.

The administration of the Jamaican Food Stamps program is done by about 150 full-time field workers. They work on a two-month cycle, with the first month devoted to identifying beneficiaries and the second month devoted to distributing the food stamps. The program has about 300,000 beneficiaries overall, of whom half are in the means-tested part of the program and half in the maternal-child health part of the program, which is not means-tested.

HONDURAN BONO MADRE JEFE DE FAMILIA (BMJF). In contrast to the Jamaican Food Stamps program, the Honduran Bono de Madre Jefe de Familia has relied on teachers to conduct simple means tests. At the beginning of the school year, primary teachers are asked to determine which of their students are from households that are headed by females and that have incomes below a set level. The teachers, in turn, ask the students' mothers what their income levels are. The teachers sometimes visit the house, and sometimes interview the mother at the school. It is assumed that, because the teachers are members of the community and have good information about the children's families, they will know whether the income reported by the mother is approximately accurate.

The teachers spend about three days at the beginning of the school year identifying the beneficiaries for the program. About 13,000 teachers are involved in the seven departments where the program operates. The program benefits about 125,000 students.

THE CONTRAST. The Honduran and Jamaican food stamp programs provide an interesting contrast in approach. In Jamaica, there is a small cadre of full-time social workers, whereas in Honduras, the program relies on the part-time effort of an army of teachers. In terms of the number of the staff days needed, some very rough calculations show the same order of magnitude of staff effort per beneficiary, though the difference in costs is slight.[1] Jamaica's total administrative costs run at about 9 percent of program costs or US$4 per year. The same costs in Honduras run at about 12 percent or US$4.50 per beneficiary per year.

Each approach has advantages. Jamaica's small-cadre approach means that training can be more thorough and the standardization of operation among social workers can be greater. It also means that the number of people who help to distribute food stamps is a fraction as large as in Honduras and the security problems are consequently more narrowly focused on providing protection to, and checking on, a few people handling large quantities of stamps. (Additional information regarding security considerations for food stamps is provided in Box 5.1)

Table 5.1 Comparison of Individual Assessment Mechanisms

Mechanism	Advantages	Disadvantages	Administrative Requirements	Appropriate Circumstances
Simple means test				
Records reported family income and size	Simplicity	Inaccuracy	Staff to conduct interviews (may be done in field or office)	Elements of self-targeting and/or geographic targeting to help to improve accuracy
No attempt to value in-kind income, seasonal income, consider individual adjustments in needs or means		Respondents have strong incentive to lie about the information	Record keeping	Low benefit levels, so absolute administrative costs must also be low
No verification of income, except optional home visit to check housing quality				
Sophisticated means test				
Adjusts family income according to family size, seasonality, costs of major items such as housing, university tuition, major medical expenses	Accuracy	Higher administrative costs	Staff to conduct longer interviews	High benefit levels (student loans, housing subsidies, large cash benefits)
Requires verification of information through third parties or by having candidates submit pay stubs, tax records, receipts, etc.		Verification may work only for literate applicants working in the formal sector	Staff time for verifying information	Applicant pool literate and in the formal sector
			Detailed recordkeeping	

Proxy means test				
Objectively calculates synthetic needs score based on a series of variables that may include housing characteristics and location, family structure, occupation, education, gender of household head, ownership of durable goods	Uniform, systematic algorithm to weight variables	Requires longer interview than simple means test	Staff to conduct interviews (may be done in field or office)	Broadly applicable
	Not clear to applicant how to lie effectively	Weighing algorithm is inflexible, may not detect special circumstances such as catastrophic illness, natural disasters	Detailed recordkeeping	Especially useful when a) large benefit levels are to go to candidate pool from illiterate, informal sector b) access to basic infrastructure is so extensive that it does not distinguish need very well in less detailed assessments
Calculation of index may be done by interviewers or computer	Calculates at permanent income without having to adjust for seasonal or in-kind income		Computerized option requires data entry capacity, sometimes at local level. Software design can be centralized	
	High marginal tax rate problem avoided	Applicants may perceive system as arbitrary	Previous analytical work and periodic updates to establish variables and weights	
Social worker evaluation				
Subjectively evaluates the same kind of information as used in proxy means test	Can detect special circumstances	Uniformity and consistency hard to ensure	Staff conduct interviews	Broadly applicable
		Mixed record in practice	Recordkeeping	
		Applicants may perceive system as allowing favoritism, influence-peddling		

(continued)

Table 5.1 (continued)

Mechanism	Advantages	Disadvantages	Administrative Requirements	Appropriate Circumstances
Nutritional status				
Weight for age	Objective, verifiable, accurate indication of need	Curative orientation, waits until child is malnourished before intervening	Growth monitoring capacity	Malnutrition widespread
Growth faltering	More preventive focus, detects problems earlier	Standards can be controversial Results very sensitive to inaccuracy in weighing and recording and to child's state of hydration	High accuracy in growth monitoring capacity	Forms part of well-established preventive health package
Nutritional risk as figured by mother's fertility history, siblings' health history, family socio-economic characteristics	Preventive focus	Adds new information requirement in health services	Prior studies to determine risk factors and their weights Training for medical staff in unfamiliar process	Forms part of well-established preventive health package

Table 5.2 Options for Verifying Information in Individual Assessment Mechanisms

Option	Advantages	Disadvantages	Administrative Requirements	Appropriate Circumstances
Performing household visits	Allows verification of housing standards and other information; Improves accuracy of targeting	Cost	More staff time; Vehicle and/or travel allowances where public transit available	Ongoing or large benefit, such as food stamps; Social worker does not know clients personally; No possibility of using written verification
Collecting information in-office, with no verification	Simplicity; Low cost	Inaccuracy	Minimal staff time	One time, small benefit needing immediate decision, such as hospital fee waivers; Interviewer knows clients well enough to detect lies, e.g. where interviewer is a village-based social worker or teacher
Collecting information in-office, with applicant submitting verifying documents (pay stubs, tax receipts, bills)	Accuracy; Places burden on applicant, not staff	Not always appropriate	Staff time to evaluate information; Information system	Large benefit; Applicant pool literate and part of formal sector
Waiting for candidates to apply for program, i.e. passive identification	Low costs	Undercoverage may be high	Normal	Participation rate already high; Available slots in programs filled
Performing outreach to identify candidates who have not applied for program	Lowers undercoverage, improves impact on poverty	High cost	Staff time to do outreach; Budget resources to give benefits to identified candidates	Adequate budget; Likely candidates clustered geographically or identifiable through their use of some social services

One of the reasons that Jamaica chose to use a small number of social workers was that the country already had two welfare programs operating in a similar way. So when the Food Stamps Program was set up in an emergency effort to compensate the poor for increased food prices arising from exchange rate changes and the phasing-out of general food subsidies, it was able to rely on existing systems and personnel to a large degree. Later the ministry needed to expand its capacity to handle the added burden of the permanent program, though there were presumably

---

Box 5.1   Cash Transfers versus Food Stamps

A strategic question that frequently arises is which method is better—cash benefits, food stamps denominated in money terms or food stamps denominated in physical quantities. The answer depends partly on the purpose of providing the benefit and partly on logistic and financial considerations. This box reviews the issues briefly. Alderman (1991) provides a fuller treatment.

Purpose of the Program

Although a link is sometimes claimed, it is doubtful whether one form of transfer is preferable to another on nutritional grounds. Most food stamp programs state an improvement in nutritional status as a goal. It is therefore hoped that providing food stamps rather than cash will encourage the purchase of food rather than other items. Economic theory holds that if the value of the food stamps is less than would be spent on food, the food stamps will result in the same additional food purchases as would a cash transfer of the equal value. The household may spend the stamp itself on food, but the money that is implicitly saved will be spent like any other income. However, some food programs contain a nutrition education component that might have the effect of persuading a household to spend more of its total income on food than it would have spent in the absence of the program. Empirical studies on the subject are contradictory. For Sri Lanka, Edirisinghe (1987) found that food stamps were used just like cash. In the United States, the conclusion varies depending on the theoretical model, statistical methods and data set used. One of the best studies methodologically by DeVaney and Moffitt (1990) showed that the marginal propensity to consume food was several times higher for food stamp income than for other income.

Food stamps may be politically more acceptable than cash transfers, especially when trying to change from untargeted to targeted programs. Almost all the food stamp programs allow stamps to be used only for certain "worthy" staple commodities. Since the food stamp is not directly spent on "unworthy" items, such as liquor, cigarettes or gambling, the possibility that it may nonetheless increase the recipients' consumption of these goods is hidden. In most countries, the items that can be purchased with food stamps are those that had previously been subsidized. In Jamaica, Sri Lanka and Zambia, the food stamp programs were an explicit move away from an untargeted subsidy to a targeted program. To increase the political viability of the change, the food stamps were linked to the same commodities that had been subsidized.

economies of scale, and using an existing system allowed the Food Stamps Program to be speedily launched.

In Honduras, the Bono Madre Jefe de Familia was also set up as an emergency effort to accompany structural adjustment. But Honduras had no network of social workers who knew how to do means tests, so schoolteachers who were already in place were used.

Logistical Considerations

The choice between cash and food stamps has little impact on the logistics of beneficiary selection, though it may have an impact on other parts of the program's administration. In general, cash transfer systems require a larger and more sophisticated institutional structure to build on, but may have lower administrative costs where that infrastructure exists.

Cash transfers are usually given not literally in cash, but rather in personalized checks. These are either picked up at welfare offices or mailed out. They are cashed at banks. The welfare agency must have a good information system to personalize the checks, and the recipients must usually show photo identification cards in order to cash them. Personalized checks will only work where the infrastructures of the welfare agency, post office and banking system are extensive and relatively sophisticated. The checks, however, require less security during transport and handling than food stamps, which circulate almost as freely as currency. Also, no expenses need be incurred for setting up a reclamation chain.

Food stamps are usually not personalized. They are handed out in face-to-face contact with the recipient or in schools, health posts, welfare offices or rotating community sites. This implies that the logistics of their distribution are more flexible than for cash transfers and that they require different security arrangements, as small concentrations of stamps are dispersed from many distribution sites. Commercial retailers must also be instructed in how to accept and reclaim the food stamps. If a serious effort is made to ensure that only the designated commodities are purchased (this is not usual and not advisable for stamps denominated in monetary terms), a detailed auditing system has to be put in place to ensure that sales of the commodity correspond to claims of sales. For food stamps denominated in physical quantities, the formula set for valuing the reimbursement to the retailer will need to be sensitive to price changes between the time of accepting and reclaiming the stamp. In high inflation economies or where prices vary seasonally, this will be particularly important but difficult to achieve.

Financial Considerations

For cash transfers and food stamps denominated in monetary terms, the real value to the consumer may erode with inflation, but the nominal budget to the government is fixed and predictable. If benefits and real budgets are to keep pace with inflation, explicit decisions must be made by the government to raise the benefit levels. In contrast, for food stamps denominated in physical terms, the real value of the program is constant to consumers, and the cost to the government will rise and fall with the price of the designated commodity. Program benefits and budgets will keep pace with inflation with no explicit adjustment needed by the government.

Furthermore, because it is easier to fool a social worker who visits the village occasionally than the teacher who lives there, it seemed that the teachers would be able to do a more reliable job of means testing. Finally, the time spent by the teachers was not a cash cost to the food stamp agency, but rather an implicit cost to the Ministry of Education. It is unclear whether the teachers were sacrificing their leisure or their classroom time. Either way, planners were happy not to have to have a budget line item for their time.

Using a large number of teachers rather than a small number of social workers, of course, has some drawbacks. It makes training, supervision and standardization of procedures extremely difficult. It provides different security challenges. In Honduras, there may be an effect on teacher-parent relations. If a parent is displeased at being excluded from the program's benefits, she is angry not at an anonymous social worker from the capital, but at her child's teacher. It is conceivable that this could impair the teacher's effectiveness in teaching. It might also encourage the teacher to include ineligible students on the rolls.

TORTIVALES AND LICONSA. Mexico also uses means testing as part of the targeting mechanism for two food subsidy programs—the Tortivales and Liconsa Milk Coupon programs. The Tortivales program allows participating households to receive one kilo of tortillas free each day from participating tortilla shops. The Liconsa program allows the families to purchase milk in participating dairy shops at one-quarter of the market price. The number of liters that can be purchased depends upon the number of children under the age of 12 in the household, but varies from 8 liters per week for families with one child to 24 liters per week for families with four or more children.

In both programs, participation is supposed to be limited to families with household incomes of under two minimum wages. The Tortivales program operates only in urban areas, and the Liconsa program has recently moved into rural areas on a limited experimental basis. Not operating in rural areas, of course, excludes the approximately 50 percent of the poor who do not live in cities.

The programs operate predominately in urban areas, partly because of the logistics involved in setting up distribution sites in the rural areas. In the case of Tortivales, towns of 50,000 inhabitants or more are included. The problem with expanding to rural areas is partly one of supervision and partly one of economies of scale. There is currently a shortage of the necessary equipment. More people can be served by concentrating the distribution sites in urban areas, and supervision costs can be kept low. Even when more equipment becomes available, the time and travel costs of supervision in rural areas would be much higher per beneficiary. Furthermore, in rural areas, there may be greater errors of exclusion. Many of the poor make their tortillas at home rather than buying them. And those who live very far from designated tortilla shops would find it difficult to use the program.

In the case of Liconsa, the milk is usually sold in liquid form. Perishability is a problem in rural areas where transport is difficult and refrigeration scarce, though there is a pilot program for distributing powdered milk in rural areas. Furthermore, there is a problem with economy of scale. The economically optimal size for a dairy store is one that sells 4,000 liters of milk weekly. Even in urban areas where the population is denser, the average in practice is 2,500 liters per week. In rural areas, the problem would be worse. In Oaxaca, there are only 188 beneficiaries per outlet and in Chiapas, 352.

The means tests used for the Tortivales and Liconsa programs are simple. They are carried out by social workers from CONASUPO (Compania Nacional de Subsistencias Populares). For the Tortivales program, candidates who want to participate are required to report to 3,500 CONASUPO offices throughout the country to be means tested. Periodic random home visits are made to reverify eligibility on a small scale. Social workers look at living conditions on an informal basis, and ask for proof of eligibility, such as birth certificates for children under the age of 12 (for Liconsa). As yet, no mechanism is in place for periodically reviewing all recipients.

The Tortivales program was preceded by the similar Tortibono program. In 1990, when the government reorganized the program, efforts were made to eliminate ineligible participants from the program roster. Through the self-selection process of registering at a CONASUPO center and the means testing verification process, the list of eligible beneficiaries in each city was reduced. In Mexico City, for example, the number of beneficiary families went down from 800,000 to 500,000. With the additional resources that were freed by this reduction, the program was able to expand to additional cities.

In addition to the means test, both programs have used poverty maps to locate poor neighborhoods in which to select participating retail outlets, a technique of geographic targeting that will be discussed in Chapter 6. The Liconsa program also has elements of self-targeting built into it. The milk must be picked up during specified appointments (a margin of 15 minutes is allowed) each day or week in centers that are open from 4:30 am to 9:30 am. The participant must also supply the container for the milk. The bother of the tight scheduling and the inconvenience of supplying one's own packaging may discourage the less needy from obtaining their milk from this source. On the other hand, the purchase requirement may act as a disincentive for the poorest. Because the household must pay 25 percent of the true cost of the milk in order to receive the 75 percent subsidy, those households who cannot afford even that 25 percent will miss out on the subsidy.

These two programs have very different methods of reimbursing stores, which is an important part of the program's administration. For the Liconsa program, the household is given a card on which is marked the number of liters of milk for which the household is eligible and the specific store to which the family is assigned. The family can then purchase milk at subsidized prices only in that one store. The store is only allowed to sell the specified number of liters to the household. The dairy outlet purchases the milk at subsidized prices from the government, and sells it for a fixed price. There is a profit margin of 3 percent built in, which the operator of the dairy store is allowed to keep, up to a maximum of two minimum salaries.

This mechanism for ensuring that families get only the specified amount of milk at the subsidized price is fairly simple. But the milk distribution outlets are dedicated exclusively to the Liconsa milk program rather than being general retail outlets. Thus, the program does not reap the advantages of relying on the private sector distribution chain. Instead, special infrastructure has to be built and maintained. So the apparent simplicity and savings do have a cost. Operating costs, without taking into account the infrastructure costs, are 28.5 percent of total program costs. This is the second highest of all the programs examined.

For the Tortivales program, families are issued with plastic identification cards that are "smart." They have magnetic strips that, when passed through a special electronic scanner, record the purchase of tortillas. The scanner keeps an accurate record of how many kilos of tortillas each shop has dispensed under the program. The shop owner must then take the card reader to a BANAMEX (a private bank) outlet once a week for reimbursement.

The Tortivales' reimbursement mechanism is administratively and technologically more sophisticated than that of Liconsa. It allows the program to work with the private sector. The Tortivales program, therefore, has no need for special factories, a transport fleet or a chain of stores. For all those needs, it piggy-backs for free on the private sector. The card reader (costing US$500) is a small investment compared to the cost of the kind of infrastructure that might be needed in other circumstances. The administrative costs of the Tortivales program are 12 percent of total costs, less than half than those of the Liconsa program.

In University Tuition Programs

The Honduran and Jamaican food stamp programs are large programs with relatively low benefit levels that use very simple means tests. The Mexican Tortivales and Liconsa programs, though they have more sophisticated reimbursement mechanisms, still use very simple means tests. In Jamaica and Colombia, more sophisticated means tests are used for the university student loan and fee waiver systems. Because the potential number of applicants is smaller and they are more likely to come from the formal sector of the economy, more sophisticated means testing is easier to do. Because the value of the benefit is higher, higher absolute administrative costs are more acceptable and less reliance can be placed on self-targeting.

COLOMBIA'S STUDENT LOANS. Colombia's ICETEX student loans are targeted according to both financial need and academic merit.[2] The assessment of need is based on family income, the size of the family and the level of education and occupations of the student's parents. Income tax returns are used to verify this information. The academic criteria used are performance on the university admission exam for new students and university grades for returning students.

The incidence information for Colombia's program is the most detailed of those of the university programs, and allows one to sort out how much of the ultimate targeting outcome is due to the three contributing factors—the characteristics of the pool of potential candidates, the individuals' decisions whether to participate or not and the screening procedure applied by the program.

The characteristics of the potential candidates can be an important factor in targeting outcomes. If those who qualify for the service are generally well off, it may be difficult to achieve incidence as good as would be the case if those who qualified were generally poor. In Colombia, 35 percent of university students come from the richest 1 percent of the population (those with incomes over 80 minimum wages—see Table 5.3). Conversely, only 2 percent of university students come from the poorest 35 percent of the population (those with incomes below 12 minimum wages). Thus, the student loan program might be expected to achieve limited progressivity in targeting because the pool of university students is generally very well off. A very small program might have progressive incidence if it helps the few poor students, but a larger program will naturally have to serve well-off students as well. In fact, the ICETEX program covers 9.4 percent of higher education enrollment, which is slightly above average relative to other student loan programs in Latin America (Carlson 1992, p. 37).

Each student must decide whether or not to apply for a student loan. Students' decisions will depend on factors such as how much trouble it is to apply, their perceptions of their chances of receiving a loan and how much they need the loan. In loan schemes, an important determinant may also be the extent to which the loan

Table 5.3   Colombian Student Loan Incidence

(percent)

Net Income from Labor in Minimum Wages	Working Population	Enrolled Students	Applicants	Benefi-ciaries	Applicant Approval Rate
0–12	34.83	1.70	35.00	37.91	70.80
13–16	22.59	3.27	9.37	9.60	66.97
17–20	11.12	6.53	9.67	9.81	66.27
21–24	7.14	4.90	7.55	7.72	66.84
25–28	5.23	3.40	5.99	6.02	65.68
29–32	4.92	6.90	4.86	4.82	64.82
33–36	1.96	5.10	4.06	3.97	64.00
37–40	1.97	2.39	3.03	2.93	63.23
41–60	5.14	20.31	9.18	8.73	62.10
61–80	5.10	10.06	4.09	3.56	56.81
81–120	<1.00	35.54	7.20	4.93	44.76
Total	100.00	100.00	100.00	100.00	65.36

Source: Betancur - Mejia (1990), p. 38.

is subsidized. If default rates are high or real interest is negative, the loan becomes more like a grant; even those who could finance their studies without the loan might like one. If the loan really must be paid back and the terms are strict, those who can do without the loan may not want to ask for one. Compared with other student loan programs in Latin America, Colombia's has relatively tough terms, such as a short repayment period, no grace period and lower than average default rates (see Carlson 1992). In Colombia, the applicants for the loans are much poorer than the general student population. Whereas only 2 percent of all students come from the poorest third of the population, one-third of loan applicants come from the poorest third of the population. Thus, the applicant pool more closely mirrors the general population.

The third factor is the effect of the actual screening process. If financial need is a criterion for receiving a loan, approval rates (or loan amounts) should be higher for poor applicants than for rich ones. This is what happens to some degree in the Colombian program. Approval rates generally fall as welfare levels rise. For the poorest group, 71 percent of applicants are approved as against an overall rate of 65 percent and a rate of 45 percent for the richest students. This is a sign of an attempt to target. But the applicant and beneficiary distributions are only slightly different. The screening process does favor the poor, but not dramatically so.

In summary, it is the self-selection into the applicant pool that has the biggest effect on reducing the negative incidence of the program overall. The administrative screening procedure is helpful, but is not the major factor. By its nature, the program is designed to serve a population that is, on average, very well off, though after self-selection and administrative screening, the end distribution of student loan beneficiaries is much less regressive than the distribution of university students.

JAMAICAN STUDENT LOANS. The Jamaican Student Loan program conducts assessments of financial need that determine both whether the student qualifies for a loan and how a large a loan the student may receive. The financial need evaluation takes into account the degree of assistance received from relatives, the number of dependents the student has, the tuition costs and whether s/he is resident on or off campus. Some verification of information is prescribed in the procedures. Students from families with net incomes above a certain threshold (which in 1989 was about three times the mean household income) are ineligible. The net income figure is derived by adjusting gross income for large expenses such as tuition and home mortgage payments.

On paper, the means testing system for the Jamaican Student Loan program is much more sophisticated than that for any of the food stamp programs. It makes many more adjustments depending on family circumstances and makes some provision for the verification of information through third-party sources. The application of these procedures in practice, however, is reported to be somewhat incomplete.

Total administrative costs, including supervision and collection efforts over the life of the loan, were about US$330 per loan or about 30 percent of program costs.

The administrative costs of vetting the applications (which is where targeting comes in) were US$40 per loan or about 2.6 percent of total costs.

In 1989, approval was granted to over 95 percent of applications, and over 90 percent of loans were for the maximum amount available for a given course of study. The high approval rate may reflect some lack of vigor in evaluating applications, but an important factor is the fact that the maximum loan available for most curricula was a fraction of the estimated annual financing required by students. Thus, many qualified for the loan. This also explains why most of the loans were for the maximum amount.

The incidence of the Jamaican program is more progressive than that of the Colombian program, but then the Jamaican student body is less concentrated among the rich—14 percent of loans go to those in the top quintile in Jamaica versus 29 percent in Colombia. But in Jamaica, 64 percent of university students fall in the top quintile, while in Colombia, the figure is even higher—80 percent.

The Colombian program has lower administrative costs both in percentage and dollar terms than does the Jamaican program. This is probably at least partly attributable to economies of scale. The Colombian program extends 14 times as many loans as the Jamaican program. The loan period is also only half as long, so the costs of tracking borrowers during the shorter repayment period is less.

SIMPLE VERSUS SOPHISTICATED MEANS TESTS. The sophistication and cost of the means tests for the student loan programs is much greater than those for the food stamp programs. They make more adjustments for family size and expenses. Also, because their applicants mostly work in the formal sector and pay taxes, the student loan programs can and do make some attempt to verify applicants' information. These procedures are more expensive, with the costs of targeting running at US$40 per recipient in the Jamaican student loan program as opposed to US$4 per recipient for total administrative costs for the Jamaican food stamp program. It should be noted that the Costa Rican university tuition waiver program carries out somewhat similar means tests (discussed below under proxy means tests) for a targeting cost of US$7 per student.

The targeting and administrative costs of the student loan programs seem high. It is, however, important to consider that the benefits they administer are many times the value of the food stamp programs. So a more costly mechanism is justified because the potential losses from leakage are much higher when benefits are higher and because self-targeting is less applicable in these circumstances.

The very simple means tests that are used in the food stamps and food ration programs are obviously quite inexact. Nonetheless, for programs with low to moderate benefit levels, they produce progressive incidence for low administrative costs. The incidence of the means-tested part of the Jamaican food stamp program is better than that for over half the programs we reviewed. The Mexican programs fall in the middle range. Compared to the general price subsidies that these programs replaced, the targeting outcomes are markedly better, even taking into account administrative costs. These means tests demonstrate that even highly imperfect targeting mechanisms can be better than none.

Social Worker Evaluation

What we shall refer to here as a "social worker evaluation" is a scheme in which a social worker interviews a prospective beneficiary and makes an assessment of eligibility for some benefit. This procedure relies on the social worker's subjective assessment of the information collected rather than on processing the information according to a pre-determined formula. The interviews typically gather information on some or all of the following—the employment status, occupation, education and gender of the head of household and sometimes his or her income; the age, sex and occupation of other family members; the location of the applicant's residence; and sometimes information about the family's special immediate difficulties such as health problems.

In many ways, the social worker evaluation resembles the means test. It requires the same kind of logistics for assessing each candidate, whether individual or household. Much of the information gathered is of the kind necessary for a sophisticated means test. The main difference is in the subjectivity of the analysis.

This subjectivity can be a good thing to the extent that the social worker makes more appropriate judgments than could result from applying strict rules or from weighting the answers to a few questions. However, it can also be problematic. Good program supervision would entail checking that each social worker correctly categorized applicants, but without an absolute standard for the categorization, it is difficult to monitor each worker's performance. It is also difficult to ensure that each social worker evaluates circumstances the same way. If this is not done, a candidate might be granted benefits by one social worker, but not by another. This would clearly be unfair. The social worker evaluation may also create an impression in the eyes of the public or of the beneficiaries that the program benefits are distributed arbitrarily or unfairly (whether this is true or not).

HOSPITAL FEE WAIVERS. In the Dominican Republic, social workers decide whether fees for diagnostic services should be waived or reduced for hospital in-patients and out-patients in several hospitals and in the national laboratory. The system is characterized by a lack of formality and uniformity at all levels. Each hospital sets its own fees and develops its own fee-waiving policy. In general, these policies are extremely informal.

The social worker evaluation in some hospitals more closely resembles a bargaining process than an investigation. Social workers interview people who are applying for a waiver in front of other patients, sometimes interviewing more than one patient at a time. Furthermore, patients do not know how much the full fee is nor what is the average frequency of waivers. This can affect their decision to seek health care and to request a waiver. It certainly affects their perceptions of the system's fairness. The conditions under which the interviews are conducted suggest that stigma discourages patients from seeking waivers. The time factor may be another discouragement. Waiting times of one to three hours are common, in addition to the time spent waiting for the health care itself.

Waivers are granted in 10 to 50 percent of cases, but inadequate data exist to assess their accuracy. In the one hospital where it was possible to quantify administrative costs, these costs were about US$0.40 per waiver approved.

In Belize, the system of user fees and the criteria for waiving fees are more formalized. A schedule of fees is in place that has five categories depending upon the patient's household income. The application of the means test is, however, still very irregular and informal. On a review of billing records, the clerks seem to charge all patients at Category I rates for x-rays and laboratory tests. Yet for most other services, Category II prices are charged. For drugs, no fees are charged, although charges are mandated for Category I and II patients. From this evidence and from observing the system, it is apparent that little real investigation or evaluation takes place.

Inadequate data exist to assess the accuracy of fee waivers within each hospital. It is clear that the share of patients paying bills and the share of costs recovered is much higher in the two district hospitals than in the referral hospital in the capital city. Given the difference in incomes between the regions served by the three hospitals, the user fee system seems to be regressive. This may be due to greater vigor in charging (and waiving) fees in the poorer district hospitals than in the central hospital rather than to inaccuracy in the waiving system when applied. If the system does not work very well, neither does it cost very much. In Belize City Hospital, the waiving mechanism costs about US$0.57 per patient.

The fee-waiving system does not work well either in Belize or in the Dominican Republic. Although the staff and the mechanisms are nominally in place, they do not do a thorough job. There is no apparent reason why the systems could not work as well as the means tests described in the preceding section, if not better. The population to be tested is captive, having already come to the hospital. Although verification may not be practical, consistent inquiries into a patient's ability to pay should not be technically or logistically very much more demanding than the system that is currently in place.

The limited implementation of these fee-waiving mechanisms may reflect some ambivalence toward the whole notion of charging fees. As yet the fees are low, so that the inconsistent and uncommitted way in which the waivers are applied does not result in the needy being turned away. Its bigger flaw is in not identifying those who can pay so that revenues can be raised. This may also indicate a circular phenomenon, as there may be resistance to raising user fees unless a good mechanism is operating for waiving them for the needy. Yet, while fees are so low, there is no real incentive to develop a good waiver mechanism.

One way to begin to make this system work would be to have a simple schedule with only one or two fee levels. Then more effort could be devoted to determining whether individuals are able to pay rather than to bargaining over very small differences in fees. It would also be important to disseminate information about the fee schedules and about the waiver system, which would increase the perception of its fairness. It might also make the waiving system easier to administer. Where fees are still quite low, the non-needy would request fewer frivolous waivers, and the needy would understand the procedure better.

COSTA RICAN FREE HEALTH INSURANCE. In Costa Rica, a rather more serious attempt has been made to ensure that the poor have access to health care. Free affiliation to the national health insurance program is granted to the medically indigent based on a social worker evaluation. The program grants the participant's family all of the regular health and maternity benefits with the exception of cash payments to the patient and transport between health care outlets. About 12 percent of the population is covered by this program. The bulk of the population, 83.7 percent, is covered by the national health insurance program, most through payroll deductions from the wages of family breadwinners. Others are covered through voluntary, income-based contributions in the case of the self-employed or by virtue of being pensioners who contributed to the insurance program during their working life. Those who are not covered can use private sector health providers or can use public providers on a fee-for-service basis.

The applicant for free health insurance must provide information on his or her head of household and the household's composition, earnings and housing conditions. S/he must bring documents that verify his or her place of residence, the age of the household members and marital status. Bills for electricity, water, rent or mortgage and telephone services are shown to substantiate claims. For those with formal hourly employment contracts, proof of contract and pay must be shown. Although random field checks are supposed to be done on a sample of applicants, in practice no field verifications are done. The reliance on documentation brought in by applicants is well suited to Costa Rica, where literacy is universal and a high share of transactions is formally documented.

The fee-waiving is carried out by permanent social workers in all clinics and hospitals. The fee-waiving system takes up about a fifth of their time. The review takes up about an hour and a half per applicant. On average, targeting costs are about US$1.30 per recipient.

In contrast to the hospital fee-waiving schemes in Belize and the Dominican Republic, the Costa Rican program for free health insurance is much better implemented. The administrative review of the applicants is methodical. The requirement that applicants bring in documentation to support some of their claims contributes to its seriousness. Although field checks are not done, the review of the documents in the office serves much the same purpose. The benefit gained is also much larger. The value of health services per beneficiary family is on the order of US$150 per year.

The incidence of the program is excellent. Indeed, the share going to the poorest quintile (55 percent of program benefits) is the third highest of all the programs reviewed. This is partly due to a meaningful applicant review process, but it may also be due in part to the extensive coverage of the national health scheme. Because coverage under the regular plan is so high, the uncovered people who form the potential applicant pool for this program are already concentrated in the lower ranges of the income distribution.

COSTA RICAN PENSIONS FOR THE INDIGENT ELDERLY. Just as Costa Rica has a system to admit indigent, noncontributing people to the health insurance scheme, it also has a pension plan for the indigent elderly who are not covered by the contributory pension scheme. Those admitted to the program receive a monthly cash payment based on the number of dependents in their household. The top of the range is US$31 per month for those with three or more dependents. The average was US$25 per month during 1990. The household also gains the same medical benefits as those granted under the free health insurance plan.

The pension program is administered by the Social Work sections of the Pension Administration units of the Social Security Institute. There are 69 local branches to which applicants apply. The work is actually done by the 18 social workers in the five regional offices. The applicant must provide information on family composition, income, regular expenses and housing conditions and ownership. A visit to the household should be performed, but in practice, this is done only sporadically.

The program is meant to reach those who are "evidently needy," but no definition or guideline is provided as to what this means. Guidelines are given on priority groups as shown in Table 5.4. Given the lack of definition of "neediness," the social workers frequently use the minimum income at which a social security contribution is required as the informal eligibility cut-off point. They also seem to give priority to the handicapped, possibly because their eligibility is verifiable. The handicapped receive 42 percent of the pensions under this program, although they are not the highest-priority group according to the program's objectives.

In addition to the lack of firm guidelines for social workers to follow in evaluating need, there is some suggestion that political pressure is brought to bear on the evaluation as well. Most of the applicants have letters from local political party' activists recommending that the pension be granted.

The calculation of administrative costs for this program is a good illustration of the methodological problems that are frequently encountered. There is no regular recertification (one of the flaws of the program). Rather, beneficiaries stay on the rolls indefinitely. There is also a ceiling on the number of participants due to a limited budget. In 1990, the number of new persons admitted was about 5,000, just one-tenth of the total program enrollment of 50,000. Taking average administrative costs for the program as a whole and dividing by the 50,000 total beneficiaries gives a cost of US$12.50 per beneficiary. Of that, the targeting cost—that is, the

Table 5.4   Costa Rican Priority Groups for Pensions for the Elderly Indigent

1. Those aged 65 and older

2. Handicapped persons of any age

3. Widows aged 55 and older

4. Orphans under the age of 15

5. Dependent elderly, handicapped or youth under the age of 15 who cannot take care of themselves

6. Indigents between 45 and 65 with limited ability to work

cost of screening new applicants—is estimated to be about one-tenth, or US$1.36. However, if only the 5,000 new enrollees are used in calculating the marginal cost of screening a candidate, the figure is 10 times higher—US$13.60 rather than US$1.36.

There is an interesting contrast in incidence between this program and the free health insurance program. Both have similar requirements. Although neither have well-specified guidelines, the variables considered in the decision are similar. Both are carried out by social workers with the same kind of background. Indeed, both are carried out by the Social Security Institute, though by different offices. And yet the incidence of the health insurance program is much more progressive than that of the pension program. Furthermore, it should be noted that the informal guidelines being used for income are different and ought to lead to the opposite incidence ranking. For pensions, the informal guideline used was the minimum pension, which in 1990 was about US$86 per month. For free health insurance, the informal guideline reported by social workers was the minimum wage, which in 1990 was about US$140 per month. Apparently, other factors account for the incidence of the free health insurance being more progressive than the incidence of the noncontributory pensions.

While the case studies do not provide answers as to why this should be the case, they suggest several tantalizing possibilities. First, there may be differences in the potential applicant pool. The pensions for the elderly indigent also confer health insurance coverage, so this group has been removed from the candidate pool of the free health insurance program. Second, there is presumably more self-targeting for the health insurance benefit. The wealthy will self-select out by using private services for much of their health care, due to the time costs incurred in applying for either program. Third, it may be that the verification of household economic status is accomplished more accurately by having the applicant present written documentation and receipts than by visiting a household. Fourth, in the pension program, it is possible that the social workers considered some elderly people as independent households where the survey identified them as members of their children's wage-earning households. Fifth, the case studies suggest that political pressure is a bigger factor in the pension program. Finally, it should be noted that the less progressive pension program makes no attempt to recertify need periodically among its beneficiaries. Since the certification is done for the household in which the elderly person lives and since the elderly in Costa Rica mostly live with their working-age children, their welfare levels may change over time. In contrast, the more progressive free health care program does have a mechanism for recertifying need.

Proxy Means Test

A proxy means test uses household characteristics other than income to categorize the household as eligible or ineligible for a social program and to determine which of several benefit levels to grant. The characteristics are chosen and weighted according to how well they predict income. They are thus proxies for income. The reason for using a proxy means test is that, while income itself can be hard to measure or verify, other kinds of information about the household are good predictors of income and are easier to collect. Proxy means tests should also cause fewer work disincentives. Since income is not the determinant of eligibility, program applicants will not have an incentive to change their work behavior in order to minimize their income.

The logistical issues for a proxy means test are largely the same as for a means test. Staff must investigate cases. There is a choice about whether to have them visit the household or not. The way the information gathered is used in deciding whether to admit an applicant may be more complex than in the means test, in that more variables are considered. It is more systematic than the social worker evaluation, which may be based on the same kinds of variables but which relies on a subjective evaluation rather than on an explicit, formulaic analysis.

Chile's Ficha CAS system is a good example of a proxy means test. Information on household characteristics is gathered on interview forms, a set formula is applied to the answers and eligibility for social programs is thereby determined. Two large cash transfer programs—the family subsidy and old age pensions for the poor—are assigned in this way, as are housing subsidies. This system was tried for both the clinic-based complementary feeding program and the school feeding program on an experimental basis, but was discontinued in both cases, as will be discussed shortly. Recently, water subsidies began to be assigned using the Ficha CAS. The information is gathered by social workers during visits to the home, which allow many of the variables to be verified. A widespread outreach effort was made when the system was first implemented. Social workers reached near census level coverage in those areas of the country where the previous poverty maps showed the poor to be concentrated.

In the first stage of the implementation of CAS, a very simple form was used to collect information on 14 variables of the location and characteristics of housing and the educational attainment and labor activity of household members. The form was constructed so that, next to each possible answer, there was a score. For example, Question 6 asked what kind of cooking fuel was used in the home. An answer of gas or electricity got a score of four, coal or paraffin, a score of two and wood or other, a score of zero. These scores were marked by the social worker in a column on the right side of the card. At the bottom of the card, the social worker totaled the score. At the end of the interview, therefore, the social worker could tell household members whether they qualified for certain social programs. For those qualifying, the social worker would then explain the application procedure and what benefits were available. The interview therefore helped to lower both leakage and undercoverage.

In an evaluation of the program, four major flaws were found. First, the simple, public formula used to weight information made it easy for the candidates to know how to bribe the social workers to falsify the information on the form. Second, the formula overestimated poverty in rural areas. Third, the information on health and education was too scant to inform decisions about such a large part of the social sector budget. Finally, the formula could not handle situations where two families shared a single dwelling. Since 1987, the survey form has been lengthened to include questions on income and wealth and on the use of health and education services or social programs. Now, rather than the scores being figured by the interviewers in the field, the answers are entered into computer databases that calculate the score and determine eligibility for programs. In some municipalities, data entry and weighting is done in-house; in many, it is contracted out to private firms.

A small unit in the Ministry of Planning oversees the CAS. It set the original formula, trained municipal staff and uses aggregate results in its sectoral planning. The household visits are organized and carried out by municipalities. At a rough estimate, about 1,100 people work on implementing the Ficha CAS system. Except for the central team of four or five staff in the planning ministry, most of these people work for the system only part-time. Their full cost cannot be ascribed to the system, but they must be trained and supervised. The total cost of the system is approximately US$5 per assessment.

Three programs use the CAS system now. For these programs, the CAS system represents from 0.5 to 5.4 percent of the program costs (figured as though the whole of the CAS cost were a cost of each program, which is, of course, an overestimate). For the two cash transfer programs that rely most on the CAS score, 72 and 62 percent of program benefits reach the poorest 30 percent of the population, the ostensible goal. These are among the best targeted programs reviewed in this work. The third program administers housing subsidies. There is a down-payment requirement in addition to the CAS selection. Since the poorest people sometimes cannot meet the down-payment, the incidence of the program is less progressive than for those programs that use the CAS alone. Indeed, the housing program's incidence is the third worst reviewed here.

Two other programs tried to use the early version of the CAS and rejected it, largely because it proved to be administratively impractical. The PNAC distributes food supplements through health clinics (see the nutritional risk and self-targeting sections). For a time, it tried to use the Ficha CAS scores to give larger benefits to those at "socioeconomic" risk of malnutrition. However, the CAS scores were kept manually by the municipalities, and the health clinics found it difficult to get access to them in a timely, easy fashion. In some cases, the nurses would interview the clients in the clinic, but this took up their time doing duties that were not really part of their jobs. In any case, the results were deemed to be inaccurate without the household visit. The school lunch program had similar problems, plus the additional problem that, for eligibility for school lunches, they needed to know the scores of all the children in school. The CAS, of course, had only been applied to roughly the bottom half of the population. In the end, both programs stopped using the system. It should be noted that some of the problems that these programs experienced may now have been solved or minimized with the introduction of CAS-II in 1987.

Costa Rica's University Tuition Waivers

Costa Rica has a system for waiving university tuition that is more sophisticated in classification and information but simpler in logistics than the Chilean system. The students applying for tuition waivers must go to the office on campus to get application forms, which they take home to fill out. The forms are long and detailed, asking questions about family composition, monetary income, housing characteristics, utility bills and ownership of real estate and vehicles. The applicant's course of study, plans and grades are included. The degree of detail is such that it asks not just whether or not the family owns a car, but what make, model and age it is. In support of some of this information, the student must bring verifying documents, such as vehicle tax receipts and utility bills.

The formula used to score all the information has gone through two iterations, as has the Ficha CAS. Originally, the formula was based on a principal components analysis, but now a regression formula is now used. The formula estimates a household welfare level. That predicted value is then used to assign to students one of eleven categories of tuition waiver. The benefits for each category and the percentage of students included in each category are shown in Table 5.5.

The program is administered by a staff of eight people in the Student Life office at the University of Costa Rica. The staff spend about 45 percent of their time reviewing applications and the rest administering the benefits. The budget of the program consists of the tuition revenue from paying students, which is then passed

Table 5.5   Costa Rican University Tuition Waivers

Category	Percentage of Beneficiaries	Percentage of Tuition Waived	Other Benefits
1	1.7	15	
2	1.7	25	
3	2.9	35	
4	4.0	45	
5	6.0	60	Discount lunch
6	9.7	75	Discount lunch
7	12.2	80	Discount lunch
8	13.3	90	Discount lunch
9	14.7	95	Discount lunch, residence
10	20.3	100	Free lunch, discount medicine, residence
11	13.4	100 + cash	Free lunch, free medicine, residence

on to poorer students in cash scholarships or the in-kind benefits that accompany the highest grades of waiver. The total administrative costs are about 16 percent of the program costs or US$14 per waived student. The targeting costs are on average about half that, 8 percent of program costs or US$7 per student beneficiary. Unfortunately, no incidence study is available.

Simulations from Other Countries

Grosh and Baker (1992) used simulations based on household survey data to see how well proxy means tests that ask only for very simple information, like the one used in Chile, could be expected to work for different countries, poverty lines and amounts of available information. The simulations used household characteristics to predict a welfare level. Then, eligibility for a hypothetical welfare program was granted on the basis of this predicted score. Finally, to assess targeting accuracy, the predicted welfare level was compared to the actual welfare reported in the survey. For most of the simulations, the poverty line was set so that 30 percent of the population would be eligible.

The simulations were done with different numbers and kinds of variables. The first set used variables that are easy to verify, such as the location and characteristics of the dwelling. Then family characteristics and the number and type of durable goods owned were added. The addition of more variables is helpful in lowering undercoverage, but is not important in reducing leakage (see Table 5.6). In Bolivia, for example, when variables on family characteristics (size, age, sex and education of the head) and ownership of durable goods are added to location and housing characteristics, leakage is nearly constant but undercoverage falls by half.

Using the full set of information regarding location, housing, family and durable goods for most scenarios, leakage is shown to be on the order of 25 to 35 percent of benefits, clearly an acceptable range when contrasted to most program experience. The one exception that has much higher leakage is the case where the poverty line is set so that only 10 percent of the population are meant to be eligible for the benefits. With such strict eligibility, it is harder to identify the targeted people correctly. Undercoverage varies more from country to country. For Jamaica, for the basic simulation, 39 percent of those who were truly poor were incorrectly identified as not being poor. In Lima, Peru, the undercoverage problem was worse, being estimated at 54 percent. This may be due to the fact that, when data from only one city are used, the variation in household characteristics is smaller than when nationwide data are used.

An important modification was carried out to reflect more accurately how programs seem to work in practice. Rather than trying to screen all households across the income distribution, one simulation assumed that only the poorest 50 percent of the population would bother to apply for a program and need screening. In that case, the predictions were better. Leakage was lowered a little, and the misclassification of the poor as nonpoor (undercoverage) occurred only a third as often.

Table 5.6   Proxy Means Test Simulations

	Leakage	*Undercoverage*
Information Bases Contrasted: Bolivia		
Location and housing	22	80
Location, housing and family characteristics	24	50
Location, housing, family characteristics and durable goods	24	40
Best 5 variables of any kind	31	57
Countries Contrasted (full information base)		
Jamaica	34	41
Urban Bolivia	24	39
Lima, Peru	35	54
Poverty Lines Contrasted: Jamaica		
10% Poverty line	67	36
30% Poverty line	34	41
40% Poverty line	25	39
Applicant Pools Contrasted: Jamaica		
All households screened	34	41
Only poorest 50% screened	28	13

Source: Grosh and Baker (1992).

Summary

In conclusion, the proxy means test represents a viable alternative to a straight income test when program administrators believe that incomes will be misrepresented or are difficult to compute because of irregular or in-kind earnings. The proxy means test requires the same kind of apparatus to gather information as the means test or social worker evaluation. In the end, it is much like a social worker evaluation. It exchanges the subjective evaluation of information for an objective (if sometimes arbitrary) one. Proxy means tests in general are computerized and thus do require that the staff administering them have the requisite computer skills and have access to the necessary equipment.

Gender of Household Head

Because female-headed households are generally poorer than male-headed households (see Gupta and others 1989), it is occasionally suggested that the gender of the household head should be used as the targeting criterion for social programs. Few programs have used this criterion, so we have little evidence of how it might work in practice, but three methodological problems indicate the limited usefulness of using the gender of headship as the sole criterion of admission to poverty alleviation programs.[3]

First, although female-headed households may, on average, be poorer than male-headed households, the correlation with poverty is not always strong enough to provide a good targeting indicator. Errors of inclusion and exclusion can both be very high.

In Jamaica, for example, the mean per capita welfare level of male-headed households is 26 percent higher than for female-headed households. Nonetheless, the probability that female-headed households will fall below the poverty line is only very slightly higher. If the poverty line is set so that 30 percent of individuals fall below it, the probability that individuals in female-headed households will fall below the poverty line is 32 percent. For those in male-headed households, the probability is 28 percent. This demonstrates some correlation, but not enough to be a good targeting indicator by itself. Indeed, the errors of inclusion and exclusion are both so high that the universal provision of services would produce the same kinds of numbers. Using female-headship as the eligibility criteria, half the population below the poverty line would be denied benefits, while, of those receiving them, two-thirds would be above the poverty line (Louat, Grosh and van der Gaag 1993).

In Honduras, the aggregate correlation between poverty and female-headship is stronger. With a poverty line set so that 30 percent of households are poor, the probability that a female-headed household will be poor is 36.8 percent. For male-headed households, the probability is 24 percent. The correlation between poverty and female-headship is much greater in urban areas than in rural areas. It is also much greater among the poorest 10 percent of households (see Winter 1992). Thus, in Honduras, female-headship is a much more promising targeting criterion than in Jamaica, especially for programs geared to the very poor in urban areas.

A second problem that limits the usefulness of using the gender of the household head as a targeting criteria is the difficulty of determining who is the head of the household and whether s/he is single.

In Honduras, the Bono Madre Jefe de Familia was targeted to female-headed households that met an income criteria and that included children attending primary schools. The teachers were assigned the duty of determining who was eligible for the food coupon. Rather than use legal marital status as the definition of headship, the program used a more flexible notion of partnership, recognizing that many women are in unions that are not legalized by formal marriage, but that do involve a male contribution to the household's welfare. Conversely, not all legal husbands are present in the household or contribute to its economic welfare. Thus, using "real" union status rather than "legal" union status may be a more accurate reflection of poverty. It is, however, problematic to determine in practice. Essentially, the teacher, with no guidelines for evaluating individual contributions to a household, had to decide whether a woman had a partner or not. This was not only somewhat arbitrary, but led to teachers looking into sensitive personal issues, sometimes using children or other community members as their source of information rather than the household itself (targeting by gossip?).

An interesting side issue was that the Catholic Church disapproved of the notion of supporting single mothers on the grounds that it might promote promiscuity or divorce. Thus, the Church, which is a powerful influence in the political arena and on the behavior patterns of households, opposed a social welfare program targeted to the needy on the grounds of its targeting mechanism.

Many of the same concerns were raised about the United States' AFDC program. Until 1988, only households without male breadwinners were eligible. Moffitt (1992) reports that the empirical studies that have tried to quantify the effect of the AFDC program on family structure have been far from conclusive.

Finally, there is a conceptual problem in some cases. Where female-headship is a criterion *additional* to income criteria, it implies that female-headed households deserve help more than equally poor households headed by men. However, on poverty criteria alone, it is clear that equally poor families deserve equal aid regardless of their gender composition.

Nutritional Status or Risk

Nutritional status or risk are obvious criteria for targeting nutrition programs. Indeed, even some programs whose objective is as much poverty alleviation as it is nutritional improvement use nutritional status as a targeting mechanism since it is an objective indicator that correlates well with poverty. Also, a mechanism is often already in place for gathering the information for medical purposes. For young children, weight for age and growth faltering are the nutrition indicators most commonly used as targeting mechanisms.

Using nutritional status or risk as determined in pre-existing growth monitoring arrangements is usually a viable and efficient system; indeed, it may be the most broadly desirable and replicable system. There are, nonetheless, some drawbacks that should be considered.

First, nutritional status may not be a perfect indicator. If the goal is to prevent malnutrition, waiting until children have become malnourished before allowing them to enter the program is not desirable. Using a nutritional risk indicator can solve this problem, but may require somewhat more complex information and decisionmaking. If the goal is actually to identify poor as opposed to malnourished families, the correlation between malnutrition and poverty is high but certainly not perfect. Using the nutritional status of children as a targeting indicator, for example, will obviously not detect poor families with no young children.

Second, the system of growth monitoring is probably not universal. Public health programs frequently have problems reaching all of the poorest members of the population. This is especially the case when outreach visits from clinics into communities are infrequent. Thus, using a health-based growth monitoring system may result in errors of exclusion among high-priority groups. On the other hand, the fact that the well-to-do tend not to use public health care introduces an element of self-targeting that helps to lower errors of inclusion.

In addition to inadequate coverage, the growth-monitoring system may also suffer from other problems. Equipment may be missing. Weighing procedures may not be standardized. Recordkeeping may not be adequate or even be designed in a way that is useful to the targeted program.

If significant amounts of benefit are targeted on the basis of growth monitoring data, the inducement to take children to be weighed may significantly increase the demand for growth monitoring. The logistical capacity will need to be increased accordingly. The experience of the pilot phase of the Honduran Bono Materno-Infantil is a case in point. Public health clinics had always administered growth monitoring. Then, the new food coupon program required children to be up-to-date on their preventive care, including growth monitoring, every month before they received their food stamp.[4] This brought more children to the health system but also increased the frequency of weighings from an average of quarterly to monthly, causing clinics to be overrun with children to be weighed. (See Chapter 7 for a more complete discussion.)

Finally, there are issues of political economy. While nurses or nurse auxiliaries have traditionally monitored children's growth, they have not always been responsible for assigning benefits to social programs. If the food or food stamps are distributed directly from the clinic (the most common practice because it both cuts administrative costs and reinforces the link between the food and preventive care), the nurses may find this responsibility unwelcome, as it leaves them open to pressures from potential beneficiaries. They may also face greater security risks if part of their job involves handling, transporting or guarding the food or food stamps to be delivered.

Chilean PNAC

The Chilean PNAC program uses growth faltering to identify children who are at risk of malnutrition. Children at risk receive bigger rations than the small basic ration assigned to those who are growing satisfactorily. Eligibility for the program in general is granted to children under the age of five and pregnant or lactating women who have demonstrated adequate prior use of preventive services. Most of the PNAC recipients use the public health system, although users of privately run but government-subsidized health maintenance organizations can also go to public clinics and receive PNAC rations. The 17 percent of participants classified as being at nutritional risk receive half of the food distributed through the program.

The combination of the regular levels of rations available to all and the large rations available to those at nutritional risk is an innovative system with several advantages. It provides some incentive for all children and pregnant or lactating women to use preventive health care services, and it may be able to maintain political support since everyone can benefit. Nonetheless, it concentrates program benefits on the neediest. (See Chapter 7 for more on the PNAC.)

The logistics of the two-tiered system have not proved unduly problematic. Children's growth was being monitored and recorded for health reasons anyway and the health system's coverage was high, so the introduction of the PNAC did not result in any new burdens being placed on the system. The only new complication has been the need to note the size of ration given to each child. This requires a sophisticated inventory and accounting system to keep track of the various benefit levels but, in the Chilean context, this has not been a major problem. Children eligible for the bigger ration are weighed monthly, more often than is standard for healthy children. But this is the norm for medical supervision and is not, strictly speaking, a requirement of the two-tiered benefit system.

There is a school of thought in Chile that holds that the growth faltering criteria are too generous. The nutrition profession still disagrees about the absolute standards to be used. Furthermore, normal variations in water retention can be large relative to expected weight gains. Because of these factors, children who are not malnourished (in other words, weigh an adequate amount for their age) can stay in the system for many months (because they gain weight slowly).

If the weight gain criterion were changed for one of absolute low weight, the size of the group receiving the extra ration would fall by about half, as the malnutrition rate in Chile is only 8 percent (using a cutoff of one standard deviation below the norm—ACC/SCN 1989). It should be noted that the program's logistics would be virtually unchanged if the growth criterion were changed in favor of a weight criterion. Children would be weighed, their weights recorded and their food ration assigned in much the same way. So what may be an important issue for medicine and for program costs is not so important administratively.

Peruvian PANFAR

The Peruvian PANFAR program uses a more complicated way of determining nutritional risk. For each child, the health worker in the participating health post fills out a form that enumerates 10 risk factors. As shown in Table 5.7, these include both socioeconomic and biomedical factors.

Table 5.7   Peru: PANFAR's Nutrition Risk Factors

Socio-economic indicators
Head of household with less than 5 years of education
Head of household unemployed or with unstable job
Father or mother missing from household
Mother's biological indicators
Pregnant woman with arm circumference of less than 8 inches
Mother with three or more children under 5 years old (living or dead)
Children's biological indicators
Underweight at birth (less than 2.5 kg)
Nutritional status (weight for age indicator)
Breastfed for less than 2 months
Serious illness in the past 3 months
Birth intervals of less than 2 years

If a child under two years old is malnourished (in other words, is less than 90 percent of the normal weight for his age), he or she is automatically selected to be a beneficiary of the program. Otherwise, the health care worker counts the number of positive answers out of the 10 variables for all of the interviewed families and ranks them in descending order. The available rations for the health post are filled in order of priority, with a high-risk family being defined as one with four or more positive answers. The allocation of rations among health posts nationwide is based on the available information on population and nutritional status as a determinant of need, with the state of the transport network and the availability of health infrastructure as possible limits to feasibility.

The system is designed to be applied to all families who use participating health posts. Extension visits are made to those families who do not come in of their own accord. Eligibility is granted for six month intervals, so the information should be updated twice a year.

In practice, a recent study showed that 89 percent of families interviewed had been assessed for eligibility. However, in half of those cases, only the socioeconomic criteria had been applied, while no assessment had been made of the biomedical risk factors. Furthermore, extension visits were relatively few, with only 16 percent of beneficiaries being identified as having received them. This faulty application of the system is probably due to insufficient emphasis being given to the biomedical risk factors in the training of program participants. With further training, it is hoped that this will improve.

PANFAR's total administrative costs consist of 22 percent of the total budget. This includes the imputed value of the time of local health workers, which accounts for a quarter of administrative costs. Transport expenses for the food account for a third of administrative expenses or about 7 percent of program costs. The transport costs are higher than in other programs. For example, in Chile's PNAC, transport is only 1 percent of costs. But many of the poor in Peru live in remote mountainous areas where access is very difficult. The high cost of transport is a direct result of trying to avoid errors of exclusion. The expenses attributed to targeting itself are about 4 percent of program costs or US$0.72 per child per year. These are for the training of health care workers, for program evaluation and for the salaries of the central supervisory staff. The cost does not include the cost of the research that led to the formulation of the high-risk criteria. Nor does it include the staff time of the health care workers doing the growth monitoring.

Dominican Republic PROMI

The PROMI program in the Dominican Republic focuses on growth monitoring, nutrition education and the donation of three kilos of staple commodities to pregnant and lactating women and children under the age of three who are at nutritional risk. The program operates in the three poorest health regions of the country. Regular health workers in the clinics in these areas identify participants as they come to the health system for medical care. Individuals who meet the risk criteria are encouraged to join the PROMI program.

A pregnant woman is deemed to be at risk of malnutrition if any of the following conditions apply to her: (a) she has an upper-arm circumference of less than 23.5 cm; (b) she had a pregnancy in the preceding year; (c) her last child died in the first year after birth; or (d) she is over 35. Children under the age of three are deemed to be at risk if they have second- or third-degree low weight for age or if they have not gained weight for two consecutive months.

Each clinic can handle up to 200 PROMI participants. They are divided into four groups that each come on specific days to get their growth monitored, to participate in a nutrition class and to receive their food ration. If a clinic has more than 200 persons at risk, priority is given to the children. Children are kept in the program for a minimum of six months in order to ensure that the mother is sufficiently exposed to the nutrition education. If after that time the child has gained weight for two consecutive months, s/he is graduated from the program. Lactating mothers and their infants are kept in the program for the first year after birth.

The program represents an interesting piggybacking of an NGO nutrition education/food program onto Ministry of Health infrastructure. The identification of the candidates, the distribution of food and the nutrition instruction are done by regular Ministry of Health staff. The clinic must provide the scales and measuring boards for growth monitoring and a clean, lockable area for food storage. The program monitoring is done by CARE staff who come to the clinics on a rotating schedule.

Although no formal assessment has been done, program workers are not greatly worried about leakage. The incidence of poverty in the three targeted regions is extremely high, and the use of public health facilities is limited almost exclusively to the poor. They are, however, concerned that the health system may not capture many of those at greatest risk, given the physical, cultural and sometimes financial barriers to health care access. The food ration does seem to be an effective device for keeping participants in the PROMI program. (During a health worker strike, no food was delivered, although the nutrition classes carried on. Without the food, attendance was low.) Since the food ration is not available to all, it probably has less impact on getting mothers in for the first visit (during which their risk status should be assessed) than in programs that give food to all pregnant women or young children.

Costa Rican CEN-CENAI Program

The Costa Rican CEN-CENAI program combines nutritional status and psychosocial risk categories with geographic location as eligibility requirements. Three kinds of benefits are provided by the program: daycare centers that offer feeding, nutrition education, growth monitoring and early childhood education; a take-home milk program; and a take-home family food basket.

Children are granted entry to the CEN-CENAI program in accordance with the following priorities: (a) those who are malnourished, those who are mistreated or abandoned, those who are referred by an institution and those who have risk scores of 40 points or higher; (b) those whose mothers work outside the home and who have risk scores of 50 points or higher; and (c) those whose mothers do not work outside the home and who have risk scores of 60 points or higher. The psychosocial risk factors and their weights are shown in Table 5.8.

The malnourished children are identified through the local health centers. When a child is found to be malnourished, the clinic refers him or her to the appropriate CEN-CENAI center. Admission is then automatic. For those entering because of psychosocial risk, the director of the local center fills out an assessment form and determines the score. Most of the applications come at the request of the family. If workers in clinics or schools find a reason to be concerned about a child's welfare, they may also ask the center director to do an evaluation on an outreach basis. In order to be admitted to the daycare centers, which have monthly benefits that are 10 times the value of the take-home food packets, the family must live within a kilometer of a center. Thus, there is also a clear element of geographic targeting.

Table 5.8   CEN-CENAI Psychosocial Risk Factors

Characteristic	*Score*
Mother or foster mother younger than 18	20
Mother's education	
Primary	10
Secondary	8
Presence of some social pathology in family	15
Mother's occupation	
None or unskilled labor	5
Semi-skilled labor	4
Skilled labor	3
No-one home during the day	10
Job security of parents	
Seasonal work	5
Both parents unemployed	5
Household income (monthly)	
Less than C 20,000	15
C 20,000–C 30,000	10
C 30,000–C 40,000	5
Marital status	
Single parent	15
Housing	
Donated, rented or informal	5
Inadequate water supply	2
Inadequate sewerage	2
Inadequate sanitation	2
Inadequate physical condition	2
More than two persons per bedroom	2

The eligibility criteria are very specifically defined for children under the age of seven. The programs, however, are also meant to serve school-age children where no school feeding centers exist. Although it is not specified how their need should be assessed, in practice, the same risk assessment is done. Finally, for pregnant and lactating women, the only general guidelines are that to participate in the take-home milk program, they should be poor, live too far from a daycare center to participate there and receive health care from the local health clinic. Pregnant and lactating women are also eligible for benefits in the centers, and 7 percent of those in the centers are, in fact, women.

It is worth noting that the risk factors are not meant to stress poverty to the exclusion of other factors. For example, it is possible for a single mother who has a semi-skilled job earning between C 20,000 and C 30,000 per month and with no one staying in the home to take care of her young child to qualify to enter the child in the full-time daycare program. This profile fits that of a middle-class public sector employee. The household's income level is certainly above the poverty line used by the Inter-American Development Bank (IDB) of C 6605 per person per month.

Program benefits (and costs) are high, but the administrative shares are not. Total administration consists of about 9 percent of program costs. The targeting costs (for the screening of applicants) are 3 percent of program costs or US$7.72 per beneficiary.

Leakages are very low according to the set goals. A survey of 546 families in the daycare programs shows that only 6 percent do not meet any of the requisite conditions (malnutrition, family pathology, low income or working mother). Thirty-five percent meet one of these conditions, 41 percent meet two and 18 percent meet at least three.

Even taking income as the only criterion, the programs compare well with most of the others reviewed. For the daycare centers, 44 percent of benefits go to the households in the first quintile and 25 percent to the households in the second quintile. The take-home food programs are even better targeted, with 56 percent of benefits going to families from the poorest quintile and 23 percent of benefits going to the second poorest quintile.

Conclusions

The blanket fear that individual assessment mechanisms are too costly or are unmanageable is unjustified. There are many ways to minimize administrative complexity. The costs run the gamut from US$0.35 to US$40 per assessment. Experience shows that some of the simplest variants can produce satisfactory targeting outcomes.

A principal determinant of the incidence outcomes is not the screening device built into the targeting mechanism itself but the characteristics of the candidate pool. The university loan programs are hard pressed to produce progressive outcomes, given that the student body is wealthy. In contrast, the incidence of Costa

Rica's free health insurance program is influenced not only by the screening mechanism, but also by the fact that the uncovered part of the population is concentrated at the lower end of the income distribution.

It is not possible to say how much more accurate the more sophisticated screening devices are compared with the simple ones. This stems partly from the fact that we do not have incidence figures for all the devices and is compounded by the unquantified but clear differences in the potential applicant pool. In general, the more sophisticated methods are used for programs where the applicant pool is concentrated at the upper end of the income spectrum and where benefits are high.

It is clear in almost all of the case studies that the programs are not administered as well as they could be. Although the systems are sensible, many programs lack the staff, equipment, training or time to implement the mechanisms well. Thus, the low administrative costs are partly the result of underspending rather than of efficiency of design. It could well be that spending more on administration would have a greater impact on poverty, would generate better incidence and, ultimately, would lower costs. Nevertheless, the quality of.administration does not appear to be any worse than is the case in most government programs. Indeed, it may well be better than the average administration of basic health care or primary education.

Looking at the various subclasses of mechanisms, some lessons emerge:

- Very simple means tests that make little or no attempt to value in-kind or seasonal income or to verify income can nonetheless produce satisfactory incidence outcomes. Elements of self-selection may play a role in this, which implies that the simple means tests will be less appropriate in circumstances where benefits are large.
- Proxy means tests seem to be a promising option. They avoid the problems of relying on reported monetary income, relying instead on more accurately reported and verifiable correlates of poverty. This avoids problems of work disincentives and the misreporting of income.
- Social worker evaluations vary widely in their effectiveness. In the Dominican Republic and Belize hospital fee waiver programs, while there is no quantified incidence, it is clear that the programs are not good at distinguishing the ability to pay. In Costa Rica, one of the programs that uses social worker evaluations has quite good incidence, while the other has an incidence outcome that puts the program near the bottom of the ranking according to the share of benefits that accrue to the bottom 40 percent of the population.
- The nutritional status and risk criteria produce good incidence. They place some demands on the staff of health clinics, but they also provide an incentive for those who are poorest to get preventive health care, and they allow a synergy of benefits among health services, health education and food or income supplements.
- The nutritional risk criteria can be used to give a low level of benefit to all comers and a high level of benefit to those at nutritional risk. This

both improves health care coverage and has the political advantage of being open to the whole population. In cases where the logistics of having more than one benefit level are not too complicated, this is an attractive option.

Notes

1. In Jamaica, there are about 150 social workers. They spend about 100 working days per year (half of a working year of 200 days) enrolling beneficiaries. The means testing is done irregularly, but an assumption of every other year might be plausible. Thus, about 75,000 means tests would be performed in a year, using 15,000 staff days. This implies a ratio of five means tests per day of social worker time. In Honduras, 13,000 teachers working three days provide 39,000 staff days to means tests about 125,000 children or 3.2 beneficiaries per day.

2. Information on Colombia's ICETEX program is taken from Betancur-Mejia (1990).

3. Of course, this is not to say that programs should not pay attention to gender and headship issues more generally. Housing programs, for example, may wish to ensure that property titles are either jointly registered or are registered to the woman rather than to the man. This can ensure that the woman and children retain property rights in the event of the dissolution of the union and can give the woman access to credit through the collateral provided by the house.

4. Eligibility was not based on nutritional status itself, but growth monitoring was required as part of the package of preventive services.

6

Targeting by Group Characteristic and Geographic Area

Group Characteristic Mechanisms

This class of mechanism gives benefits to all persons in some broad group, where membership of the group is so easy to determine that few administrative problems arise. Geographic targeting is a very common form. Another very common way in which this form of targeting is applied is through health or nutrition programs meant for young children and for pregnant and lactating women. School lunches are most commonly targeted by including some schools in the program while excluding others. Thus, instead of having students assessed individually, they are assessed in groups. Most of these programs do not rely on demographic criteria alone, but also use complementary mechanisms such as the use of health or education services. Therefore, we discuss those programs in which the complementary mechanisms are used.

Less common examples of targeting by group characteristic are fee waivers at hospitals or dental clinics for children in school uniform or for members of the armed forces. These are very easy to administer in cases where a public agency provides the service and where the assessor can tell that the client is a member of the eligible group because s/he wears a specific uniform or s/he carries an identification card certifying that s/he is a student or a member of the armed forces or other favored group. Given that so few programs use only this mechanism, no case studies were done for those programs.

Service providers who charge for their services sometimes face an incentive problem. They may try to move nonpaying users to the bottom of the queue or to avoid serving them at all. An example of this is found in Jamaica. The bus system is operated by private concessionaires, and the fares are regulated by the government. The bus fare for children in school uniform is set at below average cost, and the fare for other passengers is set at above average cost. In the aggregate, the discount and the profitable fares should average out. But each individual bus driver or company will earn more money if it can carry many adults and few school children. Moreover, buses are greatly overcrowded, so the children really do displace full-fare adults. Apparently, many bus drivers refuse to stop for children, especially at the main stops near schools. This makes commuting more difficult, time-consuming and dangerous for schoolchildren than would otherwise be the case. While this problem is not well-quantified, it is generally recognized by the public and transport authorities alike.

Geographic Targeting

In Theory

Many programs are targeted by geographic area, especially those that are provided through the use of a specific kind of physical infrastructure. For example, schools or clinics can be built in poor areas on the assumption that most of their users will, be poor. School lunches can be offered in schools in poor regions but not in wealthier regions. Food supplement programs can be tied to health centers in poor areas. Geographic targeting can be practiced at high levels of aggregation, for example, by state, or at finer levels, for example, by city or by neighborhood.

The overwhelming advantage of geographic targeting is its simplicity. No complex individual assessment mechanism is needed. Planning and budgeting are simple because the planner can easily estimate the size of the population to be served. The program can be easily understood by both the staff and the public.

The disadvantages are that geographic targeting may not be very accurate and can be politically sensitive.

TARGETING INACCURACY. The accuracy of geographic targeting will depend on the heterogeneity of the populations in the different regions. One region may be richer on average, but it will still contain some poor people. Another region may be poorer on average, but will still include some nonpoor residents. This can lead both to high leakage rates and to unsatisfactory coverage of the poor.

In order to estimate how large geographic targeting inaccuracies might be, Baker and Grosh (forthcoming) conduct simulations using household survey data from Jamaica, Mexico and Venezuela. In each case, the "poverty line" is set so that 30 percent of the population is considered to be poor. States are then ranked by mean per capita income (or consumption). The poorest states are admitted to a hypothetical transfer program until approximately 30 percent of the population is covered. Targeting errors and the impact of the transfers on poverty are calculated.

Geographic targeting at the state level results in fairly high leakage and under-coverage. Leakage rates run from 53 to 59 percent of program benefits (see Table 6.1). By comparison, an equal transfer to everyone would result in 70 percent leakage, which is not a great deal higher. State level geographic targeting fails to reach 61 percent of the poor in Mexico and Venezuela and nearly half of the poor in Jamaica.

Table 6.1   Leakage and Undercoverage for State Level Targeting in Three Countries

	Jamaica	*Mexico*	*Venezuela*
Per capita income in wealthiest state	J$9,805	M$21,823	Bs2,831
Per capita income in poorest state	J$3,721	M$ 4,970	Bs 663
Ratio of per capita income: wealthiest/poorest	2.6	4.4	4.3
Leakage rate	53.3	59.3	57.7
Undercoverage rate	48.7	61.0	61.3

Source: Baker and Grosh (forthcoming).

One way to increase the accuracy of geographic targeting is to use smaller geographic units. This is very well illustrated in Mexico. The same kind of simulation described above was run at the state level, the *municipio* level (which corresponds approximately to a county in the United States) and the *localidad* level (which corresponds approximately to a village). Both leakage and coverage improve markedly as the unit used in targeting gets smaller. At the *localidad* level, leakage is 37 percent (see Table 6.2). Compared with the uniform distribution, which implies 70 percent leakage, simply targeting by geographic area at the *localidad* level reduces leakage by almost half. The undercoverage rate also falls to 37 percent, so just over a third of the poor are missed by the program.

POLITICAL SENSITIVITY. Political sensitivities can be aroused if political entities are used as the targeting unit and if they also have voting power. Legislators can, for example, vote against funding for programs that do not include their constituencies. The potential for this is not entirely eliminated by using smaller areas for targeting than are used in the legislature. In the Bolivian Social Investment Fund, for example, the *cantons* (counties) were ranked according to a poverty index and were grouped into high and low priority groups. Because some departments were so much better off than others, they had few or no high-priority *cantons* within

Table 6.2   Mexican Leakage and Undercoverage Rates in Three Targeting Units

	State	*Municipio*	*Localidad*
Per capita income in wealthiest unit	21,823	31,302	44,469
Per capita income in poorest unit	4,970	2,981	209
Ratio of per capita income: wealthiest/poorest	4.4	10.5	212.8
Leakage rate (percent)	59.3	42.3	37.3
Undercoverage rate (percent)	61.0	46.0	37.3

Source: Baker and Grosh (forthcoming).

their boundaries. Indeed, most of the priority *cantons* fell in just three departments. The representatives of the other departments protested at funds going only to those *cantons*, especially as the broader issues of decentralization and the sharing of revenue between the national government and departmental governments were receiving much attention at the time. The priority ranking system had to be modified so that it was used to establish priorities within departments but not among them. Within each department, *cantons* were ranked according to literacy, school enrollment and infant mortality rates. Then the ranked list of *cantons* were divided into four priority groups containing approximately equal shares of the population. The cutoff point on the poverty index that delineated the difference between the first and second tiers in the priority system thus varied by department. Priority 1 *cantons* in each department were given equal treatment in project promotion and evaluation.

Now turn to several examples of geographic targeting drawn from among the case studies. Experience shows that there are a number of different ways that geographic targeting can be put into practice.

By State

The Honduran Bono de Madre Jefe de Familia (BMJF) operates only in certain states that are selected on the basis of a poverty map. A second program, the Bono Materno-Infantil, is still in its pilot phase, but it also will operate only in the poorest health regions. Both of the programs use other targeting criteria as well as state-level geographic targeting.

Mexico is another place where state level geographic targeting is being used. The primary education project—supported by a World Bank loan—focuses on the states of Chiapas, Guerrero, Hidalgo and Oaxaca. These states comprise 13 percent of the total population, but contain one-third of the nation's poor. The headcount index of poverty in these states is twice the national average.

By Municipality

The Honduran Social Investment Fund, the FHIS, uses a geographic targeting formula at the municipal level, which corresponds approximately to a county in the United States (the average population of a municipality is 15,000). The FHIS finances small infrastructure and basic needs projects that are requested and carried out by many different agencies. In allotting the funds available, the FHIS has standards for project quality and goals for the geographic distribution of projects.

The geographic goals are computed as follows. First, an allocation to each municipality is made based on its population. Then, the population-based budget is adjusted by the "poverty correction factor." The correction factors range from 1.25 to 0.83. That is, the poorest municipality would get 25 percent more than it would under a strictly proportional system, and the richest would get 17 percent less than under a strictly proportional system.

In practice, the FHIS has not financed enough projects in the poorest municipalities to comply fully with its targets. The wealthiest municipalities have fared worst, receiving approximately 50 percent of their target allocations (see Table 6.3). In contrast, the three poorest categories of municipalities have received between 60 and 80 percent of their target allocations. The next to richest category, on the other hand, has received 164 percent of its targeted allocation. The overall distribution of the FHIS budget by municipality is somewhat regressive. The poorest 20 percent of municipalities receive 19 percent of FHIS budget. The 34 municipalities rated as "acceptable" or "regular" receive 42 percent of the FHIS budget. The problem with interpreting this is that we do not know which households within in the municipalities benefit. The municipalities in the "acceptable" categories are the largest cities, and they do have significant areas of poverty. If the FHIS projects in the largest cities are in the slums, then the real targeting can be much better than it seems when municipal rather than household measures of incidence are used.

The FHIS funding, in practice, has not strictly complied with the targets because, in general, the poorer areas have fewer government or nongovernmental agencies capable of sponsoring high-quality projects. This is an inherent problem in trying to target demand-driven investment funds. The FHIS geographic poverty targeting system was, in fact, designed as a response to this problem. It serves as a brake, preventing the better-off areas from gobbling up available funds very early in the life of the FHIS. In this light, the FHIS poverty map has probably been a very favorable influence on overall targeting. Certainly, it has encouraged the outreach effort from the FHIS to poorer communities in order to encourage them to apply for project funding.

Table 6.3   Honduran FHIS Planned versus Committed Resources by Municipal Poverty Category, April 1990–September 1991

Municipal Poverty Category	*Total Population (percent)*	*FHIS Budget to Category (percent)*	*Per Capita Commit- ments ($/capita)*	*1990–91 Committed/ Planned (percent)*	*1990 Committed/ Planned (percent)*	*1991 Committed/ Planned (percent)*
Very Poor	20	19	4.9	69	60	71
Poor	21	16	4.1	61	57	62
Deficient	25	22	4.7	81	70	83
Regular	26	39	8.0	164	137	170
Acceptable	8	3	2.2	49	57	48
Total	100	100	5.3	90	79	92

Source: FHIS Mid-term Review.

By Village

The Honduran BMI operates only in the poorest health regions, and its benefits are reserved for pregnant or lactating women and children under the age of five. Because there is neither a big enough budget nor enough operational capacity in each participating health center to cover all the eligible women and children, there is an additional village-level criterion. Each village has a score on a poverty map. From a local census, the local health worker knows how many eligible women and children there should be in each village. If the center does not have enough food stamps in its allocation to serve all those women and children, it will give priority to those from the poorest villages, then from the next poorest and so on. In determining each health center's allotment of food stamps, the program planners try to cover all the eligible women and children from villages with poverty scores higher than a prescribed level.

The strict number of food stamps allocated to each health post does present problems. Although the village criterion is meant to be fair, transparent and verifiable, it is not always perceived that way. In this, as in other geographically targeted programs, there are women in villages that are not covered who are as poor as those in villages that are covered. And, in many cases, the differences in village level poverty are small enough that the residents think of the villages as being equally needy.

A further problem in the Honduran program is the occasional inability to register newborn children or new pregnancies. In a steady state, this should not be a big issue, as approximately as many children should turn five and be moved out of the program as are born.[1] But in this new program, the mechanism for graduating beneficiaries from the program when they are no longer eligible is not yet automated. Furthermore, where inscriptions were rationed and infants were given priority over older children in the original inscriptions, there will not be enough graduations to make way for new newborns. Since the newborns need more medical supervision and are at higher risk of malnutrition than are four year olds, this results in perverse targeting by age (for more on the BMI, see Chapter 7). This is not an inherent problem with the targeting mechanism, but is a result of decisions that were made to cope with underfunding. They are very appropriate in a static sense, but become difficult when program dynamics are considered.

By Neighborhood

Neighborhood level targeting is useful within large urban areas. It can enable programs with small units of service delivery to work in the poorest slums without resulting in any leakage of benefits into the better-off areas of the city.

MEXICAN TORTIVALE AND LICONSA PROGRAMS. The Mexican Tortivale and Liconsa programs use neighborhood level targeting in conjunction with other mechanisms. By only using tortilla and dairy shops which are located in poor neighborhoods, the programs help to ensure that the poor find the program convenient, that the nonpoor do not find it convenient and that the programs are able to lower costs by not setting up outlets where they are not needed.

Neighborhood-level targeting works best when the contact with the necessary structure is frequent. For example, schools, daycare centers or ration shops may be visited daily in the normal course of life, so most household members do not have to travel far to get to them. Clinics or welfare offices, on the other hand, would normally be visited only once a month or less often. People may, therefore, be willing to travel further across town for them. Accordingly, the clients they serve can be more diverse (at least geographically).

Another fact that affects the usefulness of geographic targeting is the size of benefit that is available per visit. Bigger benefits will obviously justify longer travel times.

Neighborhood level targeting is quite often used by nongovernmental organizations. Factors that are frequently associated with NGOs may contribute to this. NGOs are often too small to operate on a regional or national scale anyway. Targeting by neighborhood also fits in well with a development program that uses intensive community contacts not only to provide a given service, such as health care, but to promote community endeavors to raise living standards through a number of channels. Finally, because they are nongovernmental, these organizations are not subject to electoral pressures from the areas that they choose not to serve.

PERU'S GLASS OF MILK PROGRAM. Peru's Glass of Milk program was first started by the municipal government of Lima to combat poverty. It was shortly afterwards extended to other cities with funding from the national government. The program provides a glass of milk each day to its participants. There are three formal eligibility criteria—membership in a specific demographic group, a high level of poverty in the neighborhood and the existence of a neighborhood community organization. Since the community must organize and go through a process to get certified and then the mothers of participating households must pick up, prepare and serve the milk each day, the implied time cost induces a good deal of self-targeting as well.

Once a group organizes itself to request that it be included in the program, a municipal social worker assesses the priority of the request. There is no explicit way of weighing the priorities across the three categories, only within them. Pregnant and lactating women and children under the age of five are the first demographic priority; school-age children are the second. The neighborhood poverty level is determined by an informal visual inspection of the predominant housing materials and the availability of services. Newly settled areas with improvised housing and no services are the first priority. The second priority is poor areas with some brick construction and incomplete services. The third priority is overcrowded parts of traditional low-income areas. Other areas of the city get the lowest priority. Priority under the community organization criterion is granted based on whether there are, or have been in the recent past, active community organizations in the area.

The combination of neighborhood targeting and self-targeting has led to very low rates of leakage. Eighty-one percent of beneficiaries fall below the poverty line.[2] Alternately expressed, 72 percent of the beneficiaries are in the poorest two quintiles. The costs of achieving this are quite low. The targeting cost itself is only 1 percent of program costs or US$0.09 per beneficiary.

VENEZUELAN DAYCARE CENTERS. Venezuela has recently begun a massive expansion of a community-based daycare system that was set up in 1974. Most of the daycare centers provide care for up to eight children in the home of a community mother. Both she and her home must meet minimum criteria. The home must have running water, adequate sanitation, a cement floor and a permanent structure. The mother/caretaker must pass a brief psychological assessment, and preference is given to literate women. Mothers of the children who are looked after pay a small fee, about one-tenth of the cost of the program. The rest of the cost is provided by the national government. The center provides food during the day, a safe environment, some limited early childhood stimulation and basic health care (through a link to the Ministry of Health). The use of community homes rather than specially constructed infrastructure obviously reduces the investment cost dramatically. It also encourages community participation.

Poor areas are chosen by social workers from the Fundación del Niño, a nongovernmental organization headed by the First Lady. Within these areas, the foundation promotes the establishment of daycare centers. In addition to being targeted by neighborhood, the project also attempts to screen the enrolled children to ensure that the neediest in the neighborhood are served. In centers in the poorest areas, the family contribution is waived and the state subsidy is raised. The assessment of need is based not only on the family income, but also on the adequacy of other childcare arrangements available to the mother. Children left in the care of other young siblings, left alone or taken along to street-peddling jobs will be admitted to the daycare centers before those who are looked after by aunts, grandmothers or neighbors.

In many neighborhoods, the social workers are confronted not with the need to choose among too many eligible children, but with the need to raise participation rates. Thus, the social workers have to focus on explaining the program, its benefits and requirements to those who might qualify for the service and on identifying families whose childcare arrangements are not satisfactory.

The administrative costs for the daycare program are relatively high, at 16 percent. The targeting costs are 2 percent or US$11.22 per beneficiary. One reason the costs are relatively high is that, at least so far, the individual centers are thoroughly supervised. Rather than being high or inefficient, these costs may represent an investment in program quality. Certainly the outreach effort to those who are eligible but not yet covered is highly desirable.

SANTO DOMINGO'S ZURZA DISTRICT INTEGRATED URBAN DEVELOPMENT PROJECT. The Zurza District integrated urban development project illustrates geographic targeting using very small units of disaggregation. The program operates in only one district of the capital city. The neighborhood is very poor, with 95 percent of its population being below the poverty line, and has high rates of malnutrition and illiteracy. The Zurza program has a full range of components that include microenterprise activities, erosion and drainage infrastructure activities and a health education program.

The health education program is carried out in the homes of community members by volunteers from the community. The volunteers visit homes about once a month, focusing especially on homes where the need for health education is the greatest. The program monitors the weight of children quarterly, and provides information on, for example, nutrition, hygiene, family planning, breastfeeding, oral rehydration and vaccination. In coordination with other agencies, the program carries out vaccination campaigns and distributes oral rehydration salts.

The program's ability to arrive at the very door of target households with credible community volunteers, educational materials and a minimal backup of vaccination and rehydration supplies has meant that the program has been very successful. Malnutrition rates have fallen by half, from 50 percent of children under the age of five in 1988 to 25 percent in 1990. Likewise, the birthrate has fallen as the percentage of women who are pregnant has fallen from 18 to 9 percent, and vaccination rates have increased.

By School

School lunch programs are a natural candidate for geographic targeting. When planners know which schools are attended by poor children, they can include these in school lunch programs and exclude the better-off schools. The choice of school may be based on a formal set of criteria or on an informal assessment of which schools contain the greater numbers of indigent students. We look at four programs here—two with formal mechanisms for selecting schools and the other two with informal mechanisms. Three of the programs have unusual mechanisms for delivering the benefit provided. These innovations were introduced in order to improve cost effectiveness and to lower administrative costs.

TARGETING WITHIN SCHOOLS. The Chilean PAE targets not only at the school level, but at the individual level as well. It is the only one of the school-feeding programs that we examined that formally excludes some children within participating schools. This is possible largely due to the way the feeding is scheduled. The Chilean schools mostly operate on double shifts. The selected students who attend the morning shift get breakfast before school starts and lunch after the school day is over. The children to be fed arrive a little early or stay a little later than children not included in the program. Likewise, in the afternoon shift, children are served lunch or an afternoon snack. Theoretically, since the children who are not to be included in the program are not present while the others are being fed, the issue of stigma or jealousy is minimized. However, although the program is designed to minimize these problems, it may not have been completely successful. There are anecdotal reports that teachers, in fact, divide rations among larger numbers of students than those they were intended for so that no students are left unserved. This system may not be applicable in all countries. In some, the school day is long enough that it is necessary to feed children during the shift rather than before or after. Also, if raising children's attention span and thereby increasing learning is one of the goals of the school feeding, the meal should be before or during the school day so that the children are not hungry and therefore inattentive during class (see Lockheed and Verspoor 1991 pps. 84-85).

Another way to target formally within schools is found in the United States. All children pay some fee and receive lunch tickets. The children's parents fill out a financial statement at the beginning of the year and this is used to determine which fee on a sliding scale the family should pay. If teachers are discreet about how they collect the fees from the students, then the amount actually paid is confidential and the students and cafeteria personnel cannot tell who is getting a free lunch. Stigma is thus minimized. The administrative apparatus is, however, very complex.

Self-targeting within schools can also be encouraged since school feeding programs tend to have bland or monotonous food. Children can be allowed (and encouraged) to bring food from home. Vendors may be allowed to sell food on the school grounds during recreation periods or outside school hours. Since the foods brought from home or purchased will usually be more varied and tastier than the subsidized snacks or lunches, children whose parents can provide adequate lunch money for the private sources may opt out of the public program. Some stigma may occur for children limited only to the publicly provided lunches or snacks. In some programs, it is also possible to vary the number of portions children get. If the hungry children can get second or third servings, then within the total food allotment, informal self-targeting will occur.

CHILEAN SCHOOL LUNCH PROGRAM. The means by which schools are chosen to participate in the Chilean school lunch program, the PAE, is the most formal. Each year, schools submit information on five variables that have fixed weights as shown below (see Table 6.4). The variables and their weights are the product of a principal components analysis designed to determine which of a large group of variables will best identify poor schools.

Table 6.4   Chilean PAE: Selection Criteria

Variable	*Weight*
Incidence of low height for age	23.3
Average number of years of mothers' education	22.6
Percentage of students that teachers rate as being urgently or very urgently in need of school lunch	19.2
Repetition rates	19.0
Percentage of children with high ages for grade	15.9

In order to simplify the collection and processing of information, it is gathered only for the first graders. The child-specific data are collected as part of a long-standing census of first graders that was in place before it began to be used as part of the targeting mechanism for the school lunch program. Thus, teachers were already trained and equipment was available. The task is further simplified by using the data from the year previous to the current school year. Thus, there is no pressure to collate the information in a hurry. It may flow gradually up from the classroom to the central level, where priorities are established among the regions.

In the aggregation process, two different numbers are used for each school. The first is the overall score, which is an indication of priority. The second is the number of children that the teachers report as urgently needing the free school meals. Together, these determine total need and priority among the needy. The planners must then see how far their budget will go towards covering that need. They can both exclude schools and reduce the numbers of meals granted to participating schools. In this process, they have to take into consideration the economies of scale and the logistics of providing just a few lunches in one school.

The incidence of the Chilean PAE is among the best found in all the case studies. Seventy-eight percent of benefits accrue to the poorest two quintiles. This is presumably due both to the geographic part of targeting and to its ability to target within schools as well.

The provision of the lunch is contracted out to the private sector. Private firms participate in competitive bidding exercises for three-year contracts to provide the specified number of lunches to schools in the contract region. Currently, 10 firms hold such contracts. The firms deliver the lunches daily. Within the school, providing the personnel to serve the lunches and any necessary fuel and equipment is the responsibility of the contractor. The firms use more standardized mass production technology than did the previous individual school kitchens.

Contracting out has brought a number of advantages. Among them are that administrative costs borne by the government have fallen from 40 to 5 percent of the school lunch budget. The unit cost of the lunches themselves (which now include part of the administrative costs previously borne by the government) have fallen from US$0.60 per ration in 1980 to US$0.40 per ration in 1990. The 1980 figure was slightly higher than in years previous to the change to private contractors, but as the program's operations have been sorted out, costs have fallen markedly. Continuous evaluations of quality and content show that the industrial food technologies used in preparing the lunches have led to a higher nutritional content, and the preparation of the food is more hygienic. Also, the monitoring system has improved. The firms must report the number of rations served—information that was not known prior to the contracting out.

The change to contracting out is generally viewed as having been successful, and some lessons have been learned about what features of the system are most necessary to ensure its success. First, the contracts must be for periods that are long enough to allow for reasonable planning on the part of the private companies. In preparing their bids, firms must have detailed knowledge of the geographic location of each school, the number of rations to be served and content specifications in order to prepare realistic cost estimates. Transparency in the bidding process is essential. Finally, the state must be able to make full and timely payments to the private contractors. This may be facilitated by having the budget for the lunch program rest with a separate state entity, as is the case in Chile.

COSTA RICAN SCHOOL LUNCHES. A formal targeting mechanism has recently been introduced in the Costa Rican school lunch program. This case illustrates the problems that a long-standing universal program can have when its funding erodes. Since the 1970s, the program had operated in nearly all public schools, providing lunch (sometimes both breakfast and lunch) to all students in participating schools. As the government's real budget for school lunches fell, the overhead cost of the school cooks absorbed higher and higher shares of the budget. By 1985, about 60 percent of the funds that the central government provided for the school lunch program went on the wages of the school cooks. The program budget as a whole was not quite so unbalanced because many schools received contributions from the community to increase the amount of food served (these have not been quantified). Nonetheless, the mean calories provided had fallen by half between 1981 and 1984.

In order to address these problems, the government has undertaken two reforms. First, it has tried to target its scarce resources to schools in needy areas. All schools remain in the program, but they receive different levels of benefit according to need. For example, in 1991, Priority I schools were assigned US$0.12 per child per day; Priority II schools, US$0.08 per child per day; and Priority III schools, US$0.05 per school per day. Thus, the neediest schools get the most benefit.

The criteria for assigning priorities are clear. The first is the ranking on the Ministry of Planning's poverty map, which divides the country into three tiers of need. The poorest tier has an incidence of poverty almost twice as high as the other areas, and covers about 20 percent of the population. The second criterion used is school size. Originally, Priority I was to be assigned to all schools falling in the highest priority of the poverty map, as well as to all schools in other zones with only one teacher or fewer than 100 students. Priority II was to be assigned to all schools in the intermediate tier of the poverty map, as well as to schools in the wealthiest tier of the poverty map with between 100 and 500 students. Priority III was to be assigned to all schools in the wealthiest tier of the poverty map with more than 500 students. However, community groups and their representatives did not acquiesce willingly to their schools being assigned to the Priority III category with its low subsidy level. They exerted a good deal of pressure on the Ministry of Education, and, in 1990, most of the schools originally assigned to Priority III were upgraded to Priority II.

No evaluation has been done of how well the priority actually assigned corresponds to the criteria. The relative size of the categories appears reasonable given the combination of the school size and the poverty map criteria (see Table 6.5). No incidence study has been done since this attempt to target the resources of the

Table 6.5   Costa Rican School Lunch Program

	Share of Beneficiaries	
Priority Level	*1990*	*1991*
I	38.5	32.8
II	61.5	12.9
III	0.0	54.3
Total	100.0	100.0

Note: In 1984, the poorest tier of the poverty map accounted for about 20 percent of the population; the intermediate tier, 25 percent; and the wealthiest tier, 55 percent.
Source: Trejos (1992).

school lunch program was introduced. The figures shown in Table 4.2 refer to the pre-reform incidence. At that time, 62 percent of benefits accrued to children in the poorest two quintiles. On this evidence, the Costa Rican program was the least progressive of the school lunch programs and was well below the mean for all the targeted programs we have reviewed.

The second reform of the school lunch program was aimed at lowering the share of the budget that was being spent on overheads. Accordingly, a hiring freeze was introduced for school cook positions. Whenever a position came open due to attrition, it was eliminated. The individual schools thus had to assume the responsibility of paying a cook or organizing the parent-teacher association to provide the labor on a volunteer basis. The share of the government's school lunch expenditures that goes on salaries dropped from 60 percent in 1985 to 43 percent in 1991. This has not really redressed the imbalance in costs, but has merely disguised it by shifting part of the costs to places where they are not counted.

VENEZUELAN FOOD STAMPS. The Venezuelan food stamp programs are targeted to all children in selected primary schools. The choice of schools is left to the education authorities at the state level, though they are supposed to select schools in poor urban or rural zones. Rather than providing a set guideline or standard for defining a needy school, the officials use their "expert opinions."

While the criteria for choosing schools may not be well codified, they result in a sensible distribution of participating schools, as judged by the poverty map. The percentage of schools that participate varies from 70 percent for the state ranked poorest on the poverty map to 26 percent for the state ranked next to the wealthiest. In the poorest third of the states, about 60 percent of schools participate, while in the richest third of the states, about 40 percent of the schools participate.

It is worthwhile noting the contrast in the procedures for arriving at the beneficiary list between the Venezuelan and the Honduran school-based food stamps programs. In Venezuela, all students in the selected schools are eligible, so that the beneficiary list is basically derived from the enrollment list. This, of course, requires much less work and involves less room for dissent and discontent than is the case with the means tests in Honduras. Moreover, Venezuela has included a provision for a committee consisting of representatives from the Ministry of Education, the parent-teacher association, the neighborhood association and the school to certify the beneficiary lists. This should help to detect erroneous omissions or intentional padding.

Several aspects of the operation of the program are contracted out to the private sector in order to minimize costs and the additional workload on state agencies. The compilation of final beneficiary lists based on each school's input is contracted out to a private firm, as is the writing of individual checks. The checks are actually distributed every other month through the school system. They can be cashed at private banks on presentation of national identification papers. The private banks have an incentive to participate because they receive the deposit of money to cover the checks about a month in advance of when they are cashed. In the meantime, the banks earn interest on that money.

The use of the private banking system and of private data processing firms has helped to keep administrative costs low. Administrative costs are only 4 percent of program costs, including a rough costing of teachers' time. Because the banking system is extensive, personalized checks can be issued. This greatly reduces the security problems that must be dealt with in non-personalized food stamp programs such as those in Honduras and Jamaica.

JAMAICAN NUTRIBUN PROGRAM. As in the Venezuelan program, the choice of schools in the Jamaican Nutribun program is based on an informal knowledge of which towns or neighborhoods are poorest or have been hit hard by a recent hurricane or where school attendance or test scores are low. The choice of the poorest schools is tempered by the important logistical requirement that participating schools must be easily accessible by road. This is necessary because the Nutribun (a fortified bread product) and the liquid milk are distributed daily from five factories located around the island. The Jamaican road network is much denser than in many larger countries, but, even so, the need for the schools to be located on good roads tends to exclude those in rural areas. In Jamaica, 80 percent of the poorest two quintiles live in rural areas. Even with the informal criteria used in the selection of schools and the requirement of good road access, the incidence of the Nutribun program falls in the midrange of programs reviewed.

The Nutribun program's innovation in the provision of school lunches is its centralization of production. The idea is along much the same lines as what happens in Chile, but rather than contracting out to the private sector, a state corporation produces the snacks. There are five Nutribun factories island-wide that make the snacks using mass manufacturing technology. This provides economies of scale and ensures good hygiene in the production process, and it frees the schools from having to have cooks and kitchens and all of the administrative requirements of producing lunches in the school. Unit-costs per 1,000 calories or grams of protein delivered in the Nutribun program are about half those of the other lunch options in Jamaica.

There have been some administrative problems with the Nutribun program. Some of these can be attributed to insufficient budgets, while other problems seem to stem from general inefficiency. The daily delivery is logistically demanding under the best of circumstances. Since the fleet of trucks is poorly maintained and too small, targets are frequently not met. Many schools have used the partial and voluntary payments for the lunches to purchase refrigerators or freezers so that they can take delivery of two or three days' worth of bread and milk at once. Equipment failure and inefficient management have plagued the production process itself.

One contrast that emerges between the Chilean and Jamaican case studies is the implications of using private versus state corporations for the industrial production of school lunches. The Chilean setup seems to operate much more smoothly than the Jamaican. There are probably many causes, but it is interesting to speculate on the effect that using the private sector has on financing. Private contractors will only make a bid on the basis of a price that can accomplish the job at the set standard. The government must then decide whether to pay that price, to change the standard or to reduce the number of lunches to be served. The state corporation, in contrast, is expected to fulfill the obligation efficiently, but has no assurance of receiving sufficient funds to carry out the task. During the budgeting process, funds and expectations may not be too far apart, but the funding authorizations during the year are chronically below budgeted amounts and sometimes late. So the state corporation is left in an untenable position from which it cannot withdraw. One of the reasons that private contractors perform well is not only that the private firms have incentives to work efficiently within a budget limit, they also have the power to refuse to participate in underfunded programs.

Conclusions

Targeting by group characteristics or geographic area can be administratively simple. An inherent problem of geographic targeting is that it can be inaccurate (some of the nonpoor live in poor areas and some of the poor in nonpoor areas). There may also be difficulties of political economy. If representatives from areas that benefit little from a geographically targeted program have the power to cut its funds, it may not be sustainable.

Simulations of the accuracy of geographic targeting show that both leakage and undercoverage diminish as the size of the unit used in decisionmaking gets smaller. Most of the programs use areas smaller than the state; indeed, neighborhood, village or school targeting are much more common. The incidence of these programs covers the range of program outcomes.

While the costs of the targeting mechanism itself can be quite low for geographic targeting, a full service delivery mechanism is still needed for these programs. The range of total administrative costs, from 4 to 16 percent, is thus much the same as for other programs.

Several of the programs use very informal mechanisms for picking the schools or neighborhoods to target. This seems to work fairly well. Informality is not synonymous with imprecision.

Geographic targeting need not be an all-or-nothing proposition. For example, the Honduran FHIS is designed to spread funding to all municipalities throughout the country. But the amount of money in any municipality's "quota" is based on both their population and score on the poverty map.

Geographic targeting would seem to work especially well in the case of small local programs that need intensive community contact. Nongovernmental organizations can also use geographic targeting to good advantage. Many of their programs do not operate on a nationwide basis anyway, so placing them in the poorest regions is a good first step. Likewise, many of their programs stress integrated community development, which implies a geographic focus. And they are not subject to electoral pressures by representatives of the areas that they choose not to serve.

Geographic targeting can also be used to place services or infrastructure in parts of cities where the poor are known to be concentrated. This is most effective for services for which the frequency of contact is high. For example, schools or food shops that are visited daily will provide better geographic targeting than clinics or social security offices that are visited only every few weeks.

Notes

1.   The exact balance between children being born and children turning five will depend on demographic factors such as whether the cohort of women entering childbearing age is growing and on fertility patterns, child mortality rates and migration in or out of the area. Program factors will also affect whether mothers keep their children in the program until age of five or drop out prior to that age.

2.   The poverty line was set based on the cost of a minimum food basket, divided by the share of food in the total household budget for the decile in which mean expenditure on food was closest to the cost of the basic food basket. Both the cost of the food basket and the allowance for nonfood purchases are region specific.

7

Self-Targeting Mechanisms

The Concept and Key Factors

It is not always necessary for programs to devise some way of keeping the non-poor from benefiting. The nonpoor may elect not to participate. There are basically three factors that discourage the participation of the nonpoor—time, stigma or a product that the nonpoor are unlikely to want whereas the poor are.

Time Costs of Participation

Participating in social programs takes time, sometimes a good deal of time. Many programs require recipients to stand in line to collect the commodity or cash or to receive the subsidized service. Many require that the participants attend health education talks or that they get their children's growth monitored. These activities may involve more waiting in lines and more time. To do these things, the participants also have to get to the relevant office or clinic, so commuting time is involved. As walking and infrequent and unreliable bus services are the most common ways of getting around, the transport time can be considerable. Some programs also require the participant to work. This may involve helping to deliver the service, for example, by helping in community kitchens. It may involve providing a more general service, such as trash collecting or helping to maintain community infrastructure. Or it may be a full job in construction, as in public employment programs. Usually, it is considered more onerous to work than merely to wait. The opportunity costs in terms of time taken away from other activities may be no different, but the energy expenditures can be very different.

Time, as we know, has an opportunity cost. While the program participant is queuing, she is unable to work at a paid job or to do the myriad domestic chores that are important to family welfare and living conditions, still less to indulge in leisure. When wage rates are high, the value of the time that it takes the nonpoor to participate often exceeds the benefit to be gained in the program. The higher the wage rate is in relation to the size of the potential benefit, the more often this will be true.

While time costs can be a handy way of prompting the nonpoor to screen themselves out of programs, they can also discourage the participation of the poor. Even for the poor, the time cost is not zero. Though the hourly wage of the poor can be quite low, that money may be critical to family survival. Also, the poor have to devote long hours to processing food that the nonpoor may buy in a more processed form or to collecting and hauling water or firewood or to travelling to more distant but cheaper stores and markets. The time constraints can be especially tight for women, who are also usually the members of the household expected to queue for social services. The fact that time costs can discourage participation, including that of the poor, is demonstrated in Gertler and van der Gaag's (1990) modeling of health care demand in Côte d'Ivoire. They show that travel time elasticities are greater (*not* less) for the poor and conclude that "the opportunity cost of time is a bigger barrier to health care use for poorer individuals than it is for richer individuals. Poorer individuals can less afford to lose productive time than can the rich" (p. 88).

Another problem with time costs is that they diminish the net benefit given by the program. If a program distributes $5 worth of milk or money but requires two days' worth of walking to the clinic and waiting to get the baby weighed, listening to health education lectures or helping to pick up trash around the community, the value of those two days must be subtracted from the $5 of milk to find the true net benefit. The opportunity costs of program participation more often receive explicit analytical attention for programs with work requirements than for queuing, presumably because the time costs are highest in the workfare schemes. Newman, Jorgensen and Pradhan (1991), for example, show that workers on the Bolivian Emergency Social Fund projects gave up incomes of about 60 percent of the value of their wages from the public employment program to take their jobs on the ESF projects. Ravallion (1991) cites evidence that forgone earnings on the order of 40–50 percent of gross wages occur for the Maharastra Employment Guarantee Scheme and Bangladesh's Food for Work Program.

Time costs can sometimes be circumvented. The rich may send their maids to queue at subsidized shops, or they may bribe an official to let them jump the queue at a health care center.

In practice, programs use time costs both explicitly and implicitly to discourage the leakage of benefits to the nonpoor. An example of an explicit time requirement is found in the Peruvian Glass of Milk program (Chapter 6). Mothers are expected to share in the work of preparing and serving the milk in order for their families to be able to participate in the distribution. The Dominican Republic hospital fee-waiving scheme typifies an implicit time cost. Several hours of waiting were required simply to request a waiver, not so much by design but just by the way staffing, interviewing and querying were done.

The impression from the case studies is that, while time costs are frequently high, they are largely unintentional. Low administrative budgets or new programs with logistical problems are the main reasons for the long queues. Furthermore, attention is paid mainly to the doctors' or social workers' use of time but little to the convenience of the participants. Program managers tend to view changes in procedures that influence the time cost of participation only in terms of administrative ease or cost without taking into consideration the possible impact on targeting. Either high or low time costs may be desirable for policy reasons depending on whether the need is to reduce errors of inclusion or errors of exclusion, but policymakers should always give explicit recognition to the time costs of participation.

Stigma

Stigma is the feeling of shame that may come from an open admission that one is poor and in need of help. Stigma's most benign effect (the one most frequently considered by economists) is a degree of unpleasantness that, like standing in long lines, discourages the nonpoor from participating in programs intended for the poor. Again like the time costs of participation, stigma may also discourage the poor from using the program, and even when they do use the program, they can sometimes suffer a psychological cost that reduces the net value of the benefit distributed. In its more severe manifestations (more frequently investigated by the noneconomic disciplines), stigma can change the participants' self-image in ways that can cause their health to suffer or that can reduce their efforts to obtain education or jobs that would move them out of poverty. Quantifying either effect is a very tricky endeavor, though social scientists claim empirical evidence of each (see Moffitt 1983 and Bishop 1982 for the effect on participation rates and Rainwater 1982 for the effect on self-help).

How strongly stigma is felt will depend on a variety of cultural and program factors. The whole notion of stigma is based on the idea that being poor is not only undesirable but also one's own fault due to some moral flaw (such as sloth, stupidity or drink). In societies where this Protestant work ethic is not strong, the poor may be thought of as being just poor, rather than being guilty of something reprehensible that has brought poverty upon them. If society sees poverty as the result of fate or of unjust economic or social structures, then stigma may be less forceful. Evidence reviewed in Rainwater (1982) shows that different societies do indeed view poverty differently. In Italy, social injustice was the most often cited cause of poverty reported by 40 percent of survey respondents, while laziness or lack of willpower was cited by only 20 percent of respondents. In the United Kingdom, the ranking was reversed. Forty-three percent of respondents said that laziness or lack of willpower was the reason for poverty and 16 percent said social injustice.

Another influence on the way stigma is felt may be society's view of the role of the state. If the state has an active role in subsidizing many social services, especially across the income distribution, there may be less stigma. Rather, the recipient of a welfare program may feel justified in claiming a piece of the pie of which everyone else is also getting a piece.

Finally, the attributes of the program in question may help to determine stigma. Rainwater suggests that, although means-tested, United States' college grant and loan programs are not stigmatizing. This is partly because being in college is already evidence of hard work and merit and will lead to valued social outcomes. One can recognize parallels in the case of some of the family-oriented programs in our case studies. If pregnancy and motherhood are revered, then benefits for pregnant women and young children may not be stigmatizing even if the programs are clearly designed to benefit only the poor.

The ways in which stigma is triggered or assuaged can partly be affected by the many ways in which the program is executed. In the United States' food stamps program, for example, the need to alert the cashier that food stamps will be used to pay and the visible differences between food stamps and money alert bystanders to the fact that a food stamp recipient is going through the grocery line. This may embarrass the recipient, especially if those around him or her criticize what is in the grocery basket or voice negative views about welfare cheats and bums. Experiments are being carried out with new cards that look like credit cards and are waved over optical scanners at the check-out. If adopted, these cards will make it much less likely that any bystanders will notice that a customer is a food stamp recipient. Although the person must still acknowledge to himself that he is receiving aid, the public and third-party recognition of the phenomenon will be reduced.

In the Jamaican food stamp program, three interesting steps have been taken that minimize stigma. For the small number of beneficiaries who also receive poor relief or public assistance payments, checks are delivered by mail. They come in envelopes identical to those for old age pensions from the National Insurance Scheme (the Jamaican equivalent of social security). Thus, there are no lines to stand in, lowering both time and stigma costs, and no one at the post office knows that welfare payments rather than earned pensions are in the envelope. In the publicity campaign that launched the program, the pregnant wife of a cabinet level official was shown in a TV ad going to a public health clinic and registering for food stamps. Also, after an initial phase when they looked visibly different than money, food stamps were designed to look much like a J$20 currency note.

Although the studies are not fully comparable, two bits of evidence, one from Jamaica and one from the United Kingdom, support the notion that the importance of stigma can vary greatly. In the United Kingdom, in a sample of eligible people who do not avail themselves of free school meals for their children, stigma is given as the main reason, being cited in 39 percent of cases (Rainwater 1982). In the case of the Jamaican food stamp program, on the other hand, among nonparticipants, stigma is the sixth reason on the list of causes of nonparticipation, with only 8 percent reporting it as a cause for not receiving food stamps (PIOJ and STATIN 1989).

In the end, the policy recommendation for dealing with stigma is much like that for dealing with time costs. Because stigma can lower errors of inclusion but raise errors of exclusion, its net effect on targeting accuracy is ambiguous, but the issue should at least be given explicit attention. In situations where undercoverage is widespread and is not apparently due to inadequate service delivery capacity, measures to lower stigma are warranted. Where the biggest problem is leakage, increased stigma might improve incidence.

Product Quality

Social programs can play on consumers' preferences for differences in product amenity that do not detract from its basic function. Take, for example, finely milled white flour versus a coarser, whole wheat flour. Both provide the basic function of flour—a staple high-calorie food that can be made into bread or used in a wide variety of other forms. If consumers think the white flour tastes better or is more prestigious, they will be willing to pay more for it. If this preference is marked, then the coarse, dark flour may be a promising candidate for a price subsidy. Thus, the nonpoor with extra money to devote to extra flavor and prestige will tend to buy the white flour, while the poor, still trying to meet their basic calorie needs, will tend to buy the cheaper dark flour. Some of the nonpoor will, of course, buy the cheaper flour, and some of the poor may buy the more expensive one. The incidence of the flour subsidy will depend on the strength of preferences for the different goods, the price difference and the welfare level of the consumers (see Pinstrup-Andersen and Alderman 1988).

"Product" differences may be found in services as well as in commodities. For example, the nonpoor and poor will tend to use different health service providers on the basis of the nonmedical amenities of the services when different combinations of price and amenity are available. (See Besley and Coate 1991 for a theoretical discussion of how the quality of a public service will affect its distribution.)

Consider taking a child to the doctor for a vaccination. Although the vaccination and its effectiveness should be the same at a private doctor's office and a public clinic, other aspects may be quite different. The private doctor will have a pleasant, clean, air-conditioned waiting room and a separate examining room. An appointment will have been made at the mother's convenience and she will have to wait only minutes. There may be toys for the child to play with while s/he waits, and a lollipop after the vaccination. In the public clinic, the scenario is likely to be quite different. The clinic is likely to be ugly, uncomfortable and hot. The wait may be hours. There are no toys or lollipops. The mother has to come on the day of the week that vaccinations are given. If the clinic runs out that day, she may have to come back the next week.

Quality may also be intentionally allowed to vary for some services. The standard for subsidized daycare centers, for example, may provide for a physically safe place and plain food. Varied meals, educational toys, trained adult workers, outdoor space, field trips and general stimulus may be in short supply. Mothers who want and can pay for more stimulating early childhood education are left to find it privately.

The examples of how product choice is used in self-targeting programs are largely tied to the use of public health services, which are discussed separately below. There are two other examples, although the evidence for their self-targeted nature is more anecdotal than scientific.

In 1984, the Chilean PNAC program changed from distributing powdered milk to distributing a mixed cereal and powdered milk product. Since this change, program workers and analysts report that intrahousehold sharing of the PNAC product has been reduced. The cereal and milk product can only be made into a gruel that is reported to be viewed very much as a child's food. Thus, children under the age of five enrolled in the program or their slightly older siblings are the most likely people to eat the foodstuff. In one study, 43 percent of participating mothers report that only the enrolled child eats the milk and cereal product, while 38 percent report that it is shared with other children. Thus, leakage to adults must be less than 20 percent of the product distributed. Powdered milk, in contrast, has many uses within the household. It is used in coffee or tea by adults and can be used in baking as well. Thus, logic bears out what workers report anecdotally, that the choice of product had a significant impact on who eats it (see Munchnik and Vial 1990). Of course, none of this addresses the intrahousehold adjustments that may be made in the household's other sources of food. If the child breakfasts well on the PNAC gruel, he may not be allotted any of the family's bread. So the distribution of the net increase in calories consumed by the child would be less than the apparent gross increase available from the PNAC rations.

In most projects set up by social funds, product choice is also used as a targeting technique. The menu of activities sponsored by the funds is supposed to help to avoid leakage to the nonpoor. For example, community water taps and latrines will not appeal to well-off communities where indoor plumbing is available in each house. Nor will the no-frills schools or daycare centers appeal to those with greater means to pay for their children's education. It seems likely that the menu of project choices is enough to weed out people near the top of the income distribution. To what extent the middle is also discouraged, leaving only the poor, is still an open question. This may vary from country to country depending on the extent of the infrastructure networks.

There is one piece of evidence from the Honduran FHIS on the subject. A small survey was done of 92 households served by 18 social infrastructure projects. All the households benefiting from the projects had income levels below the poverty line used by the IDB. Intriguingly, the beneficiaries of the latrine projects and of the school desk projects were poorer than those who benefited from the rehabilitation of health centers and schools (Vargas-Olea 1992). While the survey is too small to be conclusive, this first piece of evidence on the subject suggests that indeed targeting by project type may work and may work better for some types of project than for others.

In Practice

In the Latin American experience, the self-targeting mechanisms that are most frequently used are work requirements and the use of public health services. These are discussed in turn.

Work Requirement

COMMUNAL WORK REQUIREMENTS. While fully-fledged employment programs are geared to provide a full wage income, some programs simply require participants to work for a few hours or days to help to deliver the service the program provides. This lowers the overheads of service delivery, can help to foster community decisionmaking and development and can encourage self-targeting due to the time costs of participation.

The Peruvian Glass of Milk program (Chapter 6), in addition to its geographic and demographic targeting mechanisms, requires mothers of participating children to share the work of picking up, preparing and serving the milk. Each woman works for about one and a half hours every two weeks, usually around dawn. Since this is an extra task that would not otherwise have to be done, it requires extra use of the woman's time. Those not in need will presumably find the unpleasantness of extra work at dawn too irksome to try to gain admittance to the program. It should be noted that the time of day was arranged by the participants so as not to interfere with their income-generating activities. Thus, the potential for the work requirement to discourage participation among the poor is clearly demonstrated. The Glass of Milk program has low administrative costs and good incidence.

The Peruvian Soup Kitchens are an interesting example of a program with a communal work requirement that, in the end, saves the participant time. The time saved is counted as a major benefit of the program.

The soup kitchens are organized and operated by groups of families. Each day, four or five women from the group gather the daily fees from the participating families, purchase food and cook meals in large quantities. Early in the morning, the families who want rations that day advance a small fee (about US$0.20 per ration). The money collected is used for the wholesale purchase of fuel, fresh vegetables and other daily ingredients. By noon, families pick up their meals and take them home to eat. The workers for the day finish up with cleaning and bookkeeping. Each woman works about once every two weeks from about 8:00 a.m. to 2:00 p.m.

Many kitchens actually have a built-in sliding fee scale. Families who are full partners in the soup kitchen pay about US$0.20 per ration. Families who do not share the work but wish to eat that day pay about US$0.25 per ration. Partners who are cooking that day take four or five rations without paying. The partner in whose home the cooking is done receives one free ration. Some groups have designated certain charity cases who need not pay or who pay a reduced fee.

About two-thirds of the soup kitchens receive allotments of basic staples (bulgur, corn-soy blend, lentils, rice and oil) from PRODIA or CARITAS. Both organizations have affiliation processes. They try to screen groups to ensure that they have enough cohesion to make the communal effort work. Also, they give preference to groups in the poorest neighborhoods.

The time costs of participation are about six hours every two weeks. This can actually save the women time. If they had to cook and market individually, they would spend something like three hours per day for each of the ten working days during the period. About 65 percent of women who participate in these programs work in remunerated activities such as piecework done in the home, vending or domestic service. Thus, the time saved by sharing cooking chores may allow them to generate additional earnings (as well as to qualify for food donations and wholesale prices on purchases).

It is further interesting to note that the food is taken home to be eaten in the privacy of the family. If the violation of privacy is a contributor to stigma, these families have arranged their program in a way that minimizes it. It is also a practical arrangement. The program operates not in special buildings that would require a big investment but in members' homes. The facilities of the kitchens are usually strained enough by producing the meals, so that consuming them on site as well would be very difficult.

The combination of self-targeting and neighborhood-level geographic targeting has led to very low leakage in the program. According to a 1991 survey, 93 percent of participants are under the poverty line. Coverage, however, is low, at less than 10 percent of poor households.

The administrative costs vary somewhat between the two NGOs, with CARITAS reporting its costs to be 8.9 percent or US$1.95 per beneficiary while PRODIA reports its costs to be 13.6 percent or US$3.82. The targeting costs are much lower, at 1 percent or US$0.23 for CARITAS and 0.7 percent per year or US$0.19 for PRODIA.

EMPLOYMENT PROGRAMS. Employment programs are hybrid by nature. To some degree, they are cash transfer programs with a work requirement to ensure self-targeting. To some degree, they are also infrastructure programs geared to promoting growth and welfare as a result of the improved infrastructure. It may be useful to think of a continuum of the mix of goals. At one end are the pure infrastructure investments made solely on the cost/benefit rationale of the infrastructure. The road or bridge or school is the justification and no value is given to the employment generated in building or improving it. Likewise, there are no requirements that labor-intensive methods should be used. At the other end of the spectrum are the public employment programs that focus almost exclusively on employment with little emphasis on creating anything useful with the work. Leaf-raking, street cleaning and monument painting are the stereotypical activities of this nature. In the middle of this spectrum fall the social fund projects that have sprung up in the last five years in Latin America, typified by the Bolivian Emergency Social Fund and the Honduran Social Investment Fund. These seek both to create or rehabilitate useful infrastructure and explicitly to generate employment. Labor-intensive methods are required. Here, we focus on the programs that explicitly seek to create employment and look only at the targeting of the workers, not of the projects.

How the works are contracted is the key to the targeting outcome among the workers. Broadly speaking, there are two options. Projects can be contracted out to the private sector. The firm's obligation is then to carry out the construction within budget and to the technical specifications. The managers of the firm are concerned merely with employing productive laborers, so they will follow practices typical of the construction industry.[1] They will not be concerned whether the workers are poor or not, or that they should have particular social characteristics such as being female or landless or having a low education level. The firm will want to employ laborers who are strong, disciplined and have whatever building skills are required. This mechanism is designed to produce infrastructure at a good price. If conditions in the labor market are such that wages are low for unskilled, hard labor in the construction industry relative to the rest of the economy, then this mechanism may also produce an acceptable targeting outcome for the wages paid. Alternately, projects can be carried out by a public sector body whose main purpose is to create employment. The agency may require that workers have certain characteristics, such as being poor or a head of household or a single mother. The employment of such individuals is a key goal, and the accomplishment of the physical work is secondary. It is not particularly important, then, that the workers should be disciplined or have appropriate skills or even that the work should need to be done. The agency is primarily accountable for handing out paychecks, not for producing infrastructure. This mechanism is likely to generate good targeting of wage benefits. The infrastructure, however, may not be built at the lowest cost or be of the best quality.

The Bolivian Emergency Social Fund is an interesting example of using a private sector contractor, and the Chilean Special Employment Programs provide interesting examples of the public sector management of employment projects.

BOLIVIAN EMERGENCY SOCIAL FUND. The Bolivian Emergency Social Fund (ESF) financed more than 3,000 small projects, most of which were designed to build or rehabilitate infrastructure. The projects were contracted out to private firms who hired workers. The firms had complete liberty to hire whomever they wanted. They paid the going wage for unskilled, physically demanding construction work. The projects lasted only a few months, so no worker was assured of employment for long periods. Indeed, daily or weekly work arrangements were frequent.

The decision to work through private contractors was important to the targeting outcome because it meant that market wages would be paid and that contractors would hire the kind of person who was usually employed in the construction industry. A lower-than-market wage would have meant that workers would have been drawn in even larger proportions from the ranks of the poorest. Although this was recognized at the time that the program was being designed, the market wage option was preferred. Working through private contractors greatly simplified the program administration and reinforced the introduction of market signals that were part of the larger macroeconomic adjustment program. Also, though below-market wages would have improved targeting, the net transfer would have declined.

The workers who applied to work for the ESF and were hired generally resembled those in the construction industry as a whole. Ninety-nine percent of the urban ESF workers who were surveyed were men and 71 percent were married.

Ninety-three percent reported themselves to be the head of their household. However, workers were less educated than the average for the urban work force. A simulation was done of what these men would probably have earned had they not worked for the ESF. Then, a second simulation was done of the amount that workers with similar characteristics would be likely to earn while working for the ESF. A comparison of the two simulations showed that 25 percent of ESF workers would have belonged to the poorest tenth of the urban population had they not worked for the ESF. With the ESF job, none belonged to the poorest group. Seventy-six percent of ESF workers would have belonged to the poorest 40 percent of the urban population without the ESF jobs. With the jobs, only 15 percent fell in this range.

CHILEAN SPECIAL EMPLOYMENT PROGRAMS. Chile ran several Special Employment Programs during the 1980s. They were differentiated from one another by the requirements governing what kinds of workers should be hired, the predominant type of project to be carried out by that labor and the wages and costs of the projects. Here we will look at the Minimum Employment Program (PEM) and the Occupational Program for Household Heads (POJH).

The PEM and POJH required that workers should be of working age, should be physically and psychologically able to work, should not be receiving other government welfare benefits and should work 35 hours per week. The PEM required that a worker should be the sole breadwinner in his or her family. The requirement was apparently not rigorously enforced, as a household survey showed that PEM workers on average contributed only a third of the labor income of their households. Seventy-three percent of PEM workers were women, the majority of whom had never worked before and a quarter of whom had not even been in the labor force prior to participating in the PEM. The POJH also required that the worker should be the head of the household. POJH workers contributed about half of the labor income in their households. Seventy-two percent were men, most of whom (82 percent) had worked previously, with construction being the most common previous occupation (24 percent). A fifth of POJH workers had not been in the labor force prior to joining the POJH.

The incidence of the special employment programs taken together was quite good—71 percent of participants came from the poorest 40 percent of households. Unfortunately, the study did not break down the results to reflect the differences among the subprograms.

The work was organized and managed by municipalities, while the funds to carry out the projects came from the central government. There was a requirement that labor costs should be at least 80 percent of total project costs, which helped to encourage projects that tended to be naturally labor-intensive. In practice, however, municipalities did not have enough useful work of that type. Rather, they would sometimes identify projects that they wanted to be carried out, irrespective of whether they met the labor-intensive guideline. In these cases, the municipality would estimate the cost of the materials that would be needed to do a project and multiply this cost by four to arrive at the expected labor cost. For example, a project might be produced at the lowest possible cost by spending $10,000 for materials and $20,000 for labor. Rather than rule this out, the municipality would request funds to cover $10,000 for materials and $40,000 in labor. This obviously inflated the price of the work. It also left the municipality with surplus labor on its hands.

In order to cope with the excess labor, some workers might be diverted to truly labor-intensive activities such as street cleaning. Generally, work days were shorter than stipulated, and even while workers were ostensibly working, they were not required to work hard. In a survey of project workers, it was reported that they could accomplish their work in about 27 hours as opposed to the statutory 35, meaning that the actual work done was 22 percent less than the programmed work. Finally, some "jobs" would be assigned to needy disabled persons who were not required to work. Absentee rates ran at about 12 percent. Taking all of these factors into account, the actual effective work done seems to have been about a third less than the programmed work.

By paying lower than minimum wages and sacrificing efficiency in the infrastructure's cost, the Chilean programs were able to achieve good targeting outcomes. Even with the income from their jobs, on average, PEM workers ended up in the second decile of the income distribution and POJH workers in the third decile. Discounting the PEM and POJH income (but, unlike in the Bolivian study, making no allowance for alternative activities), the families would have been in the poorest decile.

Use of Public Health Network

SHARED ISSUES. Many programs are tied to the use of the public primary health care system. This usually provides for good self-targeting as the nonpoor opt for private primary health care, which involves lower time costs or is of higher quality.[2] Even some of those who use public health care for their basic health needs choose not to participate in the add-on transfer programs with their requirements of frequent visits, queuing and possibly stigma. An additional advantage of tying eligibility to the use of the public health services is that it can increase the use of preventive health services among those who need them most and can provide opportunities for complementary health education.

The incidence of benefits from these self-targeted programs is, broadly speaking, as satisfactory as the incidence of the other mechanisms. This stems partly from the progressive nature of public health care use and partly from the additional time costs and stigma that the food programs entail. This is clearly seen in Table 7.1. The use of public health services is slightly progressive, but the targeting of the add-on nutrition programs is still more progressive.

Four of the case study programs are tied to the public health care system — the Chilean PNAC and Venezuelan PAMI, which provide food commodities, and the maternal-child portion of the Jamaican and Honduran food stamp programs. All are targeted to pregnant and lactating women and children under the age of five. All but the Jamaican program have effective requirements that preventive health

Table 7.1   Incidence of Public Health Services and Add-on Programs

	Quintiles of Participants				
	Poorest				Richest
	1	2	3	4	5
Jamaica					
Public Health Service	21	23	20	20	16
MCH Food Stamps	29	30	21	13	6
Chile					
Public Health Service	22	29	22	16	11
PNAC	41	28	18	10	3

Sources: Jamaica - original calculations from November 1989 SLC.
    Chile - Public Health Services - Petrei (1987); PNAC - Vial, Camhi and Castillo (1991).

care should be used—in other words, that children should receive up-to-date vaccinations and growth monitoring and that women should receive pre- or postnatal care. Compliance with these requirements is monitored by handing out the food or food stamp at the same time as the medical care is given or by recording the medical care on a health record card that the participant must display when picking up the food.

A common and important logistical concern is the frequency of growth monitoring or health checkups for the program participants. There is a real danger that new programs can attract so many participants that clinics will be swamped by babies waiting to be weighed to the detriment of the clinics' ability to provide other health services (which are usually limited in the first place). In Venezuela, for example, with the inception of the PAMI program, some clinics reported fivefold increases in growth monitoring. In Honduras, health care workers complain that they spend so much time on the food stamp program and its recipients that other important activities, especially tuberculosis programs, suffer.

In thinking about the consequences of increased demand for growth monitoring, it is important to make some distinctions. First, much of the increase in health service use is a good thing, indeed a goal in its own right, not merely a logistical problem to be minimized. In Honduras and Venezuela, where the coverage of the health service was low, targeting through the health centers was chosen partly with the explicit intention of encouraging their use. The deluge of babies to be weighed was a sign of the programs' success. The preventive care services in Chile, by contrast, had largely adequate coverage. Linking the PNAC to the clinics did not cause any major problems with the provision of health services.

Next, it is useful to know whether the increase in service use is due to more frequent visits by the same children who, before the food (stamp) program, were brought in every three or six months or whether it is due to children who had not previously been receiving health care. Clearly, bringing new children into the center will have more impact on health status than increasing the frequency of contact of those already there, especially if most of those in the system were already complying with standards for immunization and growth monitoring.

There are ways in which the logistical issues can be minimized while still improving the coverage of health services. The first adjustment could be the frequency of medical checkups and food distribution. In Honduras, for example, the pilot food stamp program initially required children to be weighed every month in order to get their monthly stamp. But the Ministry of Health norms require monthly weighing only for malnourished children. The frequency for weighing normal children varies by age, but averages about once every three months. So the food stamp program induced many extra weighings with little expected medical benefit.

The program's growth monitoring requirement was changed so that the children need only be weighed as often as is prescribed for their age group and nutritional status. This immediately cut to about one-third the number of weighings and medical checks that have to be carried out each month. However, the program now requires a more complicated queuing procedure. Now someone in authority must determine whether a child must get a health check or can go straight through the food stamp line.

In Jamaica, food stamps are distributed every other month rather than every month. This cuts down on administrative costs, as the officers need to travel to the rotating distribution sites only half as often. It also cuts down on the time costs for program participants. It may, however, increase congestion and anxiety at distribution sites, as missing the single distribution will mean a larger loss in benefits than would be the case under a monthly distribution scheme.

Another means of alleviating some of the logistical burden is to involve community volunteers in at least the growth-monitoring part of the health check. These people can provide extra staff power. Indeed, the use of community workers can have auxiliary benefits in helping to teach mothers that they can take an active role in monitoring their children's nutritional status and how to do so. This, of course, requires initial training and constant supervision to ensure the accuracy of the growth monitoring.

There are also a series of options regarding how to arrange the logistics. Should there be one line for both health checks and food stamps or two separate lines? Should stamps be handed out to a few people every day of the month or to everyone on one or two days? Should people be prescheduled or allowed to come at a time of their convenience? The answers to these questions will depend on such elements as the size of the physical space available, the number and mix of staff available and the degree of security necessary to safeguard the food stamps or to manage the inventory of the foodstuffs. These are issues that will benefit from conscious thought and, probably, the input of time and motion experts.

CHILEAN PNAC. Chile's PNAC program for children under the age of five and pregnant and lactating women is the longest-running and most sophisticated of the programs that are self-targeted through public health clinics. In its first recognizable form, it began in 1924. Over the years, several modifications have been made to its targeting mechanisms, logistics and benefit levels. We concentrate on the changes that have taken place during the past 10 or 15 years.

In the 1970s, little attempt was made to add an element of self-targeting to the program. Milk was distributed at many sites, including at large places of employment, such as factories and government offices. To a certain extent, this made it easier for the well-off to participate than the poor.

From 1971 to 1973, the program was expanded to cover all children up to the age of 14. The first step taken in 1973 to tighten targeting was to return the age limit to five years as it had been before 1970.

In 1981, a decision was taken to limit distribution sites to public health clinics. Furthermore, the requirement that the recipient should be up-to-date in the use of preventive health services began to be enforced, after being formally instituted in 1975. After these changes had been made, the participation rates by quintiles changed markedly, as shown in Table 7.2. Particularly as a result of the reduction in distribution sites, participation rates among the richest quintile dropped from 60 to 33 percent. Among the poorest quintile, they rose from 88 to 92 percent. One of the reasons that the participation rate for the poor can be so high is that the public health care network is extensive, and is targeted geographically to ensure that it reaches poor areas.

In 1987, members of ISAPRE (privately managed and publicly subsidized health care maintenance organizations) became eligible for PNAC foods if they came to public health clinics to receive the foodstuffs. Since ISAPRE users tend to be in the middle or upper end of the income distribution, this may tend to work against targeting. Still, the need to go to a separate location to obtain the product should continue to encourage some self-targeting.

The PNAC program is the most sophisticated of all public health-based nutrition supplement programs in terms of benefit differentiation. Benefits are differentiated by age and by nutritional status or risk (see Chapter 5). There was a time when benefits were also differentiated on the basis of socioeconomic risk categories (see Chapter 5), but this has now been discontinued. At present, normal children get 2 kilos of milk per month up to the age of one year, and 1 kilo thereafter. For children at high risk of malnutrition, there are six benefit levels by age.

The amount of administration required by the biomedical risk categorization is relatively small. All of the information required is gathered and recorded as part of the normal health check-up. The health worker merely fills in a different answer on

Table 7.2   Participation Rates in the PNAC in Chile
(percent)

Quintile	1979	1985	1987
1	88.0	91.7	94.0
2	86.0	86.1	89.0
3	81.0	80.1	78.0
4	80.0	68.0	58.0
5	60.0	32.7	26.0

Source: Vial, Camhi and Castillo (1992).

the benefit category of the card, which is then carried to the area where the food is dispensed. One logistical consequence is that bookkeeping and program evaluation data have several categories that have to be tallied separately, but this has proved to be manageable. The children identified as being at high risk must also have their growth monitored monthly. The norm for healthy children, which varies according to age, averages once every three months. But this extra growth monitoring is required principally for medical reasons, not because of the PNAC program logistics.

This use of risk levels has led to a large share of the resources being concentrated on those at risk. Half of the products distributed go to the 17 percent of children who are at biomedical risk. Simultaneously, the program continues to encourage universal use of preventive health care services and enjoys the political support that is usually accorded to a universal program.

The total administrative costs for the program are 19 percent including the time spent by medical personnel on checkups or 6 percent discounting it. Chilean analysts usually count the value of the medical time as a health benefit to the recipient rather than as a PNAC overhead expense.

VENEZUELAN PAMI. The Venezuelan PAMI is broadly similar to the Chilean PNAC. It is, however, a young program, having just been piloted in 1990, and is still in its first phase of implementation. It has, therefore, been kept simple and has only one level of benefit available to all who are enrolled in the program and does not differentiate by age or risk.

The novel feature of the PAMI is its use of private sector contractors to carry out the food distribution parts of the program. Medical staff carry out the growth monitoring as part of the health checkup and endorse the child's health card. But the person who staffs the "pantry" where the food is distributed from each health center works not for the Ministry of Health, but for the private business that has won the contract for the health district. The contractor provides the staff who distribute the food in each clinic. The contractor carries out the detailed planning for meeting the food requirements of the beneficiary groups, plans and controls the inventory and produces status reports. The contractor is responsible for transporting the food to those clinics that the food wholesaler does not supply directly.

The contractor is chosen through a competitive bidding process. Before being allowed to bid, the contractors must meet certain qualifications based on their experience in the distribution of mass consumption products, their financial capacity and the recognized scope of their operations. The terms of service are clearly specified—for example, the number of centers, the hours of operation and the transport requirements. The value of the contract is fixed. Thus, the net profit for the firm will increase the more they manage to contain costs.

The PAMI foundation is an independent government body under the Ministry of Health that is responsible for overseeing the food distribution program. As such, it sets the norms, contracts the private companies that carry out much of the day-to-day logistical work of the program and oversees these companies. While the staff of five supervisors is generally felt to be insufficient to supervise the field operations of the private contractors thoroughly, satisfaction with the contractors is high.

The Ministry of Health itself sets policy on the beneficiary selection criteria and medical check-up requirements and provides both the staff to carry out medical checks and the physical space for food storage and distribution in the clinics.

Although the costs of the four programs targeted through clinics are figured in slightly different ways, the PAMI program seems to have the lowest administrative costs, just 3 percent of program costs (including the food program alone, not the value or cost of the medical attention). Thus, the contractor mechanism seems to be both administratively efficient and cost-effective. Since the staff are not employed by the government, they can be dismissed more easily, which leads to good daily performance. And it means that, if the program later needs to be modified or cut back in such a way that it would require fewer persons to run, the lobbying power of the staff will be limited.

HONDURAN BONO MATERNO INFANTIL (BMI). The Honduran BMI operates much like the other programs linked to primary health care. Pregnant or lactating women and children under the age of five are eligible for food stamps if they stay up-to-date with their health care. Registration and distribution are done in the health centers. There is also geographic targeting at both the state and village level (see Chapter 6).

The Honduran BMI is in a pilot phase, moving towards expanding to the poorest health districts, which cover about half the country. During the pilot stage, the program has succeeded in stimulating considerable increases in the use of preventive health services, as shown in Table 7.3. Furthermore, the share of maternal-child health services in total services has gone from about one-third to about two-thirds, which is the Ministry of Health norm. Thus, the program has increased its coverage and made its actions accord more closely with the priorities it espouses.[3]

Of course, these large increases in coverage have brought logistical problems in their wake. In the pilot stage, the Ministry of Health has been able to supply the clin-

Table 7.3 Increases in Maternal and Child Health Activities after the Introduction of the Honduran Bono Materno Infantil
(percentage change)

Activity	Urban Centers	Rural Centers	Total
Well child check-up	132	171	155
Growth monitoring	137	230	186
Prenatal, first visit	108	11	46
Prenatal, follow-up	99	60	79
Postnatal	56	6	34
Family planning	6	-25	-8
Total	119	140	131

Source: PRAF.

ics with sufficient additional supplies and vaccine. Medical personnel, however, complain that they have too little time to provide quality services and that some other programs are suffering from a lack of attention. The baby weighing problem was severe enough that explicit attention has been given to the logistical issues of queuing and growth monitoring. The frequency of growth monitoring has been reduced from the initial monthly requirement to conform to Ministry of Health norms for age and nutrition status. Some workshops have been held with staff from several clinics to allow them to exchange ideas on what logistical solutions have been tried or have worked in each place. While some clinics have arrived at a fairly smooth modus operandi, others are still muddling through with less than ideal organization.

Administrative costs, including the time of the health personnel, are running at about 15 percent of program costs. If the medical time incurred is not counted, the costs are much lower at 6 percent.

JAMAICAN FOOD STAMP PROGRAM. The Jamaican program has struggled to carry out the maternal-child portion of the program despite a lack of staff input from the Ministry of Health. Most of the compromises that have had to be made as a result have minimized any link to preventive health care use. Clearly, the medical benefits of the program are fewer than in the other countries where the ties to preventive care are strong, and the targeting is probably adversely affected as well.

From the outset of the program, there was the idea that all pregnant or lactating women and children under the age of five should be registered through the health system. As in the other cases, this was to encourage self-targeting and the use of preventive services. But Ministry of Health officials and health care workers refused to take on this additional task without additional pay or staff. Their position was not entirely unreasonable given that the pay and staffing situation was so unsatisfactory that whole wings of hospitals were having to be closed down for lack of staff. Also, just before the introduction of the program, the bulk of the community health aides, a paraprofessional level of worker whose skill level made them the best candidates for the new duty, had been laid off en masse. Given that the coverage of preventive services in Jamaica was already quite good, the Ministry felt that its first priority should be to use its staff to concentrate on providing good-quality medical care rather than on producing paperwork for the food stamp program.

The impasse was first solved by paying the laid-off community health aides piece rates to register food stamp beneficiaries. Since the aides knew the community, the poor and the health users, they were very suitable for the job. And having just been laid off, many were available for work and in need of cash. They were given permission to carry out registrations in the corridors and waiting areas of clinics, and they made community visits as well.

After the initial registration period and once the whole program had settled into a workable modus operandi, staff from the Ministry of Labour, Welfare and Sport went to health clinics on a rotating basis on the days that child health clinics were scheduled. They worked in the waiting rooms and corridors and could register new beneficiaries. The arrangements were not ideal, as the infrequency of their visits made it sometimes less than convenient to register a child or prospective mother. But the program was able to operate.

In 1989, there was a reorganization of government programs. Responsibility for the Poor Relief program was moved from the Ministry of Labour, Welfare and Sport to the Ministry of Local Government. Since the Food Stamp program had relied on the Poor Relief staff to do about two-thirds of the work of running the program, this caused severe problems. Some temporary staff were hired and eventually permanent staff as well, but there was a period of over a year when food stamp operations were at least partially impaired. This led to a breakdown in the arrangements for registering mother and child beneficiaries. For children, the rule that they should be registered at clinics was de facto suspended. They were registered at food stamp distribution sites, with only the burden of standing in line remaining as a self-targeting mechanism. But there was no way to verify that women were indeed pregnant or lactating so that those categories nearly ceased to operate.

Now, the stamps are distributed by Ministry of Labour, Welfare and Sports staff once every two months. In theory, the MCH beneficiaries are supposed to get stamps at the clinics, while the means-tested participants get them elsewhere, but this has not always been honored. In many clinics, health authorities have requested that the distribution take place outside of clinic hours, as the congestion caused when stamps were distributed during clinic hours had overwhelmed the attempts to provide medical care. While this may have simplified crowd control, it has certainly lessened the link between receiving food stamps and using preventive health care.

New proposals to deal with these administrative problems in the program include distributing food stamps by mail. If this is implemented on a large scale, it will be interesting to see what impact it has on targeting. Mail distribution will considerably lower the time costs of participation, and probably stigma as well. So the elements that have encouraged self-targeting will be much reduced.

It is not possible to distinguish the difference in administrative costs between the means-tested and maternal-child portions of the Jamaican food stamp program. At 10 percent, they are about average, and the program incidence is very good. It is interesting to note that the incidence outcomes of the two halves of the program are quite similar.

Conclusions

The principal factors that promote self-targeting are time costs, stigma and low product quality. These factors all induce the nonpoor to self-select out of the program. The problem is that they may also discourage participation among the poor. Even when the poor do choose to participate, these factors lower the net benefit of the program's service.

Aside from employment programs, the time costs of participation are rarely given explicit attention. The time costs usually result from insufficient resources or inefficiency in program administration. Furthermore, important decisions about how to organize queues or how often or at what times to provide services are usually made for the convenience of program administrators rather than beneficiaries. More attention to this factor is warranted.

Stigma is culture and program specific. Like the time costs of participation, it is rarely given explicit attention. The details of how the program is designed, implemented and advertised affect the amount of stigma that may be felt by participants. These details can be manipulated to lower stigma if undercoverage is high or to raise it if that might help to lower leakage.

Many food programs have relied on low product quality as a self-targeting mechanism. New services are beginning to use the same ideas. Daycare is one example. The kind of housing, water connection and sanitation works that are funded by social investment funds is another example. While low quality is pervasive in public health and education, this is more the result of inadequate budgets or inefficiency than an explicit goal.

Because services in self-targeted programs are ostensibly available to all comers, they may have broader political support than some of the management-targeted programs. Even those who choose not to use the service know that if they need it, they can have it.

Although self-targeted programs do not need as extensive a targeting bureaucracy as management-targeted programs, they still need program administration to deliver the service. Thus, their total administrative costs tend to be in the same range as those of the other kinds of mechanisms.

An important limitation to self-selection is that it is proportionately less useful as the program benefit gets larger. People may not put up with queues or embarrassment for $5, but will be more tolerant for benefits of $500. For programs with high levels of benefit, therefore, an individual selection mechanism may be more appropriate.

Notes

1.   It would theoretically be possible to require the contractor to hire workers of specified characteristics, but monitoring this would be very difficult. No example of such a mechanism was found in practice.

2.   The nonpoor who use private primary care may revert back to the public system for hospital care, as its higher costs are harder to bear out of pocket and the private sector may not offer specialized services.

3.   There has been concern over apparent decreases in the use of family planning services. Various interpretations of the data are offered, but the truth is not yet clear. Some point out that the long lines for growth monitoring at the public health clinics are causing women to switch to the nongovernmental family planning network for those services. Since that network is the major provider of services, this does not necessarily mean that fewer services are being delivered in total. Others suggest that the increase in those availing themselves of postnatal care (which is supposed to include family planning) substitutes for visits

counted as being for family planning purposes. Still others suggest that the number of family planning visits was so small to begin with that percentage variations can be high but are actually meaningless. The indicators are being monitored closely, and training and supervision programs are being designed to improve the quality and consistency of perinatal services (including family planning).

8

Targeting and Universal Services

Strictly speaking, universal services are meant to be available to all and thus cannot be said to be targeted to the poor. As such, it may seem odd to include a chapter on universal services in a review of targeted programs. However, it is appropriate for two reasons. First, there are problems of equity in the provision of services to a greater or lesser degree in all countries. Expenditures aimed at addressing these are frequently said to be "targeted." Indeed, in World Bank documents, this is a very commonly used term. Second, the opportunity cost of putting resources into targeted programs is often what those resources could have accomplished if they had been applied to "universal" social programs. The most relevant standard by which to judge targeted programs may be these universal programs.

This chapter provides a brief discussion of the main issues of equity in universal services. We start with a review of the incidence of expenditures. We then look at differences in service coverage and quality by income group. Finally, we examine the issue of whether it is inherently more costly to try to direct services to poor groups.

Incidence of Universally Provided Programs

General Food Price Subsidies

General food price subsidies tend to benefit the rich more than the poor in absolute terms but not in relative terms. In the case of Jamaica's general food subsidies (which have now been eliminated), for example, the subsidized foods were well chosen, in the sense that they constituted a larger share of the food budgets of the poor (3.7 percent) than of the rich (1.1 percent). Notwithstanding this fact, the rich spent much more on these foods than the poor did. As a result, 14 percent of the transfer benefits accrued to the poorest quintile and 26 percent to the richest (see Table 8.1). This same pattern can be observed in the case of general food price subsidies in other countries for which incidence information is available.

The incidence of food price subsidies is determined by the income and elasticities of the commodity that is subsidized. If commodities with negative income elasticities can be found, then the incidence of the subsidy will be progressive.[1] But there are apparently few examples of food commodities with this characteristic that are also important in the food basket and have production patterns that lead to easy administration of subsidies. Governments have typically subsidized commodities with low but positive income elasticities, which has led to the incidence patterns observed above.

General food price subsidies, at least in theory, should have low errors of exclusion. Since all consumers are eligible, so long as the products chosen are consumed by all, there should be few errors of exclusion. In fact, errors of exclusion may exist. Not all subsidized products are universally consumed. Markets in

Table 8.1   Incidence of General Food Subsidies

Country	Commodity	Year	Percentage of Benefits Accruing to Quintile				
			1	*2*	*3*	*4*	*5*
Brazil	Rice	1974	19		66		15
(metro area of Belo Horizante)	Wheat		15		62		23
Jamaica	Powdered milk, wheat, cornmeal	1988	14	20	20	21	26
Mexico	Corn, sorghum, beans, wheat, rice	1984	20*			80	
Algeria	All 17 subsidized goods	1991	14	17	20	22	27
	Flour		8	12	19	25	36
	Pasteurized milk		8	14	19	26	33
	Semolina		18	19	20	21	22
	Milk powder		17	19	20	21	23
Sri Lanka	Wheat, bread	1978/79	14	17	21	23	25
	sugar		16	17	19	21	27
Egypt	Cereals		*Quartile Group*				
	Urban	1982	10	30	42	18	
	Rural		13	30	27	39	

* <1.5 min salaries, (33.7 percent of the population).

Sources: Brazil, Calegar and Schuh (1988) ; Jamaica, Statistical Institute of Jamaica and World Bank (1988) ; Mexico, World Bank (1990a) ; Algeria, World Bank (1991b) ; Egypt, Alderman (1991) ; Sri Lanka, Edirisinghe (1987).

remote areas may not be extensive enough to stock the subsidized items. Subsistence farmers may grow the crop themselves or the poor may purchase the item early in the processing chain before the subsidy is applied. For example, if tortillas are subsidized, as in Mexico, those who grow their own maize or make their tortillas from cornmeal rather than buy them ready made will not benefit from the subsidy.

General food price subsidies appear to require little administrative apparatus compared to targeted programs.[2] The logistical attractions of this are obvious. This also leads to a tendency to assume that they cost less because they do not require a large cadre of social workers. However, they can distort incentives in the economy in ways that can be quite costly but that escape measurement. Thus, the apparently low nontransfer costs can be more illusory than real. Calegar and Schuh's (1988) analysis of Brazilian wheat price subsidies, for example, estimates that the program induced economic inefficiencies (deadweight losses) worth about 15 percent of the cost of the program. Moreover, a third of the expenditures were captured by the millers rather than by the consumers.

Public Health Services

Public health services tend to have quite progressive incidence. The share of public health services accruing to the poorest quintile ranges from 11 to 58 percent (see Table 8.2). The share accruing to the richest quintile ranges from 4 to 24 percent. There are two important methodological notes here. First, these figures refer to primary health care received in public clinics or in the outpatient departments of public hospitals. As in the earlier chapters, these figures refer to the frequency with which beneficiary households fall into each quintile. They do not value the benefits or costs of these services, which often account for a relatively small share of health budgets (see Grosh 1990). Second, these numbers come from household quintiles. Population quintiles show a somewhat less progressive picture. For countries where raw data were available, we also calculated the incidence using population quintiles, since these are more appropriate for a service provided to individuals. These are presented in Table 8.3.

The progressivity of public primary health services results in large part from the fact that they tend to provide low-quality services. Those consumers who can do so tend to opt for higher-quality care at a higher cost. The public health services that are counted in Tables 8.2 and 8.3 are usually those offered by the country's Ministry of Health. In most Latin American countries, the Ministry of Health has a mandate to provide services to the whole population for free or for very low prices. Social security systems, on the other hand, usually provide health care to their affiliates, financed from payroll contributions. These services are usually of higher quality, and the affiliates tend to be in the middle or upper end of the welfare distribution. The private sector also siphons off those at the upper end of the distribution. Thus, the progressivity of the public health services, which the poor are likely to use, is the result of providing the lowest quality of care available.

Table 8.2 Incidence of Universally Provided Services by Household Quintiles

| | | | Percentage of Benefits Accruing to Quintile | | | | |
| | | | Poorest | | | | Richest |
Country	Year	Source	1	2	3	4	5
Public Health Care							
Argentina	1980	Petrei	51	17	19	8	4
Bolivia (urban only)	1989	own calculations	18	24	23	20	15
Chile	1983	Petrei	22	29	22	16	11
Colombia	1974	Selowsky	27	24	20	17	11
Costa Rica	1986	Sauma/Trejos	28	23	24	14	11
Costa Rica	1984	Petrei	30	19	21	17	13
Dominican Republic	1989	1989 Household Survey	32	25	24	12	7
Dominican Republic	1980	Petrei	41	16	20	14	9
Jamaica	1989	Author's calculations	30	28	20	13	9
Peru (Lima only)	1990	Author's calculations	14	20	25	22	19
Peru	1985	Author's calculations	11	18	24	23	24
Uruguay	1989	Author's calculations	58	24	12	4	2
Uruguay	1983	Petrei	34	30	16	8	9

Public Primary Education							
Argentina	1980	Petrei	40	25	16	11	8
Bolivia (Urban only)	1989	Author's calculations	40	28	18	10	4
Chile	1983	Petrei	37	28	19	11	5
Colombia	1974	Selowsky	32	27	20	15	6
Costa Rica	1986	Sauma/Trejos	30	27	21	14	8
Costa Rica	1984	Petrei	35	27	19	12	7
Dominican Republic	1989	1989 Household Survey	33	26	23	14	4
Dominican Republic	1980	Petrei	14	17	22	26	31
Jamaica	1989	Author's calculations	35	29	20	12	4
Peru (Lima only)	1990	Author's calculations	40	27	19	12	5
Peru	1985	Author's calculations	28	27	22	15	8
Uruguay	1989	Author's calculations	26	28	21	14	9
Uruguay	1983	Petrei	45	26	14	7	7

(continued)

Table 8.2 (continued)

| Country | Year | Source | Percentage of Benefits Accruing to Quintile | | | | |
| | | | Poorest | | | | Richest |
			1	2	3	4	5
Public Secondary Education							
Argentina	1980	Petrei	26	21	21	18	14
Bolivia (urban only)	1989	Author's calculations	30	29	22	13	6
Chile	1983	Petrei	21	27	22	19	10
Colombia	1974	Selowsky	17	22	21	25	16
Costa Rica	1986	Sauma/Trejos	18	21	23	21	17
Costa Rica	1984	Petrei	19	27	21	22	11
Dominican Republic	1989	1989 Household Survey	24	24	20	18	15
Dominican Republic	1980	Petrei	9	13	17	29	32
Jamaica	1989	Author's calculations	31	24	22	14	8
Peru (Lima only)	1990	Author's calculations	28	27	23	14	8
Peru	1985	Author's calculations	13	23	25	23	17
Uruguay	1989	Author's calculations	12	17	26	25	21
Uruguay	1983	Petrei	25	21	24	19	12

136

Public Tertiary Education

	Year	Source					
Argentina	1980	Petrei	8	9	18	27	38
Bolivia	1989	Author's calculations	8	17	24	27	23
Chile	1983	Petrei	6	7	14	20	54
Colombia	1974	Selowsky	1	5	11	24	60
Costa Rica	1986	Sauma/Trejos	10	5	14	29	43
Costa Rica	1984	Petrei	4	13	11	30	42
Dominican Republic	1989	1989 Household Survey	16	18	13	22	30
Dominican Republic	1980	Petrei	0	2	4	18	76
Jamaica*	1989	Author's calculations	5	14	9	19	53
Peru (Lima only)	1990	Author's calculations	8	22	16	33	21
Peru	1985	Author's calculations	4	12	18	30	36
Uruguay	1989	Author's calculations	3	8	19	24	45
Uruguay	1983	Petrei	7	7	17	35	34

* Public and private - separate figures not available.

Table 8.3   Incidence of Universally Provided Services by Individual Quintiles

	Year	1	2	3	4	5
Public Health Care						
Bolivia (urban only)	1989	14	20	20	25	21
Jamaica	1989	21	23	20	20	16
Peru	1990	11	18	24	23	24
Peru (Lima only)	1985	14	22	25	23	19
Uruguay	1983	45	29	16	7	2
Public Primary Education						
Bolivia (urban only)	1989	32	27	21	14	6
Jamaica	1989	24	22	22	19	13
Peru	1985	26	26	18	14	16
Peru (Lima only)	1990	15	28	25	20	12
Uruguay	1989	41	25	16	12	6
Public Secondary Education						
Bolivia (urban only)	1989	23	27	24	18	9
Jamaica	1989	21	21	21	21	16
Peru	1985	11	19	23	25	22
Peru (Lima only)	1990	12	27	26	22	12
Uruguay	1989	16	22	24	22	16
Tertiary Education						
Bolivia (urban only)	1989	5	13	21	29	32
Jamaica	1989	5	5	10	18	62
Peru	1985	2	7	20	27	44
Peru (Lima only)	1990	0	25	13	29	33
Uruguay	1989	13	13	18	16	35

Where institutional systems differ, the results may also differ. The Jamaican health system seems less progressive than those of several other countries according to Table 8.2. This is not an indictment of their coverage or programs, but is the result of the fact that Jamaica does not have a separate social security system. In effect, these numbers are equivalent to what would be seen in other countries if the coverage of the Ministry of Health and that of the social security system were combined.

While the incidence of public primary health services is generally progressive, the following section will show that they may not cover all of the poor. The incidence indicates those who do use the system, but cannot tell us who may be left out. Where the network is not sufficiently extensive, those in rural areas or newly settled slums may lack physical access to services. This is apparently why the figures for Peru for 1985 are so regressive. The poor had little access and so ended up constituting a minority of users.

Public Education

Public primary education services have much more progressive incidence than do public secondary or public university services. The percentage of public primary education services accruing to the poorest quintile varies from 14 to 45 percent (see Table 8.2). For public secondary education, the percentage of services accruing to the poorest quintile varies from 9 to 31 percent. For public tertiary education, it varies from 0 to 16 percent.

The benefits of public primary education are progressively distributed for several reasons. The poor have larger families than the wealthy. More children are, therefore, likely to be poor than wealthy. The poor are rarely able to send their children to private schools, unlike the rich. Progressivity is lower at higher levels of education largely because poor children are likely to drop out and join the labor force earlier than wealthier children.

While this picture of incidence is substantively true, two methodological qualifications must be made to it. First, none of the studies cited were able to control for quality differences within the education sector. They are based on enrollment by quintile, not expenditure per child. Thus, the benefit to a child in a good middle-class urban school was counted as being equal to the benefit to a poor child in an ill-supplied one-room school in the countryside. If it were possible to control for these quality differences, public primary education services would undoubtedly appear less progressive.

The differences of progressivity by level of education are also partly the result of using current income as the welfare variable on which quintiles are constructed for most of the studies. As discussed in Chapter 3, there is a life cycle of earnings power in which earnings rise with age. The parents of primary school children tend to be young and therefore to have relatively low incomes. The parents of college-age children will be older and are likely to have advanced farther up the earnings curve. Thus, a family may look poorer when its children are in primary school than it may do by the time the children have advanced to secondary school or university. As shown in Chapter 3 in the case of Japan, this effect can be substantial.

Coverage Differences

Health Care

There are real differences by welfare level in access to health care, despite the progressive incidence of publicly provided health services. The incidence figures presented in the previous section take all those who use public health care and organize them by welfare level.[3] Public health care use is progressively distributed largely because the well-off choose to get their health care outside of the Ministry of Health system. The incidence hides the fact that the poor are not getting care nearly as often as the wealthy, in other words, that there are errors of exclusion for a theoretically universal service.

The probability that health care is used per episode of ill health varies by income level, by rural versus urban area and by country. In Peru, for example, 20 percent of those in the poorest rural quintile who reported being ill or injured during the period of the survey sought health care of some kind (see Table 8.4). For the wealthiest rural quintile, the probability of the ill or injured seeking care was almost twice as high—39 percent. Overall, those in rural areas sought care in 29 percent of the episodes of illness or injury. In urban areas, however, the probability of them seeking care was about two-thirds higher—48 percent.

In Jamaica, the differences in access to care are much less marked than in Peru, though they do still exist. The wealthiest rural quintile seeks care about 25 percent more often than the poorest rural quintile—56 versus 44 percent of all health care provided. The overall urban rural difference is even smaller—54 versus 47 percent.

Education

There are also differences in the coverage of education, again despite the progressive nature of enrollments at the public primary level. In Peru, for example, the nationwide enrollment rate was 87 percent of children aged six to ten in 1985. For those children in the poorest 30 percent of the population, it was lower—79 percent (see Table 8.5). For those in the poorest decile, it was lower still—75 percent. The same pattern is evident in Bolivia. The size of the differences in coverage is smaller, partly because the survey covered only urban areas. The poorest children and those least likely to be in school are undoubtedly located in rural areas.

Table 8.4   Percentage of Those Ill or Injured Seeking Medical Care

	Individual Quintile					
	1	*2*	*3*	*4*	*5*	*All*
Peru (1985)						
Urban areas	35	44	48	53	57	48
Rural areas	20	20	30	34	39	29
Bolivia (1989)						
Urban areas	61	45	55	61	69	58
Jamaica (1989)						
Urban areas	43	52	57	58	60	54
Rural areas	44	41	47	46	56	47

Source: Baker and van der Gaag (1993).

Table 8.5   School Enrollment Rates by Welfare Group

	Poorest 10%	*Poorest 30%*	*Total*
Peru (1985)			
6-10	75	79	87
11-15	79	82	88
Bolivia (Urban only)			
6-10	87	89	93
11-15	87	90	94
Jamaica (1989)			
6-10	95	96	96
11-15	88	89	91

Sources: Peru - Glewwe (1989); Bolivia - author's calculations; Jamaica - author's calculations.

In Jamaica, there is virtually no difference in enrollment rates by poverty level for six to ten year olds, and only small differences begin to show up in the 11 to 15 year old range. In Jamaica, primary enrollment is truly universal. Secondary enrollment is not quite so complete, but is still quite high for the lower grades. The differences in coverage alone underestimate any differences in the quality of the services provided. Furthermore, if the poor repeat years of school more often than the wealthy, the enrollment rate unadjusted for age and grade will not reflect differences in progress or outcomes.

Differences in Quality

Even when the poor go to schools or clinics, they may receive a service that is of a lower quality than that available to the wealthy. Where funds are too limited to provide a high quality of service to all, poor areas have a tendency to get lower-quality service.

Compared with the amount of information that is available on the incidence and coverage of health and education services, there is very little evidence on how pervasive or significant quality differences are. The paucity of evidence may be due to two factors. First, policymakers usually give priority to increasing coverage over improving quality until coverage reaches satisfactory levels. So it is only fairly recently that any attention has been given to quality. Indeed, in some regions, coverage continues to be the main concern. Second, quality is harder to measure than coverage.[4] Nevertheless, there is a consensus among development practitioners that differences in quality are sizable.

Differences in the quality of services received can be due to two factors. First, quality may differ among schools or clinics of the same defined level of service. For example, Type I clinics may be defined as providing a uniform level of service. But if absenteeism among personnel is higher and supplies are delivered less often to the rural Type I clinics than to those in semiurban areas, the quality of care they actually deliver will differ. Second, the density of different levels of service may differ by area. Rural areas may be served only by Type I clinics, villages by Type II clinics and urban areas by Type III clinics, for example. (Higher-grade clinics have more highly trained staff and more sophisticated equipment.) Analogous illustrations could be given for the education sector.

Health

It is rare to be able to measure rigorously whether the quality of services actually available within a given tier of services varies systematically. In Jamaica, however, the existence of unusually detailed and linked health facility and household surveys provides such an opportunity. Forty measures of quality were used, including the adequacy of the infrastructure, the hours of service, the type of personnel on staff and present at work, the state of repair of the equipment, the adequacy of drug stocks and the existence and availability of diagnostic tests. The quality measures were used as dependent variables by Peabody and others (1993). Regression analysis was carried out to explain variations in quality, with the characteristics of the facility and its catchment area used as potential explanatory factors. Quality did not differ according to the mean welfare level of the catchment area when the facility type (public or private and level of sophistication) was taken into account. Thus, within each grade of public clinic, quality is largely uniform. Since good information on equity is both a tool for management and a demonstration of commitment to equity, it is probably not coincidental that the country that had the best available information also had good equity.

In Honduras, it appears that poor women get less adequate prenatal care than richer women due to differences in the level of public services provided in urban and rural areas. This conclusion is drawn from two pieces of evidence and an assumption. The facts are that the type of prenatal caregiver varies markedly by region and that the extent of poverty also varies by region. The assumption is that traditional midwives give less adequate prenatal care than do formal clinics or hospitals. In Tegucigalpa and San Pedro, the two major urban enclaves, 66 percent of women receive their prenatal care from institutions and 6 percent from midwives. In rural areas, 19 percent use institutions and 27 percent use midwives, with the remainder using a mix or none (from Family Health Survey 1987). Per capita household income in rural areas is only a third of that in urban areas. Women in rural areas, where highly trained providers of prenatal care are scarcer, are much poorer than women in urban areas.

Education

In education, similar differences in the quality of services used by the rich and the poor exist. They may be due to variability in quality among schools of a defined type or in the mix of school types provided in different areas of the country.

Achievement test scores from Chile show that attainment differs by the welfare level of the area even within a given level of the system, in this case, municipal primary schools. In rural areas, students from middle-wealth municipalities had mean scores of 58.1, in contrast to students from low-wealth municipalities, who had scores of 46.1, and to those from the lowest-wealth municipalities, who had mean scores of 42.6. The differences by city size within a socioeconomic stratum were smaller but still present (see Table 8.6).

Achievement test scores are an outcome measure that combines the effects of differences in service inputs and in home factors. Since poor children usually live in home environments that are less conducive to educational success than non-poor children, the differences in outcomes may be greater than the differences in educational inputs. Outcome measures are appropriate measures of quality differences if the goal of the school system is not just to provide uniform access to schooling, but to ensure that all children learn to read and write equally well.

Evidence from Jamaica shows how the mix of public schools offered to the poor differs from those available to the nonpoor. In Jamaica, there are three tracks in the general public secondary school system. They are of different quality and there is a strong correlation between income and enrollment by track. The secondary level grades of the all-age schools are of the lowest quality, the new secondary schools are of intermediate quality and the traditional high schools are of the highest quality. The per pupil expenditures in urban areas are three times as high in high schools as in all-age schools, and twice as high in new secondary schools as in all-age schools (see Table 8.9). All-age schools are generally less well supplied with infrastructure, equipment and materials. Their teachers are equally experienced but are less likely to have postsecondary training (1990 Survey of Living Conditions calculations).

There is a strong correlation between the welfare level of a student and the track of secondary school s/he attends. Traditional high schools account for 60 percent of the secondary enrollments from the wealthiest quintile, but only for 14 percent of those from the poorest quintiles (see Table 8.7). Students are placed in a track and school according to their performance in a competitive exam, which is usually taken in the sixth grade. The fact that students from poor families tend to score lower on the com-

Table 8.6   Chile: Spanish Scores in Municipal Schools by Municipal Wealth and Size

Municipal Socioeconomic Level	Size of City		
	Metro	Large	Rural
High	n.a.	n.a.	n.a.
Middle	60.8	63.2	58.1
Low	50.8	51.7	46.1
Lowest	49.2	44.2	42.6

Source: World Bank (1991a).

Table 8.7   Jamaica: Secondary Enrollment by Track and Quintile

| | Quintile | | | | | |
| | Poorest | | | | Richest | |
Type of School	1	2	3	4	5	All
All-age 7-9	28	39	25	14	7	23
New secondary	49	29	34	31	23	33
High school	14	22	30	43	60	34
Technical tracks	9	9	11	14	10	10

Source: STATIN and PIOJ (1989).

petitive examination indicates that they have received lower-quality schooling at the primary level, have home environments that are less conducive to learning, or both.

Unit-Cost Differentials

Among the constraints on improving the access and quality of either universal or targeted services offered to the poor is that the poor may inherently be more costly to reach. If this is so, then "targeting" improvements in universal services will require balancing the benefits of reaching the poor against its extra costs, just as making decisions about more narrowly defined targeting also requires balancing the costs and benefits of targeting.

The logic of why it may be more costly to reach the poor is easy to imagine. Poverty is more prevalent and more profound in rural areas. If travel times are to be kept reasonably low, a school or a clinic in a rural area will serve a smaller population than a school or clinic in a urban area. The fixed costs of the building and staff will thus be spread among fewer students or patients. Many installations will have to do without water or electricity, or a well or a generator may be needed with a commensurately higher investment cost than would be the case in urban areas. It may be necessary to pay large salary bonuses to attract high-quality staff to work in rural areas. The travel time and costs for a community health worker to make home visits is likely to be many times higher than in urban areas. Any supervision of the school or clinic by the central authorities will involve longer travel times or higher transport costs. The costs of shipping medicines and supplies to health posts or of shipping textbooks or school lunches to schools will also obviously be higher. There are, of course, some countervailing factors. Land may be a good deal cheaper in rural areas. It may be cheaper to reach an acceptable construction quality. The cost of living will be lower. Overall, however, the probable higher costs seem to outweigh the probable lower costs.

Most of the anecdotal arguments about why the costs of reaching the poor may be higher than average center around rural/urban differences. To a lesser extent, the same issues may still apply in the poorer areas of cities. Certainly where the slums are unpleasant, unsafe or poorly served by public transport and utilities, the issues will be similar, although the differentials may be smaller.

How high the cost differentials of reaching the poor may be is largely unknown. Since few countries manage to provide equivalent service quality, measuring actual expenditure differences is not an adequate estimate of true cost differences. Adjustments would need to be made for differences in quality, which, as we have just seen, are usually not measured. Here we review some limited evidence to try to get some idea of how much more it may cost to reach the poor than the nonpoor. We use rural/urban differences as the proxy for poverty, which, though not a completely accurate proxy, is the only one that is available.

Health

In Chile, service providers are reimbursed by the national health fund according to a schedule of fees for the type of services provided. The payment schedule includes a 20 percent cost premium paid to rural providers. While no good cost studies yet exist to evaluate whether the 20 percent premium is adequate, the common wisdom on the topic asserts that it is probably too low to make up for real cost differences.

A study was commissioned for this work to quantify unit-cost differences in Bolivia, and this provides a useful illustration of the difficulties involved in conducting such studies (Cisneros 1991). First, the basic data on expenditures, quantities of inputs and quantities of outputs are rarely available from health service providers. Second, the (quasi-) public health services in Bolivia are partly provided by NGOs and partly by the Ministry of Health, so they have different service philosophies, pay scales, input mixes and recordkeeping abilities. Third, the activity mix varies among the providers, probably much more as a result of their priorities and abilities than according to the health status of the population.

The most reliable comparison is the breakdown between the rural and urban costs of ProSalud, a nongovernmental organization operating in the Santa Cruz area. ProSalud is a relatively new NGO dedicated to providing basic primary health care on a self-financing basis. It charges for services, and so far it recovers its operating costs but does not yet cover its overheads, which are subsidized by donor agencies. Because of its business management orientation and because it has similar recordkeeping in both rural and urban areas, ProSalud's records were more complete and comparable than for other providers. Finally, field visits leave the impression that quality differences between ProSalud's rural and urban services are less than for the other providers.

ProSalud's expenditures per activity performed are US$3.60 in rural areas and US$3.09 in urban areas. The rural cost premium is, therefore, 18 percent (see Table 8.8). Although the activity mix is not exactly the same between rural and urban areas, it is uncertain how adjusting more rigorously for the activity mix would affect the estimate of the cost differential. The rural area has a slightly higher proportion of preventive consultations. Since preventive consultations tend to be

Table 8.8   Bolivia: Unit-Costs of Primary Health Care

	Department of Santa Cruz			
Provider	MOH Urban	MOH Rural	ProSalud Urban	ProSalud Rural
Cost per activity (US$)	2.59	9.15	3.09	3.60
Activity Mix (percent)				
Preventive	n.a.	22.7	19.5	27.6
Vaccinations	n.a.	16.9	23.3	21.0
Home visits	n.a.	4.9	2.9	6.4
Curative	n.a.	55.5	54.3	45.0
Total		100.0	100.0	100.0
Consultations/ inhabitants/year	n.a.	0.53	1.01	1.10
Staff/1,000 Population	0.64	1.27	0.77	0.55

n.a. Not applicable.
Source: Cisneros (1991), Tables 4.1, 4.2, 4.3.

cheaper to provide than curative consultations, adjusting would increase cost differences. Simultaneously, however, the rural area does more home visits, which are even more expensive. Adjusting for that might tend to diminish the cost differences.

ProSalud's market studies show that a population catchment area of about 9,000 is required to generate enough business to break even. In rural areas, this critical population mass is usually not found in the specific catchment area assigned to the NGO by the Ministry of Health. ProSalud, therefore, "poaches" patients from neighboring territories on the basis of service quality. If it served a population as small as it was originally assigned, its rural unit costs would be higher. Thus, the unit-cost differentials may be somewhat underestimated compared to a more generalizable case.

The cost differences shown for the rural and urban areas served by the Ministry of Health in the Department of Santa Cruz are much greater than those shown for ProSalud. Rural costs per activity are three and a half times as high as in urban areas. There are no data available on the activities in the urban area to allow adjustments to be made for a different case load mix.

Why the cost differentials should be so different between the Ministry of Health and ProSalud is not apparent. There are, however, some clues. First, there are twice the number of Ministry of Health staff per inhabitant in the rural areas as in the urban areas. For ProSalud, there are actually fewer. Since staff costs are a large share of total expenses, this is an important difference. Second, ProSalud provides a quality of service sufficient to attract about one consultation per inhabitant per year. The Ministry of Health's average is only half that, so the fixed costs are spread over fewer consultations even for the same size of population base. Third, the area assigned to ProSalud is less remote than many other rural areas and has a denser population.

Education

In the Chilean education system, service providers are reimbursed through a voucher system. In education, the existence of higher unit-costs in rural areas is more explicitly recognized than it is in Chile's health sector. A multiplication factor is applied to the regular per student payments, depending on the number of students in the school. This factor ranges from 2.0 for schools with one to fifteen students to 1.015 for schools with 84 to 85 students (Hoenack 1991). However, the number of schools that, in fact, receive adjustments based on their rural location is limited. In rural areas, the average primary school size is 131 students in subsidized private schools and 136 in municipal schools. For the 20 percent of municipalities that had the highest percentages of population in extreme poverty in 1982, the average school size in rural areas was 66 for subsidized private schools and 90 for municipal schools (World Bank 1990b).

The Chilean government is now considering whether to reform the reimbursement formula and whether to give more generous allowances to rural areas. This might be interpreted to mean that existing allowances are considered insufficient and may therefore be an underestimate of cost differentials. Extrapolating beyond Chile, cost differentials in other countries are probably greater. Chile's rural population is smaller and better-off than that in many other countries. The transport network is also good, though the terrain is sometimes difficult.

Another proposed reform to Chilean educational financing is an explicit premium of up to 30 percent for teachers working in "difficult conditions," in other words, in rural and poor urban areas (see Republic of Chile, Ministry of Education 1990). While this is not a scientific measurement of real cost differentials, it does give some idea of their minimum expected magnitude.

The most complete comparisons of unit-costs of education by area are those that have been made in Jamaica. For all-age schools (the lowest quality of secondary schools), the cost differential with between rural and urban areas is as high as 50 percent (see Table 8.9). Urban all-age schools have unit costs of J$529 per pupil (1988 Jamaican dollars). Rural all-age schools have costs of J$636 per pupil. Remote rural all-age schools have even higher costs—J$796 per pupil. The factor leading to the difference is the pupil/teacher ratio, which falls from 45 in urban areas to 34 in remote rural areas. For new secondary schools (which fall in the middle of the quality scale), no pattern of cost differences is found because class sizes remain the same. This is feasible partly because class sizes are already smaller than in all-age schools, so the population base need not be as high to support the ratio. In the high schools (the highest quality of the secondary school tracks), costs rise in rural areas although class size does not. This is because some of the rural high schools are boarding schools, and thus have commensurately higher costs. The average cost differential is again 50 percent. Note that no new secondary or

Table 8.9   Jamaica: Per Pupil Recurrent Expenditures by School Location and Type

		All-Age			*New Secondary*			*High School*	
Location	*No.*	*Unit-costs (J$)*	*Pupil/ teacher ratio*	*No.*	*Unit-costs (J$)*	*Pupil/ teacher ratio*	*No.*	*Unit-costs (J$)*	*Pupil/ teacher ratio*
Urban	40	529	45	26	1,255	21	25	1,634	20
Rural	279	636	38	35	1,236	22	6	2,492	21
Remote Rural	129	796	34	—	—	—	—	—	—

— Not available.
Note: All data are school averages for the 1987-88 financial year in 1988 Jamaican dollars.
Source: Ministry of Education as cited in GE Government Service et al. (1990).

high schools are available in remote rural areas at all. Even in rural areas, the proportion of the all-age schools is higher. Rather than paying higher unit costs by putting these schools in remote areas, quality in those areas is allowed to fall.

Discussion

Even on the basis of the insufficient data mustered here, it seems that the unit costs of reaching the poor are higher than average. The magnitude is still uncertain, but the observations here indicate that rural unit-costs can be at least 20 to 50 percent higher than urban unit-costs.

If the poor are more expensive to reach, then there is a dilemma about whether to spend the extra resources to reach fewer of the poorest or more of the not quite so poor. This problem can be approached analytically with the same kind of simulations presented in Chapter 3, which weighed the tradeoffs between lowering leakage and undercoverage.

In practice, such analysis is frequent but is usually qualitative rather than quantitative. In Bolivia, for example, although it is well-established that poverty and health status are both worse in rural areas, the World Bank's health project supports improvements in the coverage and quality of services in the peri-urban areas of the three principal cities. The reason for this strategic decision was very much one of cost and manageability and was qualitatively assessed. If the urban poor were not the poorest, they were still poor and numerous. The project designers felt that, with an urban-based project, there was a greater likelihood of success and a greater certainty of reaching large numbers of needy people.

Notes

1. A negative income elasticity means that if the household's income goes up, the quantity of the commodity purchased will go down. This is rare. For most staples, the share of the total budget spent on the item will decline, but the absolute quantity purchased will rise with income. It is also possible for the subsidization of commodities with high own- and cross-price elasticities for the poor but with low own- and cross-price elasticities for the rich to result in progressive incidence. Many staples do show high own-price elasticities for the poor and low own-price elasticities for the rich, and there is some evidence of similar patterns in cross-price elasticities. Of course, the same features (being an important item in the poor's food basket and having suitable production patterns) must still obtain. For a simple primer on these issues, see Chapter 7 of Foster (1992); for a more detailed treatment, see Alderman (1986).

2. State trading corporations can import the goods on the basis of their monopoly trading rights and simply sell them at below cost to the commercial distribution chain. Or prices can be regulated, leaving the producers to bear the cost as an implicit tax. Sometimes commodities are purchased from local producers at one price and then sold to the distribution chain at a lower price.

3. Typically, the information comes from a series of questions in a household survey. All individuals may be asked if they have received health care in the last three months and if so, where. Or a filter question may be introduced first, asking whether the patient has been ill or injured. Then, only those who report themselves to be ill or injured answer questions about health care use.

4. In a household survey, coverage can be verified by asking only one or two questions. To determine quality, it is necessary to ask a much longer series of questions. It also requires that the consumer must be able to report accurately on those aspects of the service s/he receives that are adequate measures of quality, and this may not be feasible. Patients, for example, may not know whether the clinics they attend have adequate equipment and supplies. They may not be able to tell how much training the service provider has had, and they may not know whether the diagnosis or treatment is appropriate. The factors that they can easily distinguish—waiting time, repair of buildings and drug supplies—may not be reliable measures of quality. These factors may affect the extent to which the service is utilized but not necessarily its medical quality. To derive quality estimates from service delivery statistics would require more disaggregated reporting than is usual. It would also require more measurement of actual inputs (texts, teacher hours) and their quality (how experienced is the teacher? how well does she integrate the text into her teaching?) rather than focusing only on expenditure as most reporting systems do.

9

Summary and Conclusions

This book began with a series of practical questions about how to target social programs. When is it appropriate? Which targeting mechanisms provide the best incidence? What are their administrative costs? What are their logistical and management requirements? Which mechanisms work in which circumstances? What standards are achievable? Where does a government start in setting up a new program? What lessons have been learned in other countries? Let us now summarize what we have learned in reviewing the experience of the 30 programs in eleven countries.

When Is It Appropriate to Target?

Whether and how to target social programs will depend on weighing the benefits and costs of doing so. The main benefit of targeting is an improvement in the cost-effectiveness of the program. In other words, for the same cost, the poor can receive more benefits. Or for fixed benefit levels, the budget can be reduced. The costs of targeting come from the administrative structure required, the possible loss of political support and possible negative incentive effects.

This study has shown that, in general, the administrative costs of targeted programs are low in both absolute and percentage terms. With the absolute magnitude of total administrative costs running at around $5 to $10, targeted programs that provide an annual benefit of $50 to $100 or more should not be precluded on the grounds of administrative expense, although of course the political economy and economic incentive costs should be factored in as well.

How much it is worth paying in administrative costs to target a program will depend on both the accuracy of the targeting and the size of the benefit to be distributed. The cost of each mechanism will depend on local conditions—whether there is a good physical, administrative and information infrastructure on which to build and the availability and cost of local staff and equipment.

151

What Are the Basic Targeting Mechanisms?

This study has used an administrative taxonomy of targeting options, with three broad classes of mechanisms:

- *Individual assessment mechanisms* require program managers to make decisions on the eligibility of individual applicants. Examples of individual assessments are means tests (is household income below the cut-off point?), using the gender of household head as the criterion (is the head of household female?) and using nutritional status as the criterion (is the child malnourished?).
- In *group or geographic mechanisms,* groups of candidates are granted eligibility on the basis of some easily identifiable shared characteristic. Geographic targeting allots benefits to states, municipalities or neighborhoods based on their average welfare level. The selection of some schools over others for participation in school lunch programs could also be considered a form of geographic targeting.
- *"Self-targeted" programs* are those in which the service or program is ostensibly available to all, but is designed in such a way as to discourage the nonpoor from using it. This can be done by requiring participants to work, as in public employment programs. Another mechanism for self-targeting is requiring people to stand in line, as this carries an implicit cost, one which the nonpoor may not be willing to tolerate. Stigma may also be used to discourage the nonpoor from accepting a benefit. Or a product of low quality may be subsidized on the assumption that a similar but higher quality product supplied by the private sector will be used by the nonpoor.

In some cases, policymakers decide not to target but rather to provide services to all. Although, *"universal"* services or subsidies are meant to be available to all, in practice they are often not used equally by everybody. Sometimes actions to improve the equity of services such as basic health care and education are also said to targeted.

How Well Do the Different Mechanisms Work?

The targeted programs reviewed in this paper cover a wide range of incidence outcomes, but even the worst examples of targeting have progressive incidence. Across all the programs we have reviewed, the share of benefits accruing to the poorest two quintiles ranges from 59 to 83 percent.

There is only a very weak correlation between the class of targeting mechanism and the incidence outcome. The difference among the incidences from a single mechanism as applied in different situations is much bigger than the differences between the averages for any two mechanisms. For individual assessment mechanisms, the median share of benefits going to the poorest two quintiles is 73 percent. For geographic mechanisms, the median is 72 percent, and for self-targeting, it is 71 percent.

The incidence outcomes are determined not only by the screening device built into the targeting mechanism itself but also by the characteristics of the candidate pool and of any self-selection effects. The university loan programs, for example, are hard pressed to produce progressive outcomes given that the student body is drawn heavily from the upper end of the income spectrum. In contrast, in Costa Rica, the candidate pool for the free health insurance program is the part of the population that has no other form of health insurance and is concentrated at the lower end of the income distribution.

The relevant comparisons are not only among targeted options but also between targeted options and universal social programs. The targeted programs have dramatically more progressive incidence than the average general food price subsidy. In each country where a comparison is possible, the incidence of the targeted programs is also more progressive than those of the public primary health or primary education expenditures. The median targeted program delivered 72 percent of its benefits to the poorest two quintiles, in contrast to the medians of 33 percent found for general food subsidies, 57 percent for primary health care and 59 percent for primary education.

In conceptual discussions of targeting, there is great concern that the targeting mechanism will erroneously exclude some eligible candidates. In practice, two of the major causes of undercoverage appear to be fairly simple to address. In several programs, budget constraints provide ceilings on the number of participants that fall well short of the targeting mechanisms' capacity to identify eligible candidates. In others, insufficient administrative budgets and the insufficient program administration that ensues make it difficult for participants to register or to receive program benefits. These problems could be solved if budgets were increased, and thus they are not a true impediment to targeting.

A third cause of errors of exclusion is that some members of the target group may not be reached by the mechanism meant to bring them into a social program. For example, the poor may have limited access to health clinics so that they would miss out on food supplement programs targeted to users of preventive health services. This is a more inherent problem and is a potentially serious one because it is often the neediest who are left out of a program.

What Do the Options Cost?

In the targeted programs reviewed, the range of total administrative costs as a share of total program costs is from 0.4 to 29 percent. The median is 9 percent. With one exception, the total administrative costs of targeted programs are below US$25 per recipient per year. The median cost is US$5 per beneficiary per year. Only a part of that cost is, strictly speaking, due to targeting (screening candidates). In the few cases where it was possible to separate out only the targeting costs, they were even lower. The median was 1 percent of total program costs. In absolute terms, the highest targeting cost was US$11 per beneficiary. The median targeting cost was US$1.36 per beneficiary.

Concern over high administrative costs is perhaps the most commonly given reason for not making serious efforts to target programs. It is also commonly given as the reason to choose some mechanism other than those requiring individual assessment. These numbers show that the concern about administrative costs has been greatly overstated. In fact, a wide variety of programs have found mechanisms that cost very little yet also produce incidence outcomes that, while imperfect, are better than those of untargeted programs.

A look at the ranges of costs for the three classes of mechanisms is also instructive. The median shares of total administrative costs as a percentage of program budgets are 10 percent for individual assessment, 7 percent for geographic targeting and 6 percent for self-targeting. Total administrative costs for individual assessment mechanisms run from US$0.39 to US$23.16 per beneficiary per year, with the exception of the student loan programs, which are well outside this range. Most of the programs targeted by individual assessment have total administrative costs of below US$10 per beneficiary per year. Group targeted programs have administrative costs from US$0.38 to US$6.92 per beneficiary per year. Self-targeted programs have administrative costs from US$4 to $6.95 per beneficiary per year.

Many factors other than the targeting mechanism affect the share of administrative costs. The type of benefit to be delivered, its size, the quality of the program's administration and possibly whether it is contracted out to the private sector or provided by the public sector are important factors. The scale of the program may also be important.

While administrative costs are generally low, this is not always a sign of efficiency. It may also be the result of scrimping on important aspects of program management and implementation. It seems likely that the quality and incidence of the services provided by the majority of programs would improve if more were spent on administration. Furthermore, it has only been possible to observe the costs of imperfectly targeted programs. It is not possible to extrapolate how much it would cost to improve targeting to near-perfect levels.

How Do We Judge Different Options?

Targeting is a tool to improve the ability of poverty programs to alleviate poverty within a given program budget. Thus, the most comprehensive means of evaluating the success of alternate targeting options is to simulate their impact on poverty. When insufficient information is available to allow such comprehensive calculations, estimates of leakage, coverage and administrative costs can be used to shed light on different aspects of the targeting outcomes.

In judging targeting accuracy, both leakage and undercoverage are important. Leakage implies that benefits are given to those who are not a high priority. Scarce resources are thus squandered. Undercoverage means that those who are most in need of benefits are not receiving them. Information on incidence and participation rates by quintile is appropriate for making comparisons among countries with different poverty lines or among programs with different subgroups of the poor as the target population. In these comparisons, it is important to use uniform methods for defining the quintiles.

In weighing the balance among targeting options, the most pragmatic method is often to calculate the amount of total expenditures, after discounting for administrative costs, that accrues to the poor. This discounts administrative costs and leakage to give a "bang for the buck" estimate. It cannot, however, factor in errors of exclusion, much less political economy or disincentive effects.[1]

The relevant standards against which to judge targeted programs are not always hypothetical uniform or perfectly targeted transfer schemes. Instead, it may be more appropriate to compare them with realistic program options, such as general food price subsidies, basic health and education services or other targeted programs.

In judging whether to expand a program, the possible differences between average and marginal incidence will be an important factor. Details of how the expansion is to occur can lead to significant differences in outcomes.

What Are the Lessons to be Learned from Specific Mechanisms?

Individual Assessment Mechanisms

The blanket fear that individual assessment mechanisms are too costly or unmanageable is unjustified. There are many ways to minimize the administrative complexity of individual assessment mechanisms. The costs run the gamut from US$0.35 to US$40 per assessment. The program experiences show that some of the simplest variants can produce satisfactory targeting outcomes.

Looking at the various subclasses of mechanisms, some lessons emerge:

- Very simple means tests that make little or no attempt to value in-kind or seasonal income or to verify income can nonetheless produce satisfactory incidence outcomes. Elements of self-selection may play a role in this, which implies that the simple means test is probably less appropriate in cases where the benefits are large.

- Proxy means tests are a promising alternative. Rather than relying on reported monetary income, they rely on other, more verifiable correlates of poverty. This avoids problems of work disincentives and misreported income.

- Social worker evaluations vary widely in their effectiveness. They seem to work best where program benefits are large and the political will exists to run a program seriously.

- The use of nutritional status or risk as targeting criteria among users of public maternal-child health care produces good incidence. Piggybacking transfer programs onto the health services places some demands on the operational staff of health clinics, but can also increase the utilization of services among the poorest and allow a synergy of benefits among health services, health education and food or income supplements.

- Nutritional risk criteria can be used to give a low level of benefit to all users of health services and a high level of benefit to those at nutritional risk. This has the medical advantage of increasing the utilization of health care services and has the political advantage of making benefits available to the whole population. In cases where the logistics of having more than one benefit level are not too complicated, this is an attractive option.

Group and Geographic Targeting

Targeting by group characteristics or geographic area can be administratively simple. An inherent problem of geographic targeting is that it can be inaccurate mainly because some of the rich live in poor areas and some of the poor in rich areas. Simulations of the accuracy of geographic targeting show that both leakage and undercoverage diminish as the size of unit used in decisionmaking gets smaller. Most of the programs examined do, in fact, use areas smaller than the state—neighborhood, village and school targeting are all much more common. The incidence of these programs covers the range of program outcomes.

Several of the programs use very informal mechanisms for picking schools or neighborhoods. To the degree that we can tell, this seems to work well. Informality is not necessarily synonymous with imprecision. While the costs of the targeting mechanism itself can be quite low for geographic targeting, a full service delivery mechanism is still needed for these programs. The range in administrative costs from 4 to 16 percent is thus much the same as for other mechanisms.

Geographic targeting need not be an all or nothing proposition. Program resources can be assigned to regions according to a formula that includes regional poverty levels as well as other indicators, such as population.

Geographic targeting would seem to work especially well in the case of small local programs that need intensive community contact. Nongovernmental organizations can also use geographic targeting to good advantage. Many of their programs are not national in scope anyway, so placing them in the poorest regions is a good first step. Likewise, many of their programs stress integrated community development, which implies a geographic focus. Also, unlike the government, they are not subject to electoral pressures from the regions they choose not to serve.

Geographic targeting can also be used to place services or infrastructure in parts of cities where the poor are known to be concentrated. This is more likely to be effective in the case of services for which the frequency of contact is high. For example, schools or food shops that are visited daily will provide more accurate geographic targeting than clinics or social security offices that are visited only every few weeks.

Self-Targeting Mechanisms

The principal factors that promote self-targeting are time costs, stigma or a low quality product. These factors all induce the nonpoor to self-select out of the program. The problem is that they may also discourage participation among the poor. Even when the poor do choose to participate, these factors lower the net benefit of the program's service.

Policymakers rarely give explicit attention to the time costs of participation. Time costs are usually the result of insufficient resources or of inefficiency in program administration. Furthermore, important decisions about how to organize queues or how often or at what times to provide a service are usually made for the convenience of program administrators rather than the beneficiaries. More attention should be given to this factor.

Stigma is country and program specific. As with the time costs of participation, this is rarely given explicit attention by policymakers. The stigma felt by participants depends upon the details of how the program is designed, implemented and advertised.

Many food programs have relied on low product quality as a self-targeting mechanism. New services are beginning to use the same idea. Daycare is one example. Another is the kind of improvement in housing, water supply and sanitation that is funded by demand-driven social investment funds. While low quality is pervasive in public health and education, this is more the result of low budgets or inefficiency than it is an explicit goal.

Although self-targeted programs do not need as extensive a bureaucracy as other targeted programs, they still need some administration to deliver the service. Thus, their administrative costs are in the same range as those of the other kinds of mechanisms.

Universal services often provide an appropriate benchmark with which to compare targeted programs in choosing a program.

General food price subsidies usually have very regressive incidence. Even when the staple foods that constitute a larger share of the food budget of the poor than of the nonpoor are chosen to be subsidized, the poor tend to consume lower quantities of food and thus receive a disproportionately low share of the transfer value. Although general price subsidies would not seem to require much administration and thus would seem likely to cost less than targeted programs, they may distort incentives in the economy in ways that are rarely measured but that may cost as much or more than the administrative costs of a targeted program would have done.

Primary health and primary education have progressive incidence. In health care, the good incidence is a result of self-targeting due to the fact that a low quality of service is offered to the poor, while the private sector and social security institutes provide higher-quality alternatives to the nonpoor who can afford to pay for them. In education, the incidence is most progressive at the primary level and becomes successively less so at the secondary and tertiary levels. Children of poor households are less likely to be able to stay in school long enough to reach the higher levels. Furthermore, private sector schools usually account for a larger share of enrollments at the secondary level than at the primary level.

Despite the progressive incidence of public health and education services, the poor may still experience problems in getting access to them. In the education sector, in countries where school enrollment is less than universal, it is the poor who are much more likely not to be in school. In the health sector, among those who report themselves as having been ill during a specified reference period, the poor are much less likely to seek medical care than the nonpoor. These differences are larger in countries where the health network is not extensive.

The poor also appear to receive public health and education services that are of lower quality than the average, though the measurement of this is far from adequate. If these differences in the quality of services received were adequately accounted for, the incidence of public health and education services would be less progressive than is commonly reported.

Unit-costs for reaching the poor, especially the rural poor, may be a good deal higher than the unit-costs of reaching the nonpoor. The limited evidence that is available for review suggests that the unit-costs of reaching the poor may be 20 to 50 percent higher than the costs of reaching the nonpoor. These differences in unit-costs should be better quantified so that policymakers with limited budgets can make more informed decisions about the tradeoff between reaching fewer of the poorest or more of the not quite so poor. The issues are analogous to those for more narrowly targeted programs.

How Do We Select and Design an Option?

When trying to decide which targeting option is the most appropriate in a given circumstance, estimates of probable administrative costs, leakage and undercoverage should be made. The program experience presented in this study can help to define the likely ranges of costs, and the qualitative information can help program designers to customize options to take into account the institutional infrastructure that is in place in the country. For example, if the school system is extensive, a program targeted through schools will have lower undercoverage than if enrollments are low. If the private health care system is well developed, the incidence of the public primary health care system may be very progressive. If a country has experience with social worker cadres or means tests, it may find these easier to implement than would be the case in countries in which they have never been tried. The kind of service to be delivered will also influence which targeting option to choose. The program designers will also have to consider themes not investigated in this study such as the political and economic incentives that may result from the various options.

In the end, there is no single right way to target. Many mechanisms can be made to work. The emphasis should be on picking one that is suitable to the circumstances and then putting diligent effort into making it work. The myriad details of how the generic targeting mechanism is put into practice matter as much as the choice of the mechanism itself.

A summary of options and considerations for each type of program is provided in Table 9.1. The planner who is contemplating whether to instigate a new program or to refine an existing one may also benefit from studying programs with similar interventions or targeting mechanisms and looking at the experience of countries that have similar administrative capacities. The case studies provide an idea of the variety of options available, why each targeting option was chosen and what implementation issues may be involved.

The following questions can be used to fine-tune both existing programs and proposals for new programs. The questions refer to the administration of the targeting mechanism and assume that the program benefit itself is already designed satisfactorily.

- Which factor is the most important in determining the targeting outcome—the nature of the candidate pool, self-selection by the potential beneficiaries or the formal targeting mechanism?
- What changes in program *design* could lower leakage?
- What changes in program *implementation* could lower leakage?
- What changes in program *design* could lower undercoverage?
- What changes in program *implementation* could lower undercoverage?
- How could the time costs of participation for the beneficiaries be lowered? What would be the effect on the targeting outcome? On administrative costs?
- How could stigma be lessened or increased? What would be the effect on the targeting outcome? On administrative costs?
- If the administrative budget could be increased by 25 percent, how could those funds best be used? What would be gained?
- If the administrative budget had to be cut by 25 percent, what would be the best way to make those cuts? What would be lost?

What Has This Review of the Experience from Targeted Programs Taught Us?

As a result of having conducted as thorough a comparative survey of targeted program as is yet available in the literature, we come to three main conclusions:

1. Targeted programs have much more progressive incidence than general food price subsidies and even somewhat more progressive incidence than basic public health and education services.
2. The administrative costs of programs with moderately good incidence need not be excessively high.
3. It is not possible to rank targeting mechanisms a priori. There are no broad correlations between the targeting mechanisms and targeting outcomes, and there is only a weak correlation with administrative costs.

Table 9.1   Selecting Targeting Options

Basic Targeting Options	Advantages	Disadvantages	Appropriate Circumstances	Information Required
Targeting Food Commodity or Food Stamps through Clinics				
Use demographic criteria only (age for children, pregnancy/lactation for women)	Administratively simple Provides greatest encouragement to preventive health care use Politically popular	Most costly due to high leakage	Malnutrition widespread Use of health services low Little administrative capacity	Age for children (birth registration) Pregnancy/lactation status for women
Use weight for age of children	Less costly due to lower leakage Preventive health care incentive provided for malnourished children	Does not *prevent* malnutrition, but treats it curatively	Malnutrition not widespread Use of preventive services high Good growth monitoring system	Age for children Weight for children
In addition to other options, limit program to geographic areas of greatest need	Lowers cost Administratively simple	Can lead to undercoverage May be politically unpopular	Program resources scarce and administrative capacity too low to use other options Strong correlation between poverty and geographic area	Poverty map
Use growth faltering for children	Focus on *preventing* malnutrition Medium leakage to children who are not malnourished	Standards controversial Requires greatest precision in weighing, recording, filing	Very good pre-existing monitoring system	Age for children Weight gain
Use biomedical determinants of risk	Focus on *preventing* malnutrition Can lower errors of exclusion	Administratively complex Limited incentive for preventive health care use	High fertility or high infant mortality	Mother's fertility history Siblings' health/nutrition history
Use socio-economic status	Accuracy	Administratively complex May have little political support May cause stigma	Low malnutrition Good health coverage Poverty variable	Household income or proxies

Give differentiated benefits according to nutritional status, risk or welfare level, with a basic level of benefits for all	Good targeting Good political support Incentives for health care use for all	Administratively complex Costly	Good administrative capacity	Depends on what criteria are used

Targeting School Lunches

Use school as unit of selection - feed all students in selected schools	Administratively simple Less stigma for selected students Less envy for non-selected students	Less accurate	Administrative capacity low Feeding timed during school shift Student welfare level homogenous within schools	Poverty map
Use student as unit of selection - feed only some students in selected schools	More accurate	Very demanding administratively May cause stigma or jealousy between student groups	Administrative capacity high Feeding before or after school shift or cost recovery mechanism in place Student welfare level heterogenous within schools	Individual students' welfare measures, such as household income or height for age
Encourage self-targeting within school by allowing children to bring food from home and/or to purchase from vendors on school grounds	Administratively simple Improves variety and taste for children using private options	Difficult to measure results May cause stigma or jealousy between student groups Private options may be high in sugars and fats but low in protein or vitamins	Vendors are abundant (e.g. in urban areas) Parent association or secondary students run co-op	None
Improve self-targeting within schools by allowing second or third servings	Administratively simple	May raise total food consumption and cost Difficult to measure results	Food abundant Hunger prevalent Portion sizes variable or serving pattern flexible	None

(continued)

Table 9.1 (continued)

Basic Targeting Options	Advantages	Disadvantages	Appropriate Circumstances	Information Required
Targeting Cash Transfers/Food Stamps				
Work through welfare agency using means test, proxy means test or social worker evaluation	Accuracy Trained personnel, standardized procedures Fits institutional mandate	No collateral benefits	Social welfare agency with good capacity	Household income or proxies
Work through health clinics	Can provide incentive for primary health care use	Can distract health personnel or budgets from higher priorities Prone to errors of exclusion May have greater security requirements Less standardized procedures	No social welfare agency Health objectives important	Depends on options (see clinic programs)
Work through schools	Can provide incentive for school enrollment and attendance	Can distract education personnel or budgets from higher priorities Prone to leakage May have greater security requirements Less standardized procedures	No social welfare agency Education objectives important	Depends on options (see school feeding programs)

Targeting Public Works/Job Programs

JOBS/WAGES

Use private sector contractors	Results in low cost construction Administratively simple Less political pressure to keep workers on payroll for long periods	No control over who is hired Contractor will pay market wage for construction workers and hire typical worker (male, young, head of household)	Infrastructure important objective Private sector focus	None
Use public agencies	Can select workers according to poverty correlates	May lead to inflated construction costs Requires supervision capacity of public sector works May lead to political pressure to make employees permanent	Cash transfer important objective Considerable public sector administrative capacity	Worker characteristics such as age, sex, employment history, household income

INFRASTRUCTURE/SERVICES

Use poverty map in selection of works	Low administrative cost	Inaccurate, especially within cities May run counter to rate-of-return criteria	Strong correlation between poverty and geographic area	Poverty map
Target by project type	Low administrative cost Low unit investment costs	Low amenity projects	Water, sewerage, road networks incomplete	Sensitivity of consumer preferences to amenity differences

Note

1.   When information on errors of exclusion is available, it is usually possible to calculate a poverty index measure.

Bibliography

Alderman, Harold (1992), "Nutritional Considerations in Bank Lending for Economic Adjustment." Paper presented at the 12th Agricultural Symposium. World Bank, Washington, D.C.

_____ (1991), "Food Subsidies and the Poor." In *Essays on Poverty, Equity, and Growth*. G. Psacharopoulos, ed. Oxford: Pergamon Press.

_____ (1987), "Allocation of Goods through Non-Price Mechanisms; Evidence on Distribution by Willingness to Wait." *Journal of Development Economics* Vol. 25, pp. 105-124.

_____ (1986), *The Effects of Food Price and Income Changes on the Acquisition of Food by Low-Income Households*. Washington, D.C.: International Food Policy Research Institute.

Alderman, Harold, M. Ghaffar Chaudry and Marito Garcia (1988), *Household Food Security in Pakistan: The Ration Shop System*. Research Report No. 4. Washington, D.C.: International Food Policy Research Institute.

Alderman, Harold, Joachim von Braun and Ahmed Sakr (1982), *Egypt's Food Subsidy and Rationing System: A Description*. Research Report No. 34. Washington, D.C.: International Food Policy Research Institute.

Anderson, Patricia (1993), "The Incorporation of Mothers and Children into the Jamaican Food Stamp Programme." Jamaican Poverty Line Project Working Paper No. 6. Planning Institute of Jamaica, Kington.

Atkinson, A. B. (1992), "On Targeting Social Security." Paper presented at the Conference on Public Expenditures and the Poor: Incidence and Targeting. World Bank, Policy Research Department, Washington, D.C.

Avila Seifert, G. F., Fernando Campero Prudencio and J. Patino Sarcinelli (1992), *Un Puente Sobre la Crisis: El Fondo Social de Emergencia*. La Paz: Fondo de Inversion Social.

Baker, Judy L., and Margaret E. Grosh (forthcoming), *Poverty Reduction Through Geographic Targeting: How Well Does It Work?* Living Standard Measurement Study Working Paper. Washington, D.C.: World Bank.

Baker, Judy L., and Jacques van der Gaag (1993), "Equity in the Finance and Delivery of Health Care: Evidence from Five Developing Countries." In *Equity in the Finance and Delivery of Health Care*. Eddy van Doorslaer, Adam Wagstaff and Frans Rutten, eds. London: Oxford University Press.

Ballenger, Nicole, and Courtney Harold (1991), "Revisiting Surplus Food Programs after Surpluses: The Temporary Emergency Food Assistance Program and Its Role in the District of Colombia." Discussion Paper Series No. FAP91-01. National Center for Food and Agricultural Policy, Resources for the Future, Washington, D.C.

Bentancur-Mejia, Gabriel (1990), "Colombian Institute of Educational Credit and Training Abroad: Assessment of its Experiences over 40 Years and Their Replicability." World Bank, Latin America and Caribbean Technical Department, Washington, D.C.

Besley, Timothy, and Stephen Coate (1991), "Public Provision of Private Goods and the Redistribution of Income." *American Economic Review* Vol. 81, No. 4, pp. 979-984.

Besley, Timothy, and Ravi Kanbur (1990) "The Principals of Targeting." Policy, Research and External Affairs Working Paper Series, No. 385. World Bank, Research Administrator's Office, Washington, D.C.

Binswanger, Hans, and Jaime Quizon (1988), "Distributional Consequences of Alternative Food Policies in India." In *Food Subsidies in Developing Countries*. Per Pinstrup-Andersen, ed. Baltimore: Johns Hopkins University Press.

Bishop, John (1982), "Discussion: Modeling the Decision to Apply for Welfare." In *Income-Tested Transfer Programs: The Case For and Against*. I. Garfinkel, ed. New York: Academic Press.

Calegar, Geraldo M., and G. Edward Schuh (1988), *The Brazilian Wheat Policy: Its Costs, Benefits, and Effects on Food Consumption*. Research Report No. 66. Washington, D.C.: International Food Policy Research Institute.

Carlson, Sam (1992), "Private Financing of Higher Education in Latin America and the Caribbean." Latin American and Caribbean Technical Department Regional Studies Series No. 18. World Bank, Washington, D.C.

Castaneda, Tarsicio (1990), *Para Combatir la Pobreza*. Santiago, Chile: Centro de Estudios Publicos.

Cavallo, Domingo (1982), *Agriculture and Economic Growth in an Open Economy: The Case of Argentina*. Research Report No. 36. Washington, D.C.: International Food Policy Research Institute.

Chaudhuri, Shubham, and Martin Ravallion (forthcoming), "How Well Do Static Welfare Indicators Identify the Chronically Poor?" *Journal of Public Economics*.

Cisneros, Rodrigo (1992), "Bolivia: Costos Unitarios de los Servicios de Salud Primaria." In "From Platitudes to Practice: Targeting Social Programs in Latin America," Volume II. Margaret Grosh, ed. Latin America and Caribbean Technical Department Regional Study Series, Report No. 21. World Bank, Washington, D.C.

Cox, Donald, and Emmanuel Jimenez (1992), "Social Security and Private Transfers in Developing Countries: The Case of Peru." *The World Bank Economic Review*, Vol. 6, No. 1, pp. 155-170.

Datt, Gaurav, and Martin Ravallion (1990), "Regional Disparities, Targeting, and Poverty in India." Policy, Research and External Affairs Working Paper Series, No. 375. World Bank, Agriculture and Rural Development Department, Washington, D.C.

de Janvry, Alain, A. Fargeix and E. Sadoulet (1989), "Economic Welfare and Political Consequences of Stabilization Policies: A General Equilibrium Approach." Background paper for the *World Development Report 1990*. World Bank, Washington, D.C.

Departamento de Economia Agraria, Universidad Catolica de Chile INTA, Universidad de Chile (1990), *Experiencias y Dilemas en la Focalizacion de Programas de Salud y Nutricion*. Santiago, Chile: Pontificia Universidad Catolica de Chile.

Devaney, Barbara, and Robert Moffitt (1990), "Assessing the Dietary Effects of the Food Stamp Program." In *Food Stamp Policy Issues: Results from Recent Research*. Carole Trippe, Nancy Heiser and Harold Beebout, eds. Washington, D.C.: United States Department of Agriculture, Food and Nutrition Service.

Dreze, Jean, and Amarty A. Sen (1989), *Hunger and Public Action*. Oxford: Clarendon Press.

Economic Development Institute, World Bank, and Agencia Espanola de Cooperacion Internacional (1992), "Reasignacion del Gasto Social para el Alivio de la Pobreza." World Bank, Washington, D.C.

Edirisinghe, Neville (1987), *The Food Stamp Scheme in Sri Lanka: Costs, Benefits, and Options for Modification*. Research Report No. 58. Washington, D.C.: International Food Policy Research Institute.

Foster, James, J. Greer and E. Thorbecke (1984), "A Class of Decomposable Poverty Measures." *Econometrica* Vol. 52, No. 3, pp. 761-765.

Franklin, Ralph (1990), "Targeting Poverty Groups in Honduras: Some Preliminary Estimates and Scenarios." World Bank, Regional Unit for Technical Assistance, Washington, D.C.

Garfinkel, Irwin (1982), *Income-Tested Transfer Programs: The Case For and Against*. New York: Academic Press.

Gattgens, Xinia (1987), "El Programa de Comedores Escolares: Analasis Evaluativo de una Politica Social." Documento de Trabajo Numero 105. Universidad de Costa Rica, Instituto de Investigaciones en Ciencias Economicas, San Jose.

G.E. International Service Corporation (n.d.), "Unit Cost Study: Ministry of Education, Jamaica." Kingston.

Gertler, Paul, and Paul Glewwe (1989), *The Willingness to Pay for Education in Developing Countries*. Living Standards Measurement Study Paper No. 54. Washington, D.C.: World Bank.

Gertler, Paul, and Omar Rahman (1991), "High Risk Pregnancies and Maternal Health Services in Jamaica." Santa Monica, California: Rand Corporation.

Gertler, Paul, and Jacques van der Gaag (1990), *The Willingness to Pay for Medical Care*. Baltimore: Johns Hopkins University Press.

Gill, Indermit, Emmanuel Jimenez and Zmarak Shalizi (1990), "Targeting Consumer Subsidies for Poverty Alleviation: A Survey and a Primer of Basic Theory." World Bank, Policy Research Department, Washington, D.C.

Glewwe, Paul (1990), *Efficient Allocation of Transfers to the Poor*. Living Standards Measurement Study Working Paper No. 70. Washington, D.C.: World Bank.

_____ (1988), *Distribucion del Bienestar Economico en el Peru en 1985-1986*. Living Standards Measurement Study Working Paper No. 42S. Washington, D.C.: World Bank.

Glewwe, Paul, and G. Hall (1991), *The Social Costs of Avoiding Structural Adjustment: Inequality and Poverty in Lima, Peru from 1985-1986 to 1990*. Living Standards Measurement Study Paper No. 86. Washington, D.C.: World Bank.

Glewwe, Paul, and O. Kanaan (1989), "Targeting Assistance to the Poor: A Multivariate Approach Using Household Survey Data." Policy, Planning and Research Working Paper No. 225. World Bank, Population and Human Resources Department, Washington, D.C.

Glewwe, Paul, and Jacques van der Gaag (1988), *Confronting Poverty in Developing Countries*. Living Standards Measurement Study Working Paper No. 48. Washington, D.C.: World Bank.

Gordon, Derek (1989), "Identifying the Poor: Developing a Poverty Line for Jamaica." Jamaican Poverty Line Project Working Paper No. 3. Planning Institute of Jamaica, Kingston.

Gomez, Sergio (1992), "La Realidad en Cifras Estadisticas Sociales." FLASCO, Santiago, Chile.

Graham, Carol (1992), "The Politics of Protecting the Poor During Adjustment: Bolivia's Emergency Social Fund." *World Development* Vol. 20, No. 9, pp. 1233-1251.

_____ (1991a), "The APRA Government and the Urban Poor: The PAIT Programme in Lima's Pueblos Jovenes." *Journal of Latin American Studies*, Vol. 23, Part I, pp. 91-117.

_____ (1991b), "From Emergency Employment to Social Investment: Alleviating Poverty in Chile." Brookings Occasional Papers. Washington, D.C.: Brookings Institution.

Griffin, Charles (1989), "Means Testing in Developing Countries." Urban Institute, Washington, D.C.

Grosh, Margaret E. (1993), "Five Criteria for Choosing Among Poverty Programs." Paper prepared for Brookings Institution Conference on Confronting the Challenge of Poverty and Inequality in Latin America. World Bank, Policy Research Department, Washington, D.C.

_____ (1992a), "From Platitudes to Practice: Targeting Social Programs in Latin America," Volumes I and II. Latin American and Caribbean Technical Department Regional Study Series, Report No. 21. World Bank, Washington, D.C.

_____ (1992b), "The Jamaican Food Stamp Programme: A Case Study in Targeting." *Food Policy*, Vol. 17, No. 1, pp. 23-40.

_____ (1990), *Social Spending in Latin America: The Story of the 1980s*. World Bank Discussion Paper No. 106. Washington, D.C.: World Bank.

Grosh, Margaret E., and Judy L. Baker (forthcoming), "Proxy Means Tests: Simulations, Sensitivity and Set-Up." World Bank, Policy Research Department, Washington, D.C.

Gupta, Geeta, Adrian Maraviglia and Florence Yagoda (1989), "Summary of Research Findings on Women-Headed Households: The Relationship with Poverty and Consequences for Children." In *Notes from the Seminar Series: The Determinants and Consequences of Female-Headed Households*. Lisa McGowan, ed. Washington, D.C.: Population Council and International Center for Research on Women.

Haddad, Lawrence, and Ravi Kanbur (1991), "Upper-Limit Indicator Targeting and Age-Based Nutritional Interventions: Optimality, Information and Leakage." International Food Policy Research Institute, Washington, D.C.

_____ (1990), "Is There an Intra-Household Kuznets Curve?" Policy, Planning and Research Working Paper No. 466. World Bank, Research Administrator's Office, Washington, D.C.

Haddad, Lawrence, Joan Sullivan and Eileen Kennedy (1991), "Identification and Evaluation of Alternative Indicators of Food and Nutrition Security: Some Conceptual Issues and an Analysis of Extant Data." International Food Policy Research Institute, Washington, D.C.

Haindl Rondanelli, Erik, Ema Budinich Besoain and Ignacio Irarrazaval Llona (1989), *Gasto Social Efectivo*. Santiago, Chile: ODEPLAN and Unversidad de Chile.

Hoenack, Stephen (1991), "Chile's Voucher System." University of Minnesota, Hubert Humphrey School of Public Affairs, Minneapolis.

Honduras, Ministerio de Salud Publica (1987), "Encuesta Nacional de Epdemiologia y Salud Familiar Honduras." Tegucigalpa, Honduras.

Hopkins, Raymond (1988), "Political Calculations in Subsidizing Food." In *Food Subsidies in Developing Countries*. Per Pinstrup-Andersen, ed. Baltimore: Johns Hopkins University Press.

Horton, Susan (1991), "Unit Costs, Cost-Effectiveness and Financing of Nutrition Interventions." University of Toronto, Department of Economics, Toronto, Canada.

Instituto Cuanto (1991), *Ajuste y Economia Familiar 1985-1990*. Lima, Peru.

Jamaica Ministry of Education (1991), "Social Sectors Development Project, School Incentive Awards Scheme." Minutes of Committee Meeting on May 2, 1991. Kingston, Jamaica.

James, Estelle, and Gail Benjamin (1987), "Educational Distribution and Income Redistribution through Education in Japan." *Journal of Human Resources* Vol. 22, No. 4, pp. 469-489.

Jimenez, Emmanuel, Marlaine Lockheed, Eduardo Luna and Vicente Paqueo (1989), "School Effects and Costs for Private and Public Schools in the

Dominican Republic." Policy Research and External Affairs Working Paper Series No. 288. World Bank, Population and Human Resources Department, Washington, D.C.

Jorgensen, Steen, Margaret Grosh and Mark Schacter (1992), *Bolivia's Answer to Poverty, Economic Crisis, and Adjustment.* World Bank Regional and Sectoral Studies. Washington, D.C.: World Bank.

Kanbur, Ravi (1991), "Children and Intra-household Inequality." Policy, Research and External Affairs Working Paper Series No. 685. World Bank, Development Economics, Washington, D.C.

Kanbur, Ravi, Michael Keen and Matti Tuomala (1992), "Labor Supply and Targeting in Poverty Alleviation Programs." Paper presented at the Conference on Public Expenditures and the Poor: Incidence and Targeting. World Bank, Washington, D.C.

_____ (1991), "Optimal Nonlinear Income Taxation for the Alleviation of Poverty." Policy Research and External Affairs Working Paper Series No. 616. World Bank, Development Economics, Washington, D.C.

Kanbur, Ravi, and Michael Keen (1989), "Poverty, Incentives, and Linear Income Taxation." In *The Economics of Social Security.* A. Dilnot and I. Walker, eds. Oxford: Clarendon Press.

Kawas, M. Celina, Rita Dignora Liza, Dora Costillo Brown, Virginia Quintana Sosa and Antonio Ugalde (1992), "Estudio de la Percepcion que los Usuarios y Proveedores Tienen de los Servicios de Atencion Primaria en Honduras." Tegucigalpa, Honduras.

Kennedy, Eileen, and Harold Alderman (1987), *Comparative Analyses of Nutritional Effectiveness of Food Subsidies and Other Food-Related Interventions.* Washington, D.C.: International Food Policy Research Institute.

Lewis, Maureen, Margaret Sulvetta and Gerard La Forgia (1990a), "Estimating Public Hospital Costs by Measuring Resource Use: A Dominican Case." Urban Institute, Washington, D.C.

_____ (1990b), *Measuring Costs, Efficiency, and Quality in Public Hospitals: A Dominican Case.* Latin America and the Caribbean Region Internal Discussion Paper. World Bank, Washington, D.C.

Lockheed, Maureen, Adriaan Verspoor and associates (1991), *Improving Primary Education in Developing Countries.* New York: Oxford University Press.

Louat, Frederic, Margaret Grosh and Jacques van der Gaag (1993), *Welfare Implications of Female-Headship in Jamaican Households.* Living Standard Measurement Study Working Paper No. 96. Washington, D.C.: World Bank.

Lustig, Nora (1986), *Food Subsidy Programs in Mexico.* Research Report No. 3. Washington, D.C.: International Food Policy Research Institute.

Mackintosh, Fiona J. (1989), "Notes on Means-tested Poverty Programs in the U.S." World Bank, Policy Research Department, Washington, D.C.

Mansilla, Cesar O., and Rony L. Alcayaga (1991), "Estudios de Financiamiento de Salud Publica Sistemas de Recuperacion de Costos." Chile.

Mardones, Francisco and Rafael Zamora (1990), "Evaluacion Socio-Economica de la Entrega de Leche 'Purita' a la Embarazada en Chile." *Revista Medica Chilena* Vol. 118, pp. 1043-1051.

_____ (1989), "Evaluaciones Socio-Economicas del Programa Nacional de Alimentacion Complementaria: Ques es lo Que se Ha Hecho?" *Revista Chilena de Nutricion* Vol. 17, No.3, pp. 169-174.

Mardones-Santander, F., Pedro Rosso, Rafael Zamora, Francisco Mardones-Restat, Nicolas Gonzalez and Dick Uiterwaal (1991), "Cost Effectiveness of a Nutrition Intervention Program for Pregnant Women." *Nutrition Research* Vol. 11, pp. 295-307.

Mardones-Santander, F., Pedro Rosso, Abraham Stekel, Eugenia Ahumada, Sandra Llaguno, Fernando Pizarro, Judith Salinas, Isabel Vial and Tomas Walter (1988), "Effect of Milk-Based Food Supplement on Maternal Nutritional Status and Fetal Growth in Underweight Chilean Women." *American Journal of Clinical Nutrition* Vol. 47, pp. 413-419.

Mateus, Abel (1983), *Targeting Food Subsidies for the Needy, The Use of Cost-Benefit Analysis and Institutional Design.* World Bank Staff Working Paper Number 617. Washington, D.C.: World Bank.

McGowan, Lisa, ed. (1990), "Notes from the Seminar Series: The Determinants and Consequences of Female-Headed Households." Population Council and the International Center for Research on Women, Washington, D.C.

McLure, Charles E., Jr. (1975), "General Equilibrium Analysis: The Harberger Model After Ten Years." *Journal of Public Economics* Vol. 4, No. 2, pp. 125-162.

Meerman, Jacob (1979), *Public Expenditure in Malaysia: Who Benefits and Why.* New York: Oxford University Press.

Miranda, E., V. Loyola and O. Reyes (1991), "Estudio Asignacion de Recursos Financieros al Interior del Sector Publico de Salud." Chile.

Moffit, Robert (1992), "Incentive Effects of the U.S. Welfare System: A Review." *Journal of Economic Literature* Vol. 30, No. 1, pp. 1-61.

_____ (1983), "An Economic Model of Welfare Stigma." *American Economic Review* Vol. 73, No. 5, pp. 1023-1035.

Muchnick, Eugenia, and Isabel Vial (1990), *Impacto del P.N.A.C. en Preescolares de Santiago.* Santiago, Chile: Ediciones Mar del Plata.

Munnell, Alicia H. (1986), *Lessons from the Income Maintenance Experiments.* No. 30. Melvin Village, New Hampshire: Federal Reserve Bank of Boston and the Brookings Institute.

Musgrove, Phil (1991), "Feeding Latin America's Children, An Analytical Survey of Food Programs." Latin America and the Caribbean Technical Department Regional Studies Series Report No. 11. World Bank, Washington, D.C.

Newman, John, Steen Jorgensen and Menno Pradhan (1991), "How Did Workers Benefit?" In *Bolivia's Answer to Poverty, Economic Crisis and Adjustment: The Story of Bolivia's Emergency Social Fund.* Steen Jorgensen, Margaret Grosh and Mark Shacter, eds. Washington, D.C.: World Bank.

Nieto de Aguilar, Mabel (1992), "Sistema de Indentificacion, Seleccion, y Registro Unico de Beneficiarios de los Programas Sociales." Instituto Mixto de Ayuda Social, San Jose, Costa Rica.

Peabody, John W., Omar Rahman, Kristin Fox and Paul Gertler (1993), "Public and Private Delivery of Primary Health Care Services in Jamaica: A Comparison of Quality in Different Types of Facilities." Rand Corporation, Santa Monica, California.

Pechman, Joseph A. (1985), *Who Paid the Taxes, 1966-85?* Washington, D.C.: Brookings Institution.

Petrei, Humberto (1987), *El Gasto Publico Social y sus Efectos Distributivos.* Rio de Janeiro, Brazil: Programa de Estudios Conjuntos sobre Integracion Economica Latinoameriana.

Pinstrup-Andersen, Per, ed. (1988), *Food Subsidies in Developing Countries.* Baltimore: Johns Hopkins University Press.

Pinstrup-Andersen, Per and Harold Alderman (1988), "The Effectiveness of Consumer-Oriented Food Subsidies in Reaching Rationing and Income Transfer Goals." In *Food Subsidies in Developing Countries.* Per Pinstrup-Andersen, ed. Baltimore: Johns Hopkins University Press.

Presidencia de la Republica de Honduras, Fondo Hondureno de Inversion Social (1991), "Presupuesto de Inversion 1991, FHIS." Direccion de Proyectos, Tegucigalpa.

Programa de las Naciones Unidas para el Desarrollo (1992), "Documento de Proyecto: Sistema de Seleccion de Beneficiarios para la Focalizacion del Gasto Social." Proyecto del Gobierno Costa Rica. San Jose, Costa Rica.

Raczynski, D. (1991), "La Ficha CAS y La Focalizacion de los Programas Sociales." Estudios Cieplan No. 141. La Corporacion de Investigaciones Economicas para Latinoamerica, Santiago, Chile.

Rainwater, Lee (1982), "Stigma in Income-Tested Programs." In *Income-Tested Transfer Programs: The Case For and Against.* I. Garfinkel, ed. New York: Academic Press.

Ramirez, Noel (1991), "Illusion y Realidad en America Latina." Instituto Centroamericano de Administracion de Empresas.

Ravallion, Martin (1993), "Poverty Alleviation through Regional Targeting: A Case Study for Indonesia." In *The Economics of Rural Organization: Theory, Practice and Policy.* K. Hoff, A. Braverman and J. E. Stiglitz, eds. New York: Oxford University Press.

_____ (1992), *Poverty Comparisons: A Guide to Concepts and Methods* Living Standards Measurement Study Working Paper No. 88. Washington, D.C.: World Bank.

_____ (1991), "Reaching the Poor through Rural Public Employment: Arguments, Evidence, and Lessons from South Asia." *The World Bank Research Observer* Vol. 6, No. 2, pp. 153-176.

_____ (1989), "Land-Contingent Poverty Alleviation Schemes." *World Development* Vol. 17, No. 8, pp. 1223-1233.

Ravallion, Martin, and Kalvin Chao (1989), "Targeted Policies for Poverty Alleviation Under Imperfect Information: Algorithms and Applications." *Journal of Policy Modeling* Vol. 11, No. 2, pp. 213-224.

Republica de Chile, Ministerio de Educacion (1990), "Proyecto de Ley que Establece Nuevas Normas Sobre Estatuto Docente." Ministerio de Educacion, Santiago, Chile.

Sancho, Antonio (1991), "Participacion del Sector Privado en la Prestacion de Servicios Sociales." Inter-American Development Bank, Washington, D.C.

Sauma, Pablo, and J.D. Trejos (1990), "Evolucion reciente de la Distribucion del Ingreso en Costa Rica (1977-1986)." University of Costa Rica, Instituto de Investigaciones en Ciencias Economicas, San Jose.

Selden, Thomas M., and Michael J. Wasylenko (1990), "Benefit Incidence Analysis in Developing Countries." Policy Research Working Paper Series, No. 1015. World Bank, Country Economics Department, Washington, D.C.

Selowsky, Marcelo (1979), *Who Benefits from Government Expenditure? A Case Study of Colombia.* New York: Oxford University Press.

Sigma One Corporation (1990), "Targeting Poverty Gaps in Honduras: Some Preliminary Estimates and Scenarios." Washington, D.C.

Statistical Institute of Jamaica (STATIN) and the Planning Institute of Jamaica (PIOJ) (1989), "Preliminary Report: Survey of Living Conditions, July 1989." Statistical Institute of Jamaica, Kingston.

Statistical Institute of Jamaica (STATIN) and World Bank (1988), "Living Conditions Survey: Jamaica." Preliminary report. Statistical Institute of Jamaica, Kingston.

Trejos, Juan Diego (1992), "Costa Rica: Los Comedores Escolares." In "From Platitudes to Practice: Targeting Social Programs," Volume II. Margaret Grosh, ed. Latin America and Caribbean Technical Department Regional Study Series Report No. 21. World Bank, Washington, D.C.

Ugalde, Antonio (1984), "Where There is a Doctor: Strategies to Increase Productivity at Lower Costs. The Economics of Rural Health Care in the Dominican Republic." *Social Science and Medicine* Vol. 19, No. 4, pp. 441-450.

United Nations Development Program (1992), *Human Development Report 1992.* New York: Oxford University Press.

Universidad de Chile, Facultad de Ciencias Economics y Administrativas Departamento de Economia, (n.d.), "Estudio Sobre Los Programas Especiales de Empleo." Santiago, Chile.

Vargas-Olea, Sergio (1992), "Evaluacion Ex-Post de Proyectos Financiados por el Fondo Hondureno de Inversion Social." Inter-American Development Bank, Tegucigalpa, Honduras.

Vial, Isabel, Rosa Camhi and Antonio Infante (1992), "Chile: El Programa de Alimentacion Complimentaria (PNAC): Su Evolucion y Mecanismos de Focalizacion." In "From Platitudes to Practice: Targeting Social Programs in Latin America," Volume II. Margaret Grosh, ed. Latin America and Caribbean Technical Department Regional Study Series, Report No. 21. World Bank, Washington, D.C.

Waiselfisz, Jacobo (1990), "Relatorio de Aplicacao Piloto do Sistema de Avaliacao do Ensino Publico de Primero Grado." Instituto Interamericano de Cooperacao para a Agricultura, Brasil.

Winter, Carolyn (1992), "Honduras Women's Country Assessment Paper." World Bank, Latin America and Caribbean Country Department III, Washington, D.C.

_____ (1990), "Target Efficiency in Health and Education: Developing Country Experience." World Bank, Policy Research Department, Washington, D.C.